THE
Archive Photographs
SERIES

YORKSHIRE
COUNTY CRICKET CLUB

Herbert Sutcliffe and Percy Holmes – Yorkshire's most celebrated opening pair, together they shared 69 century partnerships for the county and laid the foundations for many White Rose triumphs.

THE
Archive Photographs
SERIES

YORKSHIRE
COUNTY CRICKET CLUB

Compiled by
Mick Pope

CHALFORD

The Chalford Publishing Company
St Mary's Mill, Chalford,
Stroud, Gloucestershire, GL6 8NX

ISBN 0 7524 0756 2

Typesetting and origination by
The Chalford Publishing Company
Printed in Great Britain by
Redwood Books, Trowbridge

Three of Yorkshire cricket's legendary figures. From left to right: George Hirst, Wilfred Rhodes and Lord Hawke at the Scarborough Cricket Festival in 1930.

Contents

Leonard Hutton, a batsman of peerless skill on difficult pitches. His grace and style enriched the game; his cover drive was one of cricket's glories.

Foreword

by Sir Lawrence Byford CBE, QPM, LLD, DL

Whilst writing the foreword to Mick Pope's fascinating photographic record of Yorkshire County Cricket Club's history, I was reminded of my boyhood in a West Riding community in the 1930s, where during the season, playground conversation inevitably turned to cricket and the feats of that great side led by Brian Sellers.

A vivid memory for me was my first visit to Lord's in May 1937 when Len Hutton, ably supported by Maurice Leyland for part of his innings, scored his first century for a representative first-class side other than Yorkshire. It was for the North against the South during the MCC Centenary celebrations. Ken Farnes (killed during the war) and Alf Gover of Surrey were the South's outstanding front-line attack and Len's superb batting that day left an indelible impression on a Yorkshire schoolboy.

As youngsters, we were proud to feel part of Yorkshire's great cricketing traditions, expecting them to win the County Championship every year and we were rarely disappointed. If by chance the evening newspaper reported that the team had had an indifferent day, this prompted initial surprise, then disappointment, coupled with an earnest desire to have matters put right before the end of the match.

The well-known maxim that, 'when Yorkshire is strong, so will England be' was clearly manifested during that period and later again when a similar phase of triumphs in the County Championship came in the 1960s. Needless to say, we now impatiently await the dawning of another successful era for our great Club. With the impact of overseas players it is likely to prove more difficult to have such a sustained pattern of success at one Club, although with the crop of home-grown young players currently coming to the fore, there is good reason to believe that we should become a team as much to be feared as those in earlier times.

I wish Mick Pope every success with this timely reminder of Yorkshire's great years and its personalities, and I very much hope that it will give as much pleasure to you as it has to me.

Acknowledgements

The author would like to express his thanks to the following for their assistance in the compilation of this book. Many of the old and rare photographs loaned from collectors and private sources have been skilfully reproduced by David Mangham. Special thanks to Sir Lawrence Byford CBE, QPM, LLD, DL for kindly consenting to write the foreword; David Buxton at Chalford Publishing for his help and guidance throughout the project; and a particular thank you to my girlfriend Tracy Smith, whose word processing, computer and proof reading skills were put to good use during the production of the book. A large number of other people and organisations have given considerable assistance with photographs and information and my thanks go to the following: Arthur Bower, Michael Burns, County Print Services, Paul Dyson, Keith Farnsworth, John Featherstone, David Frith, Albert Gamble, Ian M. Goddard, Ian Hall, Alan Hill, Andrew Johnson, the late Bob Jones, R.F. Kirby, Mrs M. Kilner, Peter D. Kilner, Leeds Central Library, Alec Lodge, John Lodge, Revd Malcolm Lorimer, Pat Mangham, Laurie Milner, David Musgrave, William A. Powell, Colin Shakespeare, Sheffield Library and Information Services, *The Cricketer*, Dr John Turner, Ken Utley, G. Vidlen, J. White, Roy Wilkinson, Wombwell Cricket Lovers' Society, Tony Woodhouse, Peter Wynne-Thomas, Yorkshire CCC, and *Yorkshire Post Newpapers Ltd*. I have tried, wherever possible, to consult and acknowledge possible owners of copyright. Any oversight is inadvertent, and the author will examine any further claims that might arise if called upon to do so.

Bibliography

Who's Who of Cricketers, Hamlyn 1993, Philip Bailey, Philip Thorn and Peter Wynne-Thomas. *England Test Cricketers*, Collins Willow 1989, Bill Frindall. *The Wisden Book of Test Cricket 1877 to 1977 4th Edition*, Headline 1995, Bill Frindall. *The Wisden Book of Test Cricket vol II 1977 to 1994 4th Edition*, Headline 1995, Bill Frindall. *John Wisden's Cricketers' Almanack* various years. *Playfair Cricket Annual 1948 to 1996. The Yorkshire CCC Yearbook 1893 to 1996. First-Class Cricket in Australia vol I 1850/51 to 1941/42*, Ray Webster 1991, Ray Webster and Allan Miller. *Who's Who of Yorkshire CCC*, Breedon Books 1992, Anthony Woodhouse. *Yorkshire Cricketers 1863 to 1985*, ACS 1986. *The Daily Express. The Daily Mail. The Yorkshire Evening Post. The Yorkshire Post. The Cricket Statistician. The Cricketer International 1921 to 1996. The Playfair Cricket Monthly. The Twelfth Man. The White Rose. Wisden Cricket Monthly. Express Deliveries*, S. Paul 1949, William Eric Bowes. *F.S. Jackson – A Cricketing Biography*, Crowood Press 1989, James Coldham. *Before and After Bramall Lane*, Private Publication 1988, Keith Farnsworth. *Cricket Grounds of Yorkshire*, ACS 1995, Steven Draper. *Pageant of Cricket*, Macmillan London Ltd 1987, David Frith. *The Golden Age of Cricket 1890-1914*, Lutterworth Press 1978, David Frith. *The Wisden Book of Cricket Obituaries*, Queen Anne Press, Macdonald and Co. Publishers Ltd 1986, Benny Green. *Recollections & Reminiscences*, Williams and Norgate Ltd 1924, Lord Hawke. *Johnny Wardle: Cricket Conjuror*, David and Charles 1988, Alan Hill. *Herbert Sutcliffe: Cricket Maestro*, Simon and Schuster 1991, Alan Hill. *The Official History of Yorkshire County Cricket Club*, Crowood Press 1989, Derek Hodgson. *The History of Yorkshire County Cricket 1833-1903*, Archibald Constable and Co. Ltd 1904, The Revd R.S. Holmes. *History of Yorkshire County Cricket 1924-1949*, Yorkshire CCC 1950, J.M. Kilburn. *The Complete Who's Who of Test Cricketers*, Queen Anne Press 1987, Christopher Martin-Jenkins. *History of Yorkshire County Cricket 1903-1923*, Chorley and Pickersgill 1924, A.W. Pullin. *Talks With Old Yorkshire Cricketers*, Yorkshire Post 1898, A.W. Pullin. *Tragic White Roses*, Private Publication 1995, Mick Pope. *The Laughing Cricketer of Wombwell – A Biography of Roy Kilner*, Darf 1990, Mick Pope. *Yorkshire's 22 Championships 1893-1946*, Edward Arnold and Co. 1949, E.L. Roberts. *Yorkshire Cricketers 1839-1939*, Hodgson 1973, Peter Thomas. *Hirst and Rhodes*, Epworth 1959, A.A. Thomson. *The History of Yorkshire CCC*, Christopher Helm 1989, Anthony Woodhouse. *Cricketers of Wombwell*, Wombwell Cricket Lovers' 1965, A. Woodhouse, R.D. Wilkinson and J. Sokell. *Yorkshire Cricket: A Pictorial Survey*, Dalesman 1974, A. Woodhouse and Ron Yeomans. *The Hamlyn A-Z of Cricket Records*, Hamlyn 1983, Peter Wynne-Thomas.

Introduction

*'Yorkshire cricket is a thing of which not only every Yorkshireman
but every Englishman must feel proud.'*
Lord Hawke

Childhood habits and influences often linger into adulthood and in my case a love of cricket, its rich tradition and its glorious history, has remained my constant passion into manhood. Equally, a fascination with the pictorial image was developed at an early age.

As my love affair with the summer game developed through my teens, so my thirst for knowledge brought out the 'bookworm' in me as I sought to absorb as much information as possible about the giants of long ago. I suppose, looking back, being born in Yorkshire it was natural that I should develop a close affinity with cricket, the County Club, and the deeds of its cricketers from Sheffield's early 'champion', Tom Marsden, to Darren Gough in modern times.

I was only four years old when Yorkshire CCC last won the County Championship and the intervening years have, for the most part, been barren and devoid of success; so I suppose, in an attempt to share in the glories of yesteryear, I turned to the chronicles of Yorkshire's cricket past to find my solace. Through the ages the history of the White Rose county has been faithfully documented by a host of dedicated writers and historians: Revd R.S. Holmes, A.W. Pullin, Neville Cardus, A.A. Thomson, Jim Kilburn and, more recently, Tony Woodhouse and Derek Hodgson. Through the written word the triumphs of ages past can be relived, great cricketers recalled and memorable moments retold. Yet for me, however good the creative scribe, there remained a missing link, a sense of unfulfilment; that is, until now.

Time travel remains, even in the last decade of the twentieth century, an improbable dream, yet there are alternatives. The pictorial image can, to some extent, recreate a long lost era, freezing as it does a small moment in time: a glance backwards into the past.

Cricket spread steadily from its southern cradle during the eighteenth century and the first certain reference to the game in Yorkshire was recorded in 1751. Sheffield became the early focal point for Yorkshire cricket in the years before and, for sometime after, the formation of the county club. Indeed as early as 1771, Sheffield could boast a cricket XI, and that year they met Nottingham in the first of a long running and eventful series of fixtures that stretched into the mid nineteenth century.

On 8 January 1863 at the Adelphi Hotel, Sheffield, the Yorkshire County Cricket Club was officially formed. The early Yorkshire teams were full of characters and talented cricketers like John Thewlis, Joseph Rowbotham, the bowling partners Hodgson and Slinn, and George Anderson, one of the best batsmen of the day. Yorkshire were crowned Champion County in 1867 and 1870.

The county's twenty-nine 'official' Championship crowns fall conveniently into three distinct periods of cricket history. Under the influence and control of Lord Hawke, Yorkshire emerged as a powerful force during cricket's Golden Age. Between 1893 and 1908 Hawke led the county to eight Championship titles and before the First World War swept away the age of innocence, Yorkshire, under the leadership of Sir Archibald White, were champions again in 1912. The players under Hawke's command were a new generation of champions, none more so than the two all-rounders from Kirkheaton, near Huddersfield: George Herbert Hirst and Wilfred Rhodes, both right-handed batsmen and left-arm bowlers, both legendary figures in the history of Yorkshire cricket. There were others who played their full part in ensuring the club's rise to power: David Hunter, Yorkshire's regular wicket-keeper between 1888 and 1909; David Denton, attacking middle-order batsman who scored over 36,000 runs in first-class cricket; the opening pair of 'Long John' Tunnicliffe and J.T. Brown; all-rounder Schofield Haigh, and Sir Stanley Jackson, an amateur who epitomised the spirit of the Golden Age.

Between the wars, Yorkshire were all-conquering, winning the Championship twelve times in the twenty-one seasons from 1919 to 1939. In the early 1920s new heroes emerged: Sutcliffe, Holmes, Kilner, Macaulay, Waddington, Oldroyd, and Leyland; they continued where the giants of the Golden Age had left off. In 1933 Yorkshire's second 'great' captain took the reigns. Brian Sellers was a formidable, authoritative, single-minded leader who guided the county to five Championships during his first seven seasons in charge. Even greater jewels emerged in the shape of Bill Bowes, the spearhead of the Yorkshire bowling attack in the '30s, Hedley Verity, who succeeded Rhodes as the side's premier left-arm slow bowler and from Pudsey, a batsman called Hutton.

The inter-war period of Yorkshire supremacy was summed up by J.M. Kilburn in his *History of Yorkshire County Cricket 1924-1949*, 'Yorkshire were sometimes a magnificent team, sometimes less than great, but never, throughout the whole period, were they without a great player, one whose name was known as well in Sydney as in Sheffield. It was the time of Sutcliffe, Verity, Bowes, and Hutton, when those were at the peak of power; it joined a generation gone through the link of Wilfred Rhodes, and made its contact with the future through the batsmanship of Leonard Hutton.'

The first postwar English cricket season of 1946 saw Yorkshire crowned Champions for the twenty-second time, their sixth title under Sellers. In the 1950s a new power forged ahead of the White Rose as Surrey claimed the Championship outright seven years in succession between 1952 and 1958. Yorkshire's re-emergence in the late '50s was sustained throughout the 1960s, which brought the county a further six Championship titles under Vic Wilson and then Brian Close at the helm, as well as double success in the new one-day Gillette Cup competition in 1965 and 1969. The nucleus of the team that had lived in Surrey's shadow during the 1950s had been broken; Hutton, Willie Watson, and Bill Sutcliffe had all retired as had Bob Appleyard, and Johnny Wardle was exhibiting his craft in other circles. But Trueman, Close and Illingworth remained, and around them gathered the next generation of Yorkshire cricketers: from Fitzwilliam came Geoffrey Boycott, the most prolific batsman of his age; Doug Padgett, right-handed correct batsman; opening bat and brilliant fielder Ken Taylor; left-arm spinner Don Wilson; Philip Sharpe, akin to Tunnicliffe as a slip fielder and an aggressive batsman; and Jimmy Binks, Yorkshire's regular wicket-keeper from the mid '50s until David Bairstow's arrival in 1970.

At 4.55 pm on 30 August 1968, Yorkshire were crowned County Champions for the twenty-ninth 'official' time in the club's history, having beaten Surrey at Hull by 60 runs. Well over a quarter of a century has now elapsed since that last Championship conquest. The storm clouds that gathered over Headingley during the 1970s and '80s brought an era of bitter and regrettable internal conflict. The John Player Sunday League in 1983 and the Benson and Hedges Cup win over Northamptonshire in 1987 heralded several false dawns of a hopeful return to the top flight.

What follows here is an attempt to turn back the hands of time and relive again some of the White Rose County's greatest moments of glory.

One
Sheffield Beginnings

The cricket ground at Darnall, Sheffield, which was the first purpose built cricket venue in Yorkshire and was opened in 1822. It quickly became one of the largest and best appointed in the country, being regarded as second only to the great Lord's. There, in 1826, local left-hander Tom Marsden hit 227 for the combined Sheffield and Leicester side against Nottingham. In 1827 the first 'experimental match' to test round-arm bowling was played there.

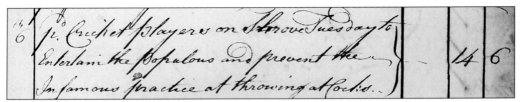

This extract from the Burgery of Sheffield Town Trustee's Account Book 1757 contains one of the first known references to cricket in Yorkshire. The entry reads, 'Paid cricket players on Shrove Tuesday to entertain the populous and prevent the infamous practice of throwing at cocks 14s 6d'.

The Hyde Park Cricket Ground was opened in 1826 and, following the decline of Darnall, became the home of Sheffield and indeed, Yorkshire cricket, in the 1830s and '40s. In 1833 it staged Yorkshire's first county match against Norfolk, whose side included Fuller Pilch, the finest batsman of the period. In 1846 Hyde Park hosted the inaugural match of William Clarke's touring All England XI, who were beaten by twenty of Sheffield. The game attracted a crowd of over 16,000; but by the 1850s the ground was in a state of decline and the opening of Bramall Lane in 1855 signalled the beginning of the end for Hyde Park.

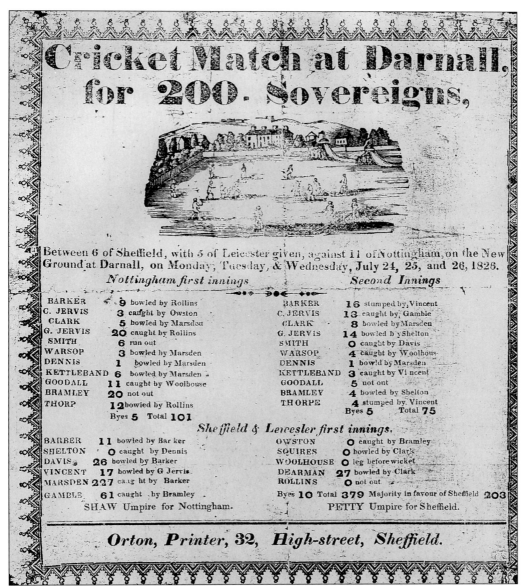

A famous scorecard recording the historic performance of Yorkshire's first champion, Tom Marsden, at Darnall, in 1826 when he became only the second player, after William Ward, to reach the dizzy heights of a double hundred. He batted for over eight hours in compiling his final total of 227. Marsden's fame, like that of Darnall Cricket Ground, was short-lived and in 1843, at the early age of 38, he died – many of his greatest deeds long since past.

Henry Sampson took over the mantle left by Tom Marsden during the 1840s and '50s. Born at Hallam, Sheffield, in 1813, he was a small, stout man, an excellent batsman and round-arm bowler. As early as 1841 he won lasting fame by defeating the 'Champion of Yorkshire' Marsden in a single-wicket clash. Earlier that year, on 8 February, he established a most unusual record by scoring 162 during a match played on ice! His cricket career spanned twenty-five years and he was the landlord, for over twenty years, of the Adelphi Hotel in Sheffield, birth place of Yorkshire CCC.

The Adelphi Hotel. It was there, on 7 March 1861, that the Sheffield Public Match Fund Committee was formed and on 8 January 1863, where Yorkshire County Cricket Club became a reality.

Michael Joseph Ellison, born 1 June 1817, was indeed 'the Father of Yorkshire and Sheffield cricket'. He served as Treasurer of Yorkshire CCC from 1863 until 1893 and was President between 1864 and 1897. He urged the foundation of the short-lived Public Match Fund Committee in 1861 and was influential in the development of the Bramall Lane ground, persuading the Duke of Norfolk to lease the land in his capacity as the Duke's agent. Ellison's contribution to Yorkshire cricket in its formative years is immeasurable.

Joseph Beckett Wostinholm was the Secretary of Yorkshire from 1864 to 1902. Like Ellison, he had a passion for cricket and together they formed an autocratic partnership which ruled the Club for over thirty years. He had a somewhat brusque manner; and while he may not have been the most popular of men, he was very single-minded and had the ability to get things done. Originally he was paid ten per cent of all subscriptions and then, between 1870 and 1882, his remuneration became a fixed £10. After 1882 the Committee deemed that his value had increased sufficiently to pay £25 per annum. Significantly when he did retire, the Club was forced to offer his successor the huge sum of £350.

15

Roger Iddison, Yorkshire's first official captain from 1863 to 1872. Under his leadership Yorkshire were acclaimed Champion County in both 1867 and 1870. A hard-hitting batsman, right-hand fast round-arm bowler, and occasional slow lob bowler, he played his first important match in 1853 and ended his career in 1876. He represented Lancashire in sixteen matches between 1865 and 1870, assisted the Players against the Gentlemen, helped form the United North of England XI and toured Australia on the first trip 'down under' in 1861/62.

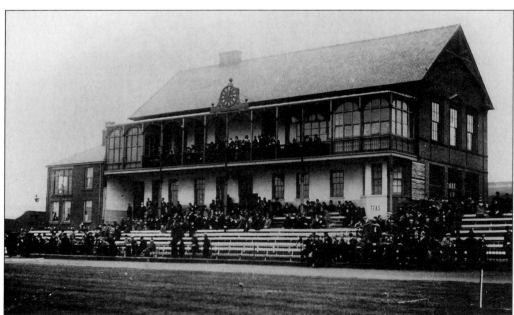

The old pavilion at Bramall Lane, pictured in its Victorian heyday. In August 1855 Yorkshire played their first game there, and were heavily defeated by Sussex, for whom John Wisden (founder of *Wisden Cricketers' Almanack*) scored 148.

First Lancashire v. Yorkshire Match

Played at Whalley, June 20th, 21st, 22nd, 1867.

Lancashire, 1st Innings.	
A. N. Hornby c Stevenson b Freeman.	2
J. Ricketts b Greenwood	3
J. F. Leese c Freeman b Greenwood.	22
C. Coward b Greenwood	13
A. B. Rowley b Greenwood . . .	0
G. Holgate c Anderson b Freeman .	8
Arthur Appleby b Freeman	1
W. Hickton c Anderson b Freeman .	2
E. Leventon b Freeman	0
E. B. Rawlinson not out	1
— Hibbert b Freeman	2
Extras	3
Total	57

Lancashire, 2nd Innings.	
A. N. Hornby b Freeman . . .	3
J. Ricketts b Freeman	0
J. F. Leese b Freeman	4
C. Coward c Iddison b Greenwood	5
A. B. Rowley b Freeman . . .	0
G. Holgate run out	21
Arthur Appleby b Greenwood . .	18
W. Hickton b Freeman	0
E. Leventon c Iddison b Greenwood	6
E. B. Rawlinson b Greenwood . .	14
— Hibbert not out	2
Extras	2
Total	75

Yorkshire, 1st Innings.	
J. Rowbotham c Hornby b Appleby .	7
J. Thewlis b Appleby	1
E. Stevenson b Leventon	54
Roger Iddison b Appleby	14
J. E. Lee b Appleby	0
E. Dawson b Hickton	11
G. Anderson b Leventon	6
G. Freeman c Rawlinson b Hickton .	28
J. Berry c Hibbert b Appleby . . .	27
L Greenwood c and b Appleby . . .	19
G. Atkinson not out	14
Extras	7
Total	188

Yorkshire won by an innings and 56 runs.   **Umpires: Wright and Rostron.**

The Whalley Cricket Ground in Lancashire staged the first Yorkshire v Lancashire match (its only first-class fixture) in June 1867. Yorkshire won the first Roses encounter comfortably. Ned Stephenson (spelt incorrectly on the scorecard above) top scored for Yorkshire with 54 and Freeman captured 12 wickets in the match for only 51 runs.

George Freeman, born at Boroughbridge in 1843, was Yorkshire's first great fast bowler, considered by W.G. Grace the best fast bowler he ever faced. He had a short but meteoric career, captured 209 wickets for the county and played a large part in Yorkshire being declared Champion County in 1867 and 1870. He toured America in 1868/69, under the leadership of Edgar Willsher, where he met with considerable success and was engaged by George Parr for the All England XI. After 1871 he practically gave up cricket, having become a successful auctioneer in Thirsk. He died there in 1895 at the early age of 52, having suffered from Bright's disease for two years.

The Yorkshire side of 1875. Back row, left to right: G. Martin (umpire), John Thewlis. Middle row, left to right: George Pinder, George Ulyett, Tom Armitage, Joe Rowbotham, Allen Hill, Andrew Greenwood. Front row, left to right: Tom Emmett, John Hicks, Ephraim Lockwood and Charlie Ullathorne. This was a talented but ill-disciplined team, possessing, as Yorkshire cricket historian Revd R.S. Holmes later commented, 'all the eccentricities of genius'.

G. ULYETT.

'Happy Jack' – George Ulyett, who was born at Pitsmoor, Sheffield, in 1851, was one of the most popular cricketers ever to play for Yorkshire. He made his county debut in 1873 and in a twenty year career scored over 20,000 first-class runs and took 653 wickets with his right-arm fast bowling. He played in the inaugural Test match at Melbourne in 1877, and his innings of 149 at Melbourne in 1881/82 was the first Test hundred for England in Australia. He toured Australia five times, as well as North America and South Africa. He was a complete all-round cricketer and was considered one of the best batsmen of the Victorian era, scoring 1,000 runs in a season on ten occasions. A practical joker, he once filled Tom Emmett's socks with snails under Niagara Falls and on another occasion rode an ostrich bare back! A warm, cheerful sportsman, Ulyett was goalkeeper for Sheffield Wednesday FC until 1883. He died of pneumonia, contracted after watching Yorkshire play Kent at Bramall Lane in 1898.

Revd Edmund Sardinson Carter was born 3 February 1845 at Malton. He was educated at Durham Grammar School and Worcester College, Oxford. An unorthodox batsman, fast and lob bowler, and wicket-keeper, he won blues at cricket and rowing whilst at Oxford. He played fourteen times for Yorkshire between 1876 and 1881 and he represented the Yorkshire Gentlemen from 1864. Whilst recovering from pleurisy in Australia he appeared in one match for Victoria in 1869. He introduced the slow left-arm bowler Ted Peate to the Yorkshire ranks and was influential in bringing the name of Martin Bladen Hawke to the attention of the club.

Yorkshire team 1884. Back row, left to right: E. Peate, T. Emmett, H. Turner (scorer), W. Harris, J. Hunter. Middle row, left to right: J.T. Rawlin, F. Lee, L. Hall (captain), R. Peel, G. Ulyett. Front row, left to right: W. Bates and I. Grimshaw. The one notable absentee from this line-up is Lord Hawke, who succeeded Tom Emmett as county captain in 1883.

Two
The Golden Reign of Lord Hawke

Yorkshire team 1900. Back row, left to right: T. Mycroft (umpire), J.B. Wostinholm (secretary), W. Rhodes, J. Tunnicliffe, D. Hunter, L. Whitehead, J. Hoyland (scorer), A. Shaw (umpire). Middle row, left to right: E. Wainwright, T.L. Taylor, Lord Hawke (captain), S. Haigh, G.H. Hirst. Front row, left to right: J.T. Brown and D. Denton. Yorkshire were unbeaten champions having won 16 of their 28 matches and drawn the remaining 12. It was the first of a hat-trick of Championship wins under the all powerful Lord Hawke.

Martin Bladen Hawke was born at Willingham Rectory, Gainsborough in the county of Lincolnshire on 16 August 1860. He came from a family with a rich heritage: one of his ancestors was Admiral Lord Hawke, while his father was Rector of Willingham. The young Hawke received the classic education: Eton and then Cambridge University. He made his first appearance for Yorkshire in 1881 and assumed the captaincy of the county in 1883, a position he held until 1910. As a cricketer, he was a hard-hitting middle order batsman and although not in the highest class, he scored 16,749 runs in first-class cricket at 20.15. He played in five Test matches and captained England in four of those games as well as touring North America, India, South Africa, Australia, the West Indies and Argentina. His prime concerns, despite all his achievements, lay with Yorkshire CCC. It was Hawke who introduced the Yorkshire cap and colours and he is credited with the decision to institute winter pay for players. In 1898 he succeeded Michael Ellison as the club's President and remained in charge of virtually all the county's affairs until his death in 1938. His contribution to Yorkshire, and indeed English cricket, is awesome.

David Hunter, Yorkshire's regular wicket-keeper between 1888 and 1909, succeeded his brother Joseph behind the wickets. Tall for a wicket-keeper, *Wisden* described him as 'quiet, sure, neat'. A gritty right-hand batsman of limited ability, he shared a last wicket stand of 148 with Lord Hawke against Kent in June 1898, a county record until 1982. Outside cricket, he was a man with a wide range of interests including breeding canaries and pigeons, boxing and clog dancing.

George Herbert Hirst, a young all-round cricketer from Kirkheaton, near Huddersfield, made his first appearance for the county in 1891. A shortish, but strongly built figure, he was a forcing right-handed batsman and a high-class left-arm swerve bowler, destructive in helpful conditions. Over the next thirty years lay a golden career for one of cricket's truly great all-rounders.

Robert (Bobby) Moorhouse was a brave right-hand batsman, fearless against the quick bowlers of the age. He was never a prolific batsman but in a career for Yorkshire, which spanned twelve summers, he scored over 5,000 runs including three hundreds. He stood up to the mighty Surrey bowlers Tom Richardson and Lockwood in one famous encounter on a poor wicket at Bramall Lane, Sheffield, in 1893. He made match scores of 39 and 38 not out in Yorkshire's innings totals of 98 and 91 – modest perhaps, but on a wicket 'where the ball took great pieces of turf away with it' this was a fine achievement. After his playing days, he coached at Sedbergh School. He died at his native Berry Brow, Huddersfield, on 7 January 1921.

Edward (Ted) Wainwright, born at Tinsley, Sheffield, in 1865, played a vital all-round role in the Yorkshire team of the 1890s. He was a useful middle-late order right-hand batsman, good enough to score 1,000 runs in a season on three occasions, his top score being 228 against Surrey at The Oval in 1899. He bowled right-arm medium pace and took 100 wickets in a season five times during his career, made five Test appearances for England and toured Australia with Stoddart's team in 1897/98. Wainwright coached for many summers at Shrewsbury School, where for some time his assistant coach was one Neville Cardus, who would later immortalise his times and memories of Ted in his book *Close of Play*. The craggy all-rounder from Sheffield died at his home on 28 October 1919, after a long illness.

Yorkshire team 1893. Back row, left to right: E. Wainwright, J. Tunnicliffe, H. Turner (scorer), D. Hunter, R. Moorhouse. Middle row, left to right: G. Ulyett, F.S. Jackson, Lord Hawke (captain), A. Sellers, R. Peel. Front row, left to right: J.T. Brown, E. Smith, and G.H. Hirst. Yorkshire secured the county's first 'official' Championship title with twelve victories from their sixteen matches played.

Joseph Thomas Mounsey was a hard working middle order batsman who played over ninety matches for Yorkshire between 1891 and 1897. A brave cricketer, he stood firm along with Moorhouse on a savage Sheffield wicket against Surrey's bowling in 1893 to score 27 not out. His contribution helped Yorkshire to victory by 58 runs. He made his highest score for the county in 1896, a stubborn 64 against Hampshire at Southampton following his first innings' 55. Both knocks helped save Yorkshire from a crushing defeat after Hampshire's E.G. Wynyard had made 268. In 1899 Mounsey became coach at Charterhouse School, a position he held until 1927 after which he served as groundsman until 1938. This much respected player passed away in the spring of 1949.

John Thomas Brown of Driffield was a short, stylish batsman who scored 16,380 runs for Yorkshire with 23 hundreds. He batted in the middle order during the county's first Championship season of 1893; in the decade ahead he moved up the order to form, with John Tunnicliffe, an outstanding opening partnership, the first of Yorkshire's great top order combinations. He died at the early age of only 35 on 4 November 1904, from heart failure, congestion of the brain and asthma.

John Tunnicliffe was born at Lowtown, Pudsey in 1866. He was a tall (6 ft 2 in) right-handed opening batsman and exceptional slip fielder. 'Long John' as he became known, tempered his youthful aggressive style of batting to become the dour, stubborn, and sometimes tediously slow foil for his pugnacious opening partner Brown. Tunnicliffe's limitations meant that he was overlooked by England despite 20,310 first-class runs between 1891 and 1907, to say nothing of the 695 catches. Following his retirement, he became coach at Clifton College and later became a committee member at Gloucestershire CCC. A highly respected man, he was also a Methodist lay preacher.

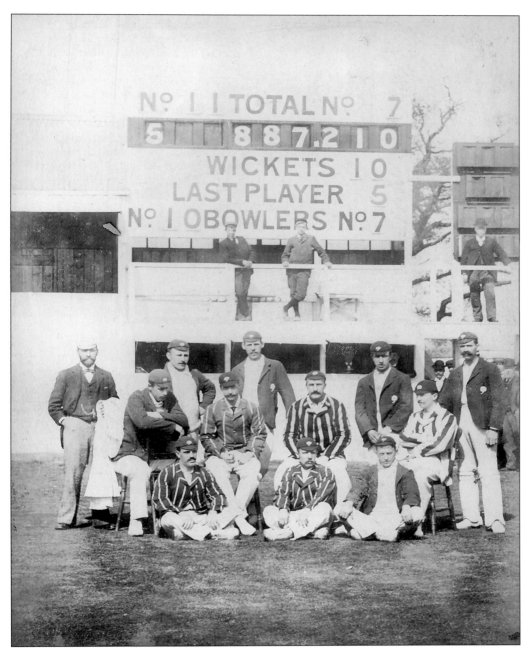

The Yorkshire team of 1896, underneath the Edgbaston scoreboard displaying their record-breaking innings total of 887 against Warwickshire. Back row, left to right: R.G. Barlow (umpire), G.H. Hirst, E. Wainwright, D. Denton, D. Hunter. Middle row, left to right: J. Tunnicliffe, F.S. Jackson, Lord Hawke (captain), F.W. Milligan. Front row, left to right: J.T. Brown, R. Peel and R. Moorhouse. The Yorkshire total took 11 hours to complete and included centuries from Jackson (117), Wainwright (126), Lord Hawke (166), and Bobby Peel (210 not out). Their total remains a County Championship record, but despite the size of Yorkshire's 'mountain', Warwickshire escaped with a draw.

The successor to Edmund Peate as Yorkshire's slow left-arm bowler was Bobby Peel who played his first match for the county in 1882. Summer upon summer, Peel bowled an immaculate length, collecting 100 wickets or more in seven seasons. In 1896 he also scored 1,193 runs to complete the 'double' of 1,000 runs and 100 wickets for the first, and only time during his long career. He seemed at the height of his powers, when in 1897, he appeared on the field after a heavy drinking session still far from sober. Lord Hawke instantly dismissed him and suspension for the remainder of the season soon followed – Peel's career was at an end. An excellent cover-point fielder and a good batsman, Peel played twenty times for England taking 101 wickets and scoring 427 runs at 14.72, despite collecting a 'pair' in successive Tests against Australia in 1894/95. He scored over 12,000 runs in his career and picked up 1,775 wickets.

David Denton, the slightly built but stylish, right-handed batsman from Wakefield, made his debut for the county in 1894. An attacking batsman and brilliant fielder, he was nicknamed 'Lucky' as he often gave the bowlers a chance to claim his wicket. Strong wrists meant that he was a powerful player of the cut shot. In 1905 he scored 2,258 runs, thus becoming the second Yorkshire cricketer to pass 2,000 runs in a season, George Hirst having first achieved the feat the previous season. His 36,440 career runs included over 33,000 for Yorkshire. After his retirement in 1920, he umpired at first-class level from 1925 to 1930 and, for a time, acted as county scorer. Without question one of Yorkshire's premier batsmen, he passed away on 16 February 1950 at his home in Wakefield.

Chesterfield, August 1898. J.T. Brown and John Tunnicliffe are in front of the historic scoreboard which displays to the cricket world their record-breaking opening stand of 554 against Derbyshire. Together they had scaled new heights, in 1897 sharing an opening partnership of 378 against Sussex at Bramall Lane, but at Chesterfield reaching the summit of their many great achievements together. Tunnicliffe batted 5 hours, 5 minutes for his 243 whilst Brown's innings of 300 occupied 5 minutes longer. Derbyshire were crushed by an overwhelming innings and 387 runs.

Alfred William Pullin, who wrote under the pseudonym of Old Ebor was, together with Revd R.S. Holmes, one of Yorkshire's earliest cricket writers. As a travelling journalist he averaged two columns a day on cricket for the *Yorkshire Post* and *Yorkshire Evening Post,* and covered rugby football in the winter (he never missed a rugby international involving England for nearly forty years). He travelled the length and breath of the country with the Yorkshire team; Lord Hawke called him the 'non-playing member of the side'. He wrote four books on cricket: *Alfred Shaw, Cricketer: his Career and Reminiscences* and *Talks with Old English Cricketers*, an expansion of perhaps his most significant work, *Talks with Old Yorkshire Cricketers*, published in 1898. This brought to the public's attention the plight of old cricketing heroes like John Thewlis, long since forgotten by the county club, living their later years in abject poverty. His *History of Yorkshire County Cricket 1903-1923* was published in 1924. He devoted his life to sport and it is perhaps fitting that he passed away whilst travelling to Lord's to watch the 1934 England v Australia Test match.

The dismissal of Bobby Peel in 1897 left Yorkshire without a proven left-arm spin bowler at the beginning of the 1898 season. That problem was quickly resolved with the arrival of Wilfred Rhodes, another product of Kirkheaton; like his team-mate George Hirst, he batted right-handed and bowled left. Born on 29 October 1877, Rhodes made a remarkable entry into first-class cricket at the age of 20 taking seven for 24 in his first Championship appearance against Somerset, thirteen for 45 in the match. By the end of that first season, he had captured 154 wickets at 14.60 each. His rise was indeed rapid; his 1898 performances won him instant acclaim with selection as one of *Wisden's* Cricketers of the Year in the 1899 edition. A rich jewel in cricket's golden crown had entered the world stage.

The Yorkshire team at Bramall Lane 1898. Back row, left to right: S. Haigh, W. Rhodes, R. Moorhouse, J.B. Wostinholm (secretary), D. Denton, J.T. Brown, D. Hunter. Front row, left to right: G.H. Hirst, F.S. Jackson, Lord Hawke (captain), E. Wainwright and J. Tunnicliffe. County Champions by a comfortable margin from Middlesex, this side possessed great all-round ability.

'Long John' Tunnicliffe was a master slip fieldsman and ranks among the best in the history of the game in that specialist position. He took 7 catches in a match on two occasions, both against Leicestershire in 1897 and then 1900. He took 50 or more catches in a season four times, none better than his tally of 70 in 1906, a Yorkshire total equalled only by Philip Sharpe in 1962.

A sparse crowd at Park Avenue, Bradford, in the early years of the twentieth century. Perhaps the most Yorkshire, and indeed Victorian of all the county's grounds, Park Avenue was opened in July 1880 and from the outset housed both cricket and rugby. The venue was soon established as one of Yorkshire's three major venues, together with Sheffield and Leeds.

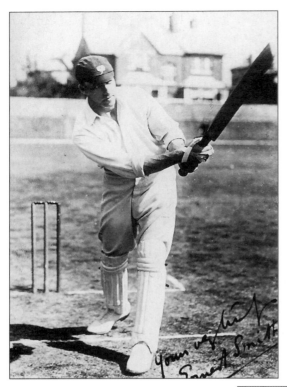

Ernest Smith, born on 19 October 1869 in Morley, was a more than useful amateur cricketer. He made his debut for Yorkshire in 1888 and continued to play, on and off, until 1907. His duties as a schoolmaster meant that his appearances each summer were restricted, but he was an attacking right-hand batsman and right-arm fast bowler and he often led Yorkshire in Hawke's absence. He averaged just over 20 with the bat for the county and took 248 wickets at 25.31 each.

Francis Stanley Jackson (later Rt Hon F.S. Jackson), was born in Leeds on 21 November 1870. Jackson packed more than most into his lifetime. He played cricket for Harrow, Cambridge University and as an amateur for Yorkshire between 1890 and 1907. An attacking right-hand batsman and fluent right-arm fast medium bowler, he did the 'double' only once in 1898, but was rarely able to play a full first-class season. He hit 1,000 runs in a season ten times. He saw active service in the Boer War and after his cricketing days were over, he became a well-known politician for Howdenshire between 1915 and 1926. In his role as Governor of Bengal from 1927 to 1932, he narrowly escaped assassination. He was President of the MCC in 1921 and Yorkshire President after Lord Hawke from 1939 to 1947. Stanley Jackson died on 9 March 1947 in Knightsbridge, London, aged 76, having failed to recover after being knocked down by a taxi.

Schofield Haigh was a right-arm fast medium bowler from Berry Brow, Huddersfield, who first played for the county in 1895. Throughout a long career, he perhaps lingered in the shadow of George Hirst and Wilfred Rhodes but his record with the ball remains exceptional: 2,012 wickets in first-class cricket at 15.94, 1,876 of those for his county as well as over 11,000 runs. He played eleven times for England and following his retirement went to coach at Winchester College. His son Reg became President of the Huddersfield Cricket League in 1961 and also served on the Yorkshire CCC Committee. Outside cricket, Schofield Haigh's passion was billiards. The Yorkshire cricket writer A.W. Pullin described Haigh as 'the sunshine of the Yorkshire XI'.

A newcomer to the Yorkshire ranks in 1900 was William Arthur Irving Washington, a stylish left-handed batsman from Wombwell in South Yorkshire. Apart from an innings of 86 against Hampshire at Hull, Irving did little of note in his first season of county cricket and failed to win a first team place at all in 1901. However, in the wet summer of 1902, he scored over 1,000 runs for the county and a bright future seemed assured but no sooner had the season ended, then so did Washington's career. Tuberculosis drove him to South Africa to seek recovery, but he was destined not to play again for Yorkshire. He died in 1927 at the age of 47; by then his nephews Roy and Norman Kilner had both enjoyed long and successful county careers.

A large crowd at Bramall Lane. Opened in 1855, the ground became the home of Yorkshire cricket until Headingley, welcomed first-class fixtures in the early 1890s. The Sheffield ground established a reputation for its knowledgeable crowds, which were sometimes hostile but often also full of humour and fun. They valued their low wages and were concise in their criticism of players or team if they felt they weren't getting their money's worth. In 1902 the ground staged its one and only Test match, when Australia beat England by 143 runs. Clem Hill scored 119 for the tourists and Victor Trumper blazed his way to 62 in 50 minutes.

How the mighty fall – Somerset inflicted Yorkshire's only Championship defeat in the summer of 1901, so ending an unbeaten run of 48 games which had started in August 1899. Beginning their second innings 238 runs in arrears, Somerset ran up 630 with hundreds from Palairet (173), Braund (107), and Phillips (122). Yorkshire, still bewildered by Somerset's onslaught, were swept aside for 113, losing the match by an enormous 279 runs – a result Yorkshiremen found hard to comprehend. Back in Taunton, Sammy Woods and his men were heroes.

Headingley, Leeds, was officially opened on 27 May 1890 and Yorkshire first used the ground in 1891. Despite problems with the wicket in its first few years, Headingley quickly became an established venue for Yorkshire cricket. Popular with spectators, huge crowds were commonplace like the one in this photograph from around the turn of the century. In 1899, the ground staged its first Test match and by 1903, the Yorkshire Committee had made the decision to leave Bramall Lane and move their offices to Leeds.

The 1902 Yorkshire team. Back row, left to right: W.A.I. Washington, D. Hunter, J. Tunnicliffe, L. Whitehead, W. Rhodes. Middle row, left to right: G.H. Hirst, F.S. Jackson, Lord Hawke (captain), T.L. Taylor, S. Haigh. Front row, left to right: J.T. Brown and D. Denton.

Another view of Headingley under Edwardian skies, as Schofield Haigh and George Hirst gather further runs against Sussex. In Yorkshire's 1902 fixture with the southern county at Leeds, snow and rain interrupted the match which predictably ended as a draw; the sun didn't always shine during the Golden Age of cricket!

Charles Henry Grimshaw first played for Yorkshire in 1904 and enjoyed an extended run in the first XI in the Championship season of 1905. An opening left-handed batsman, he failed to make a significant breakthrough, scoring just over 450 runs for the county at 18.20 in 1905. Despite playing for Yorkshire until 1908, he did little to further his playing career. He continued to play for Bowling Old Lane in the Yorkshire Council and Bradford League and in 1915, made a record score of 230 not out in the Priestley Cup against Great Horton.

Frederick Charles Toone succeeded Joseph Wostinholm as County Secretary in 1903, having established his reputation during a five year spell at Leicestershire CCC. He remained in office at Yorkshire for twenty-seven years, during which time the county membership doubled. Toone revised many of the club rules, as well as organising the players benefits and editing the county yearbook. He managed the MCC tours to Australia in 1920, 1924, and 1928 and was knighted for his services to cricket. He died in June 1930 at the age of 62.

Lord Hawke (centre) with two of the county stalwarts: John Tunnicliffe (left), often considered as Hawke's right hand man and Tom Lancelot Taylor (right), an amateur middle order right-hand batsman, who represented Cambridge University from 1897 to 1900 and made his debut for Yorkshire in 1899. Taylor hit 1,000 runs for the county three times, his best being 1,517 runs at 37.92 in 1902. Much later in life he was honoured with the Presidency of Yorkshire CCC.

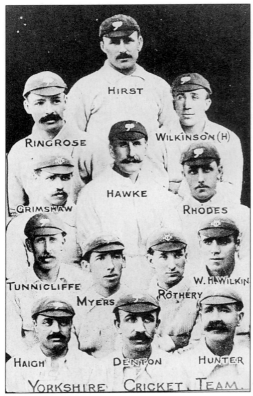

HIRST

RINGROSE   WILKINSON (H)

HAWKE

GRIMSHAW   RHODES

TUNNICLIFFE   W. H. WILKIN

MYERS   ROTHERY

HAIGH   DENTON   HUNTER

YORKSHIRE CRICKET TEAM.

The Yorkshire team of 1905, in an unusual head and shoulders line-up. The County Champions that year, they regained the crown with 18 wins from their 28 matches after two years off the top. Still greatly reliant on the likes of Hirst, Tunnicliffe, Denton, Haigh and the youthful Rhodes, the side began to take on board the next generation of Yorkshire cricketers: James Rothery, Henry and W.H. Wilkinson, Grimshaw and Myers. They were amongst a group of hopefuls who never quite made the grade.

William Ringrose was a regular member of the Yorkshire Championship winning team during the summer of 1905. He made his debut for the club in 1901 as a left-handed batsman and right-arm fast bowler but his health broke down in 1906, and further injury brought his career to an end in 1913. He played most of his cricket in Scotland from 1907 onwards, but after his injury he returned to his native county and served as Yorkshire's scorer from 1923 until the outbreak of the Second World War.

George Hirst was at the height of his powers as an all-rounder during the seasons 1904, 1905 and 1906. In each of these he achieved the 'double' with consummate ease. In 1904 he became the first Yorkshire player to pass 2,000 runs in a season in all matches, not to mention 132 wickets. In 1905 he again passed the 2,000 run mark and completed another 'double' with 110 wickets. His five first-class hundreds that summer included a 7 hour innings of 341 against Leicestershire, a score which remains the highest individual innings for Yorkshire. In 1906 he rewrote the record books with perhaps the greatest domestic all-round performance of them all by accomplishing the 'double' 'double', making 2,385 runs at 45.86 and taking 208 wickets at 16.50, at the tender age of 35!

Benjamin Wilson, born at Scarborough in December 1879, was a dour, right-handed batsman who made his county debut in 1906 but did not join the regular first team ranks until 1909. Tall and powerful, he often took a long time to gather his runs. His best season was 1914, when he scored 1,608 runs at 32.74. His only double century also came that season: 208 against Sussex at Bradford. He coached at Harrow, York and in New Zealand.

Hubert Myers (left) and William Wilkinson – two of Yorkshire's 'nearly' players. Myers, a right-handed batsman and medium pace bowler, made his county debut in 1901. His potential was never quite fulfilled and he left the Yorkshire side after the 1910 season, emigrating to Tasmania where he played cricket for the island and became coach of the Tasmanian Cricket Association. W.H. Wilkinson was a hard-hitting, left-handed batsman from Rotherham, South Yorkshire, as well as being a noted soccer player for Sheffield United before his county cricket days. He enjoyed his best season in 1908, scoring 1,282 runs, but like Myers his form declined rapidly and he made his final appearance for Yorkshire in 1910. He became a stocktaker in Birmingham where he lived until his death in 1961 at the age of 80.

Sir Archibald Woollaston White. Born at Tickhill near Doncaster in 1877, he captained Yorkshire from 1912 until the outbreak of the First World War. Championship success came in his first season in charge, much to many people's surprise. White made his debut in 1908 and led Yorkshire occasionally in 1911 in the absence of E.J. Radcliffe. He was a positive skipper and only ordered defence as a last resort. His modest first-class record reads 1,471 runs at 14.42, with a highest score of 55 against Nottinghamshire at Headingley in 1920.

The Yorkshire team take the field at Trent Bridge in June 1912. The players from left to right: D. Denton, Sir Archibald White, B.B. Wilson, S. Haigh, M.W. Booth, H. Watson, G.W. Bayes, W. Rhodes, J. Tasker (hidden), and Alonzo Drake. The Yorkshire player not pictured is Roy Kilner. Champions again after a four year spell, this team had a blend of youthful potential and vast experience – a bright new era seemed imminent.

Alonzo Drake had a meteoric rise to fame in the Yorkshire side. After a successful debut in 1909, the left-handed all-rounder from Rotherham, latterly of Honley near Huddersfield, became a regular member of the county line-up. In 1911 he scored over 1,000 runs and in 1913 performed the 'double' by hitting 1,056 runs and taking 116 wickets. He reserved his greatest efforts though for the season of 1914, when his 158 wicket tally for the summer included a stunning bowling display against Somerset at Weston-Super-Mare. On a poor wicket he took fifteen for 51 in the match, including all ten of Somerset's second innings wickets to become the first Yorkshire cricketer to capture 'all ten' in a first-class fixture. The coming of war brought a premature close to the career of this giant, obsessive cricketer. Rejected by the military during the war on health grounds, he passed away on 14 February 1919 at the age of only 34. In a brief, but dazzling career he scored 4,816 runs and took 480 wickets.

Cricketers down the ages have become well versed in finding activities to amuse themselves whilst bad light or rain holds up play. Here several members of the Yorkshire team relax over a game of whist at Tunbridge Wells in July 1913, during their match with Kent. The players from left to right: R. Kilner, G.W. Bayes (looking out of the picture), T.J. Birtles, J. Hoyland (scorer), A. Drake and D. Denton.

The Golden Age of Edwardian cricket came to a sudden and tragic end in August 1914 with the beginning of the First World War. Several members of the county staff and former players saw active service, and Lieutenant-Colonel Harold Kaye was one of those. Kaye made only eighteen appearances for Yorkshire in 1907 and 1908, although he played for the Yorkshire Gentlemen for many years and later became a member of the Yorkshire CCC Committee. During the war he served in France and Belgium; in 1916 he was awarded the DSO and MC and was mentioned in despatches on three occasions. He lived long after the horror in Europe, right through the Second World War, before passing away in November 1953 at his Wakefield home.

Eric Rockley Wilson, born at Bolsterstone near Sheffield, in March 1879. Rockley Wilson was the youngest of five brothers, a sound lower order right-handed batsman and a right-arm slow bowler of immaculate length and flight. He made his debut for Yorkshire in 1899, but only played occasionally until 1902, not playing again until 1914. A schoolmaster at Winchester, he answered Yorkshire's call for help during the August holidays after the First World War. He proved so successful that he was selected as vice-captain for England in the ill fated 1920/21 tour of Australia, which England lost 5-0. During the war, Wilson was commissioned into the Rifle Brigade, qualified as a Turkish interpreter and served in Palestine. His commanding officer described him as one of the untidiest subalterns he had ever known.

Members of the Leeds Pals battalion enjoy a break from the war effort at Headingley in June 1915, when a specially arranged fixture between the Pals and a Yorkshire XI took place. The match was used as something of an experimental trial for the use of 29 inch stumps and eight ball overs. The Yorkshire XI won by a comfortable 81 run margin.

Roy Kilner, a cheerful young left-handed batsman and slow left-arm bowler from Wombwell near Barnsley, made his Yorkshire debut in 1911. He showed great promise in 1913, scoring over 1,500 runs and in 1914, made more than 1,300. Corporal Kilner was injured in France shortly before 'zero hour' on 1 July 1916 when countless thousands of soldiers were slaughtered. One of the many men who lost their lives during the Somme offensive was Major Booth, Kilner's close friend and Yorkshire team-mate. Kilner made a full recovery from his injury and went on to forge a successful county cricket career during the 1920s.

Major William Booth, born in Pudsey on 10 December 1886, first played for Yorkshire in 1908. He quickly blossomed into one of the best all-rounders in England. A right-handed batsman and medium fast bowler, he demanded a regular first team place from 1910 onwards; in the seasons to 1914 he passed 1,000 runs twice and took 100 wickets on three occasions. His best return came in 1913 when he took 181 wickets at 18.46 each; that summer he also completed the 'double' for Yorkshire. He toured South Africa in 1913/14 with the MCC and played his only two Test matches for England. Shortly after dawn on the morning of 1 July 1916, Lieutenant Booth led his Number 10 machine gun team 'over the top'. He was amongst the first of thousands to lose their lives that fateful day. It took nine months to recover his body and he was only identified then by an MCC cigarette case which was found in his pocket. He is buried in Serre Road cemetery, France. His sister refused to accept her brother's death and kept Booth's room in their family cottage undisturbed for over 40 years in the hope of his return. In his short but successful career, Major (his christian name, not rank in the army) captured 603 first-class wickets and scored 4,753 runs.

Three
Inter-War Dominance

Yorkshire team, 1925. From left to right: A. Waddington, G.G. Macaulay, R. Kilner,
E. Robinson, P. Holmes, M. Leyland, W. Rhodes, A. Dolphin, Major A.W. Lupton (captain),
H. Sutcliffe and E. Oldroyd. Champions for the fourth successive year, they were unbeaten in
the process, winning 21 of their 32 matches.

Herbert Sutcliffe – a young, determined and technically sound batsman who made an immediate impression in the Yorkshire side of 1919. Born in Summerbridge, near Harrogate in 1894, Sutcliffe played for the Yorkshire Second XI in 1914 and learned much of his cricket at Pudsey. A right-hand batsman, he possessed an unperturbable temperament and a good defence which became tighter and more difficult to penetrate as the years passed. A fierce driver of the ball on the off side, he also played the hook shot with a dismissive air. He started the 1919 season in the Yorkshire middle order, but by the end of June he was opening the batting alongside Percy Holmes. The successors to Brown and Tunnicliffe had been found. Herbert Sutcliffe's career spanned the inter-war period, and he reached heights as a batsman that few of his contemporaries could match.

George Hirst batting against the MCC at Lord's in 1919. His innings of 180 not out was the 54th century of his staggering career and helped Yorkshire escape with a draw. Hirst's career finally came to a close in 1921 when, at the age of 50, he bid farewell to take up a coaching engagement at Eton where he stayed until 1938. In first-class cricket, Hirst made 36,356 runs and took 2,742 wickets. No fewer than nineteen times he hit 1,000 runs in a season, going on to 2,000 on three occasions. In fifteen seasons he topped 100 wickets and once exceeded 200. In all, he performed the 'double' fourteen times.

On 2 July 1919, Yorkshire introduced Abraham Waddington into the side for the match with Derbyshire. This left-arm fast medium bowler made an immediate impact by taking four for 26 in 26 overs. By the close of that season he had picked up 100 wickets at 18.74 each. His best season was 1920 when his tally of wickets reached 140, but after 1925 his form declined following a shoulder injury and he left the county at the close of the 1927 season. A man of fiery temperament, he often sparked controversy and was a volatile character in many ways; but in his relatively short career his rhythmical, flowing left-arm deliveries brought him 852 first-class wickets at 19.75.

Arthur Dolphin became Yorkshire's regular wicket-keeper in 1910 following the retirement of David Hunter. A native of Wilsden, near Bradford, Dolphin was generally regarded as one of the best keepers of the age but played only once for England during the disastrous tour of Australia in 1920/21. After his playing career, he became a first-class umpire. Dolphin passed away on 23 October 1942.

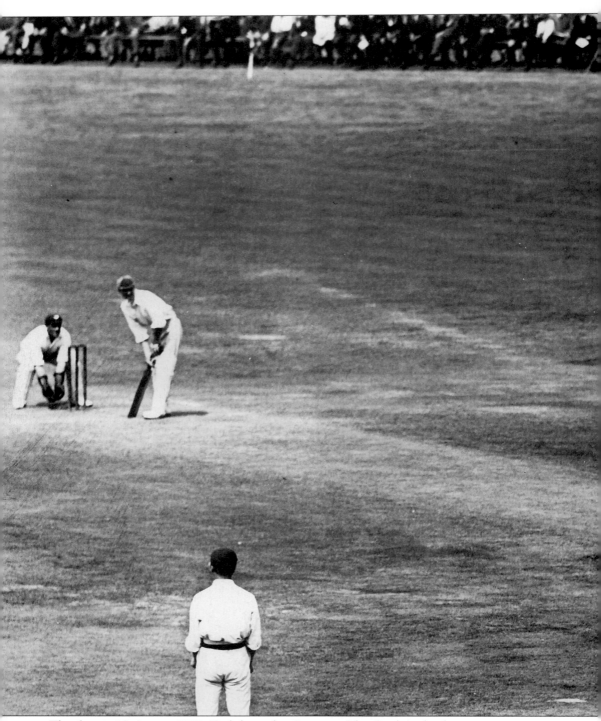

The date is 12 August 1919. Yorkshire play Surrey at The Oval in the first post-war summer which saw an experimental two-day Championship competition. Abe Waddington's left-arm bowling (pictured in action above) was instrumental in Yorkshire securing their tenth county

title since 1893. The game with Surrey ended as a draw, although in their first encounter earlier in the season at Bradford, Yorkshire had secured a ten wicket win.

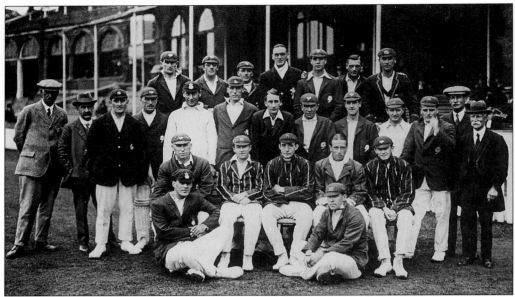

Yorkshire v Rest of England at The Oval in September 1919. Yorkshire won 12 of their 26 Championship fixtures that summer which were played over a two-day duration, an experiment which proved hugely unpopular. The traditional three-day Championship game returned in 1920. The Rest of England crushed Yorkshire by ten wickets in The Oval match to quickly dispel any thoughts of invincibility in the White Rose camp.

Edgar Oldroyd made his debut for Yorkshire in 1910, although in those pre-war days he was primarily a defensive batsman. During the 1920s his style of batting became much less restrained and he developed into a strong, hard-hitting middle order batsman. His best season was 1922, when he scored 1,690 runs including five centuries. He retired in 1931, at the age of 42, having registered 15,925 first-class runs at an average of 35.15. Still a model of consistency he played for Pudsey St Lawrence, where he opened the batting with a future Yorkshire batting star by the name of Len Hutton. Oldroyd lived in Harrogate before retiring to Falmouth in the early 1960s. He died in Truro, Cornwall, in 1964.

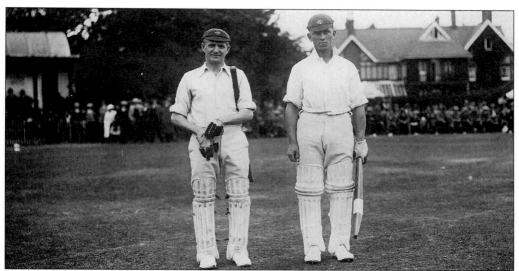

A young Morris Leyland (right), whose first name was nearly always spelt Maurice, alongside stalwart Yorkshire cricketer Emmott Robinson. Robinson, an all-rounder from Keighley, came into the Yorkshire side in 1919 at the age of 35, when most cricketers are thinking of retirement. He stayed on to become a regular part of the team until 1931. A right-hand batsman, he bowled at an accurate medium pace and despite his age was an excellent fielder with a keen tactical knowledge of the game. Leyland, born at Harrogate in 1900, made his county debut in 1920, but it took until 1923 for him to be considered a regular member of the Yorkshire side. A forcing left-handed batsman, he passed 1,000 runs for the first time in Championship cricket in 1923, a sequence which continued unbroken to 1939. A broad shouldered, oak-like man, he was a vital member of the Yorkshire XI until the outbreak of the Second World War.

George Gibson Macaulay was a fiery, hostile medium pace bowler from Thirsk, devoted to Yorkshire's cause. He made his debut in 1920, took his first haul of 100 wickets in 1921 and climbed to the peak of his career in 1925, becoming only the third Yorkshire bowler to claim 200 wickets in a season. He played eight times for England and made a remarkable entry into Test cricket, taking a wicket with his first ball (G.A.L. Hearne) against South Africa in Cape Town on the 1922/23 tour. He died whilst serving with the Royal Air Force in December 1940, having caught pneumonia when on duty in the Shetland Islands and was buried at Lerwick Cemetery.

Cec Tyson, born at Brompton-by-Sawdon near Scarborough in 1889. Tyson had a remarkable, if brief career for Yorkshire. On his debut for the county against Hampshire at Southampton in 1921, at the age of 32, he hit 100 not out in the first innings and followed that with 80 not out in the second. Yet he played only two more games for the Club as payment terms could not be agreed upon. An exceptional left-handed batsman, Tyson made two further first-class appearances, not for Yorkshire, but for Glamorgan in the 1926 season. He died in 1940 leaving behind a career record for Yorkshire which read: 3 innings, 232 runs at an average of 77.33.

A group of the all-conquering Yorkshire side of the early 1920s, gathered here for an informal team photo. From left to right: N. Kilner, A. Waddington, M. Leyland, E. Oldroyd, E. Robinson and P. Holmes. Beaten only twice in thirty Championship matches, Yorkshire regained the Championship crown from Middlesex (Champions in 1920 and 1921) in 1922.

The season of 1922 was the first for Yorkshire under the leadership of Geoffrey Wilson, who captained the side until 1924. His record as skipper was outstanding as the Championship title returned to the county in the three seasons of his leadership. A right-handed batsman, Wilson scored 1,801 first-class runs at a modest 16.22, although he was an excellent cover fielder. His record as captain might have ranked alongside that of Lord Hawke and Brian Sellers, but for a display of ill-discipline by the side in a match against Middlesex in 1924 after which Wilson resigned from the captaincy.

YORKSHIRE'S CHAMPIONSHIP. By TOM WEBSTER

G-R-R-R-R

THE COUNTY CHAMPIONSHIP

THE YORKSHIRE TYKE

(NOTE. A MUZZLE HAS BEEN USED BEFORE BUT VERY FEW HAD THE ABILITY TO APPLY IT THIS YEAR.)

Tom Webster's 1922 cartoon of Yorkshire supremacy was emphasised to even greater effect in the summer of 1923, with the White Rose county winning 25 of their 32 Championship fixtures (a 78 per cent success rate and still a county record). They were beaten only once, by Nottinghamshire, and then only by three runs.

The powerful Yorkshire side of 1923 and 1924: the dominant force in county cricket during the first half of the new decade. Back row, left to right: M. Leyland, G.G. Macaulay, A. Waddington, N. Kilner, H. Sutcliffe, W. Ringrose (scorer). Middle row, left to right: A. Dolphin, W. Rhodes, E.R. Wilson, G. Wilson (captain), E. Robinson, P. Holmes. Front row, left to right: E. Oldroyd and R. Kilner.

Percy Holmes, a short right-handed opening batsman, made his debut for the county in 1913 and immediately won a place in the side after the First World War. He formed, with Herbert Sutcliffe, one of the finest county opening partnerships in the history of the game. Holmes, an attractive batsman and a strong player of the square-cut and hook, was unfortunate to win only seven Test caps; his contemporaries Hobbs and Sutcliffe denied him further international honours. By the conclusion of his career in 1933, Holmes had compiled 26,220 runs for Yorkshire at 41.95 per innings. After his retirement he played for a time as a professional at Swansea and then coached at Scarborough College until 1959. He died on 3 September 1971 at Marsh, Huddersfield.

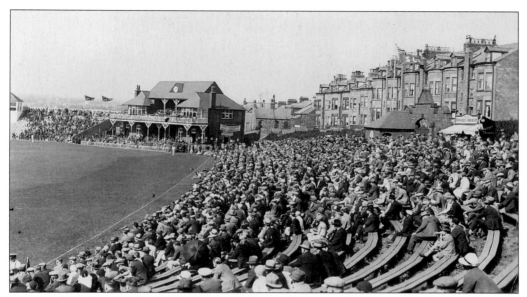

A view of the Popular Bank, North Marine Road, Scarborough – as crowded as ever between the wars. The ground has witnessed Yorkshire cricket since 1874. The Scarborough Festival began in Victorian times and enjoyed a huge popularity during the inter-war period. Each August and September, as today, cricket lovers gathered to meet old friends and enjoy the special atmosphere that Scarborough has to offer.

The Yorkshire side in 1925. Top row, left to right: A. Waddington, E. Robinson, P. Holmes. Second row, left to right: H. Sutcliffe, Major A.W. Lupton (captain), R. Kilner. Third row, left to right: G.G. Macaulay, W. Rhodes, A. Dolphin. Fourth row, left to right: M. Leyland and E. Oldroyd. This was the last 'Test free' summer of English cricket and, able to concentrate solely on domestic affairs, Yorkshire claimed their fourteenth 'official' Championship title since 1893.

The death of Roy Kilner in the spring of 1928 was a grievous loss, not only to the Yorkshire club, but also to cricket in every sense. Kilner had accepted an invitation by the Maharajah of Patiala to coach in India during the winter of 1927/28, but shortly before returning home he was taken ill and upon his arrival back in England, was rushed to the Kendray Fever Hospital near Barnsley. He died there on 5 April 1928, at the age of 37. His condition had been diagnosed as a form of enteric fever contracted on the Indian trip. In his career (1911-1927), Kilner scored 13,018 runs for Yorkshire and took 857 wickets, but he was remembered for much more than statistics alone. A warm and friendly character, he was loved by thousands and his death brought a show of affection from the public which was seldom seen.

The funeral procession for Roy Kilner through the packed Wombwell streets was led by the Wombwell Town Band, followed by local corps of the St John Ambulance Association and the Wombwell Church Lads Brigade. Never before had the small mining village witnessed such a gathering. Contemporary estimates suggested that well over 100,000 people attended Roy's funeral that sombre April day.

> Dear Mrs Kilner,
>
> I don't know you, but I knew your husband. and I have loved him as a typical Yorkshireman. an ideal Englishman. which means a _true gentleman_ I never spoke to him, but like many others. (Thousands) I am very very sad that we have lost _a man._ in every meaning of the word. I don't know what denomination he belonged to. but in my humble opinion, he was a real Christian character in his every day life. Would to God there were more men like him
>
> Yours Very Sincerely, a man in the street.

Roy Kilner's loss was felt by many: friends, family, and his Yorkshire colleagues who attended the funeral to say their own goodbyes. Thousands of others who followed Roy from afar, men and women alike, sent messages to the Kilner family expressing their own feelings. One such message which was signed simply, 'A man in the street', summed up the county's loss.

William Arthington Worsley (front left) leads Yorkshire out at Headingley during his time in charge of the side. He captained the county in 1928 and 1929. Worsley is accompanied by Yorkshire's senior pro Wilfred Rhodes, followed by E. Oldroyd, E. Robinson, P. Holmes, G.G. Macaulay, W. Barber and Frank Dennis (brother-in-law of Len Hutton and himself a right-arm fast medium bowler).

Wilf Barber came in to first-class cricket at the relatively late age of 25 in 1926. A defensive middle order/opening right-hand batsman, he was an above average out fielder, and he gave loyal service to the county until 1947. In his twenty years of service, Barber scored over 16,000 runs at 34.38 in first-class cricket. Later in life he became coach and groundsman at Ashville College near Harrogate, before his death in September 1968.

The Yorkshire team in 1928 at Scarborough. From left to right: E. Robinson, E. Oldroyd, G.G. Macaulay, W.A. Worsley (captain), A. Wood, M. Leyland, W. Rhodes, W. Barber, F. Dennis, H. Sutcliffe and P. Holmes. That season the county finished fourth in the Championship as their Red Rose rivals from across the Pennines claimed their third successive title.

A tall, bespectacled right-arm fast medium bowler made his debut for Yorkshire in the 1929 match against Oxford University. William (Bill) Eric Bowes took two for 28 in Oxford's first innings and in all, took 45 wickets for the club that season at a respectable 19.22. Not an out and out quick in the mould of contemporaries Harold Larwood and Gubby Allen, Bowes had a tremendous control of length and both in and out swing. He didn't win a regular first team place until 1932, but quickly became one of Sellers' main weapons.

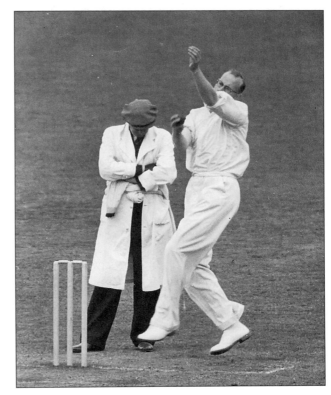

Arthur Mitchell (left) and Wilf Barber walking out to bat for Yorkshire against MCC at Scarborough in 1929. Mitchell made his first team debut in 1922 but didn't become a regular member of the side until 1928. His team-mates gave him the nickname of 'Ticker' after his habit of talking whilst play was in progress. An outstanding close to the wicket fielder, he was to become an integral part of Brian Sellers' all-conquering side of the 1930s.

Alan Theodore Barber, born Ecclesall, Sheffield, in 1905, succeeded William Worsley as Yorkshire captain in 1930. A fine all-round sportsman, Barber captained Oxford University at both cricket and soccer and was also a golf blue. He made his debut for Yorkshire in 1929 and in all, made forty-two appearances as an amateur leading the county to third place in the Championship in 1930, his only season as skipper. He gave up the game to teach at Ludgrove School, one of the leading preparatory schools in the country and eventually became headmaster there until retiring in 1973. He passed away on 10 March 1985.

At the age of 52, Wilfred Rhodes' magnificent career finally came to an end in the summer of 1930. His achievements left an impregnable mark on cricket's record book. Twenty-three times he took over 100 wickets in a season, three times going on to 200 or more. Twenty times he passed 1,000 runs in a season and in sixteen summers he did the 'double'. His final tally of first class runs was 39,969; add to that 4,204 first class wickets and you have the record of a monumental cricketer. After his retirement he became coach at Harrow School, passing on his skills to mortals far less gifted than himself. Despite failing sight in his later years, Rhodes still attended county matches and maintained a close interest in the game which he had dominated for over thirty years right up until his death in July 1973.

The Yorkshire team at Scarborough in 1931. Left to right: A. Wood, W. Barber, M. Leyland, G.G. Macaulay, H. Verity, W.E. Bowes, F.E. Greenwood (captain), H. Sutcliffe, E. Robinson, E. Oldroyd and P. Holmes. Yorkshire achieved their 15th Championship crown since 1893 with an overwhelming superiority that suggested a return to the dominant days of the 1920s.

The next of Yorkshire's spin wizards was Hedley Verity who followed Peate, Peel, and Rhodes as the left-arm spinner. He made his debut in 1930 playing in twelve matches, several alongside his distinguished mentor, Rhodes. Taller than Rhodes, Verity delivered the ball with greater speed, but his rise, like that of the Kirkheaton giant, was swift and decisive. As one great master departed so a new one emerged; the link had been made and a rich tradition was continued without fault or failing.

A year after Verity had captured all ten wickets in an innings against Warwickshire, Headingley again played host to an even greater piece of bowling from the young Hedley Verity in the match against Nottinghamshire in July 1932. Verity, who had taken two for 64 in the first innings, set about a total destruction of Nottinghamshire's second innings in the post lunch session of the final day. The visitors crumbled from 44 for no wicket to 67 all out – Verity claimed a hat-trick (Walker, Harris, and Gunn) and in two successive overs took two wickets with consecutive balls. Verity's final analysis of 10 wickets for 10 runs came in 19.4 overs of magical left-arm spin bowling.

YORKSHIRE v. NOTTINGHAMSHIRE, at Headingley.

NOTTINGHAMSHIRE.

		1st Innings		2nd Innings	
1.	Keeton b Rhodes	9	c Macaulay b Verity	21
2.	Shipstone b Macaulay	8	c Wood b Verity	21
3.	Walker c Barber b Bowes	36	c Macaulay b Verity	11
4.	A. W. Carr c Barber b Verity	0	c Barber b Verity	0
5.	Staples (A.) b Macaulay	3	c Macaulay b Verity	7
6.	Harris lbw b Leyland	35	c Holmes b Verity	0
7.	Gunn (G. V.) b Verity	31	lbw b Verity	0
8.	Lilley not out	46	not out	3
9.	Larwood b Leyland	48	c Sutcliffe b Verity	0
10.	Voce b Leyland	0	c Holmes b Verity	0
11.	Staples (S.) b Leyland	0	st Wood b Verity	0
	Extras b 8, lb 6, w 2, nb 2	18	Extras b 3, nb 1.	4
	Total	234	Total	67

Total runs at fall of each wicket

15 35 40, 46 67 120 159 233 233 234 | 44 47 51 63 63 63 64 64 67 67

Bowler	Overs	Maidens	Runs	W'kts	Overs	Maidens	Runs	W'kts
Bowes	31	9	55	1	5	0	19	0
Rhodes	28	8	49	1	...	...	...	
Verity	41	13	64	2	19.4	16	10	10
Macaulay	24	10	34	2	23	9	34	0
Leyland	8.2	3	14	4	...	...	...	...

Umpires : Messrs. Baldwin & Reeves.

Scorers : Messrs. Ringrose & Carlin.

Arthur Wood (right), walking out to bat with his Yorkshire skipper Brian Sellers at Scarborough in 1933, was a stocky and cheerful wicket-keeper batsman from Bradford. He became the first Yorkshire wicket-keeper to score 1,000 runs during one season, hitting 1,249 runs in 1935. He made his Test debut for England just a few days short of his 40th birthday in the famous Oval Test of 1938.

The Daily Mail   JUNE 17, 1932.

Sutcliffe 313, Holmes 224,

34-YEARS-OLD FEAT
ECLIPSED

Yorkshire Innings Win in Sight : Essex Failures

By H. J. HENLEY

The newspaper headlines proclaim the feat of Herbert Sutcliffe and Percy Holmes, who shared an opening partnership of 555 against Essex at Leyton in June 1932 to overhaul Brown and Tunnicliffe's 554 record from 1898. The pair batted for 7 hours and 25 minutes, Holmes scoring 224 not out and Sutcliffe 313 (his career best) before being dismissed. Their partnership remains in the record books as the landmark to which all other county opening pairs aspire.

Above: Nervous young fans wait patiently for the signature of Brian Sellers. Appointed Yorkshire captain in 1933, Sellers from Keighley was a natural leader. A tall, strong batsman he led by example and was a brilliant close fielder. He inherited a side with vast talent and he led them with a firmness and purpose that few other counties could match.

Left: Cyril Turner, another born in Roy Kilner's home village of Wombwell, was a left-handed batsman who bowled right-arm medium pace. A modest man, he served the county for over thirty years as a player, a coach, and a scorer. A superb close to the wicket fieldsman, he was a team man in every sense of the word. He scored 1,000 runs in a season only once (1934), but chipped in with important contributions throughout his long career such as his fine all-round performance against Derbyshire in 1937, when he scored 81 not out and took five for 45 and three for 63 with the ball. He looked after the boy prodigy Hutton when Len first came into the Yorkshire side and was responsible in later years for introducing Fred Trueman to the county.

Herbert Sutcliffe narrowly escapes being run out by a fine return from A.H. Bakewell in the Yorkshire v Rest of England game at The Oval in September 1933. Sutcliffe's anxious batting partner is Maurice Leyland. Wally Hammond looks on and Ames is the wicket-keeper. Despite scores of 114 not out and 41 from Sutcliffe in the match, Yorkshire were beaten by an innings.

Surrey's E.A. Watts is caught by G.G. Macaulay off Hedley Verity for 0 (to complete a pair) against Yorkshire at The Oval 1934. Cyril Turner looks on from second slip and Arthur Wood is the wicket-keeper. Yorkshire won the match by an innings and 157 runs.

Len Hutton made an inauspicious start to his first class career in 1934 at the age of 18 when he was dismissed for 0 at Fenner's. He followed that with half centuries at The Parks and Edgbaston, and he announced his arrival before the season was through with 196 against Worcestershire. Born in the cricket nursery of Pudsey, in the line of Tunnicliffe, Major Booth, and Sutcliffe, Hutton, a slightly built right-hand batsman, was to become England's master batsman in the late '30s and post-war period.

Yorkshire, 1935. Back row, left to right: B. Heyhirst (masseur), L. Hutton, H. Verity, W.E. Bowes, T.F. Smailes, C. Turner, A. Wood, W. Ringrose (scorer). Front row, left to right: W. Barber, H. Sutcliffe, A.B. Sellers (captain), M. Leyland and A. Mitchell. In 1935 they were Champions again, after dropping to an unprecedented sixth position in 1934. This was a Championship won, to use the words of Yorkshire cricket writer Jim Kilburn, by '...a business-like side.'

Ellis Pembroke Robinson, an off-break bowler from Denaby in South Yorkshire, first played for the county in 1934 but failed to secure a regular place in the first XI until 1938. In addition to his bowling, Robinson was a useful left-handed late order bat and an excellent close to the wicket fielder. Against Leicestershire at Bradford in 1938 he took a Yorkshire record of 6 catches in an innings and 7 in the match, a feat equalled by Tunnicliffe twice (1897 and 1900) and Sellers once (1933). Robinson stayed with Yorkshire until 1949 and then had three seasons with Somerset before returning to his native South Yorkshire.

The first outdoor practice at Headingley, April 1937. Arthur Mitchell (left), Wilf Barber (centre), and Herbert Sutcliffe brave the cold spring air.

Thomas Francis Smailes, born at Ripley near Harrogate, in March 1910. Frank Smailes was a hard hitting left-handed batsman and right-arm medium paced bowler who played 262 times for Yorkshire between 1932 and 1948. In 1938 he became the first all-rounder for twelve years to achieve the 'double', scoring 1,002 runs and taking 113 wickets. In late June 1939, Smailes became the third Yorkshire bowler to take all ten wickets in an innings when he recorded figures of ten for 47 against Derbyshire at Bramall Lane. He played one Test for England against India in 1946.

Yorkshire team, 1937, at Scarborough during their match against the MCC. From left to right: H. Verity, W.E. Bowes, N.W.D. Yardley, A.B. Sellers (captain), H. Sutcliffe, T.F. Smailes, W. Barber, A. Wood, M. Leyland, C. Turner and L. Hutton.

Yorkshire v Lancashire at Bradford, June 1938. Smailes is bowling to John Iddon, who made 28 and 66 in the match. Arthur Wood collects behind the wicket and Wilf Barber is in the field. Yorkshire won the match by eight wickets.

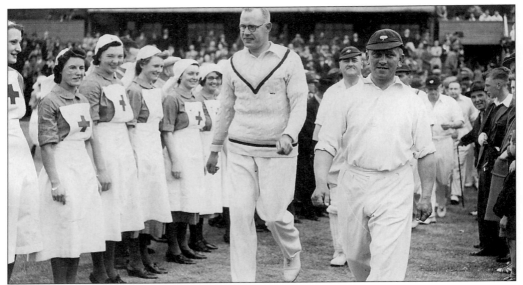

Hitler sentenced cricket to another enforced isolation in the late summer of 1939, as the guns of war again sounded out over Europe. Yorkshire cricketers once more played their part in the conflict. Maurice Leyland (right) and Bill Bowes take the field during a Red Cross cricket match at Headingley in June 1940. Both players served during the Second World War – Leyland went into the Royal Artillery together with team-mates Frank Smailes and Brian Sellers, but was destined to spend much of his wartime service in East Anglia and East Yorkshire. Bowes was captured in North Africa in 1942 whilst on active duty. He spent three years as a prisoner of war until the thankful release from oppression in 1945.

Many of the English cricket grounds were used by the military authorities during the Second World War. Bramall Lane did not escape the German bombing during the blitz on Sheffield in December 1940. Part of the John Street stand was destroyed, while the Shoreham Street roofing and terracing in front of the scorebox were badly damaged. Further bombs fell on the football pitch and at both ends of the cricket square – the Luftwaffe were certainly not lovers of cricket! Despite its wartime scars, Bramall Lane, like the world, emerged in 1945 and welcomed England and Australia when the second of the Victory Tests was played there in June that year.

Four
Test Tykes and Tourists

England v India at Headingley, June 1952. On the eve of the first Test of the summer, the players inspect the Leeds' wicket. From left to right: V.S. Hazare (Indian captain), Len Hutton (the newly appointed England captain), P. Sen, D.G. Phadkar, and Yorkshire captain Norman Yardley adds to the debate. England went on to a convincing seven wicket win with Yorkshire debutant F.S. Trueman claiming seven wickets in the match.

George Anderson, born at Bedale in January 1826. Anderson was a powerfully built batsman, coached by William Clarke of Nottingham. He was a member of George Parr's tour party that made the trip to Australia in 1863/64. The voyage from Liverpool lasted sixty-one days and Melbourne was reached nine days before Christmas. The journey was largely pleasant, but George Anderson proved a poor sailor and suffered a great deal from sea-sickness. He played thirty-three matches for Yorkshire between 1850 and 1869. He was also a noted billiards and whist player.

Frank William Milligan – the ideal late nineteenth century cricketer. A Yorkshire player from 1894, he toured South Africa with Lord Hawke's team of 1898/99, playing in both the Tests without much success. Afterwards he decided to stay on in the country, only to be killed in his prime whilst serving under Colonel Plumer, in the bid to relieve Mafeking during the Boer War. In his short career, this cavalier amateur cricketer represented the Gentlemen v the Players in 1897 and 1898 and also toured North America in 1895. He was only 28 years of age when he died.

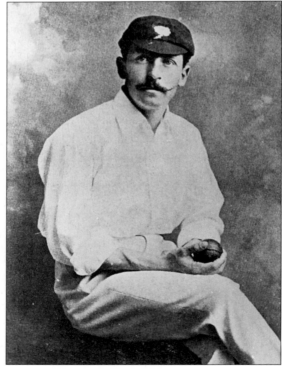

Frank Mitchell, a powerfully built right-hand batsman, played only two full seasons with Yorkshire in 1899 and 1901, having made his county debut in 1894. He scored well over 1,000 runs in both of his completed summers for the county, his best being 1,807 runs in 1901 which included seven centuries. Amongst the select group of players in Test history to have represented two countries, Mitchell played twice for England in 1898/99 and captained the 1904 and 1912 South African tours of England, playing three further Tests. This outstanding amateur cricketer toured North America in 1895, 1898, and 1901 and served during the Boer war in South Africa.

Scarborough cricket ground in the 1950s. The Scarborough Festival has down the years played host to many of the touring sides who have visited England, together with Women's Test cricket and two one-day International matches – England v West Indies in 1976 and England v New Zealand two years later. During the inter-war years and indeed, for sometime afterwards, the H.D.G. Leveson-Gower's XI v Tourists match was often referred to as the 'Sixth Test Match'. The Australians, the most eagerly awaited visitors to Scarborough, first played there in 1878.

J.T. Brown, Yorkshire's opening batsman during the golden era, played eight times for England. He toured Australia with A.E. Stoddart's party of 1894/95. In the deciding Test at Melbourne, Brown shared a third wicket partnership of 210 with A. Ward to secure a six wicket win for England to clinch the rubber. Brown's first 50 came in 28 blistering minutes, and his century took just 95 minutes in all. He was finally dismissed for 140.

Stanley Jackson basked in his own glory during the summer of 1905. Appointed England captain, he led the side to a 2-0 victory over the Australians, winning the toss in each match as well as topping both the batting and bowling averages with 492 runs at 70.28 and 13 wickets at 15.46. England retained the Ashes and 'Jacker' reached the pinnacle of his illustrious career.

Tykes in India. Yorkshire players Maurice Leyland (second from left) and Roy Kilner (centre) get away from the cricket in January 1927 at Patiala in India. Both cricketers were out there coaching when due to injury, Leyland was drafted into the touring MCC party. Hampshire cricketer George Brown (second from right), another of the MCC tourists, was one of those unfortunate enough to be injured on the trip.

David Denton played only eleven times for England between 1905 and 1910, J.T. Tyldesley of Lancashire often being preferred to him. His debut came on home soil at Headingley in July 1905 against Australia. He was dismissed for 0 in his first innings and made just 12 in the second. He was somewhat overshadowed by the other England debutant A. Warren, who took five wickets in the first innings of his only Test match. Denton toured South Africa in 1905/06 and 1909/10. In the third Test at Johannesburg in March 1910, he scored 104 in only 100 minutes at the crease; it was his sole Test century.

Maurice Leyland, probably the finest left-handed batsman Yorkshire have produced, had a real pedigree for Test cricket which exceeded even his county record. Despite a poor start in international cricket, a duck against the West Indies on his debut in 1928, he made 137 and 53 not out in his first encounter against Australia at Melbourne in 1928/29. He toured Australia three times and enjoyed an outstanding Test record against the 'old enemy' – 1,705 runs at 56.83 per innings. In England's record total of 903 for 7 declared at The Oval in 1938, Leyland contributed 187, sharing a second wicket stand of 382 with his Yorkshire team-mate Len Hutton. That was to be the last of his 41 Test appearances in which he made 2,764 runs at an average of 46.06, including nine centuries. As well as Australia, Leyland also toured South Africa, the West Indies and India.

Sutcliffe's famed opening partner, Jack Hobbs, wishes the Yorkshireman well for his benefit match at Headingley in 1929. For England, Sutcliffe and Surrey's master batsman Hobbs, shared fifteen century stands, two of exceptional quality – 172 at The Oval on a 'glue pot' against Australia in 1926 and 105 on a sticky Melbourne track in 1928/29.

Wilfred Rhodes, somewhere in India in the early 1920s. Rhodes first played for England at Trent Bridge against Australia in 1899: W.G. Grace's last Test appearance. The last of Rhodes' 58 Test caps came during the Caribbean tour of 1929/30. He batted in all 11 positions for England and shared opening stands of 221 with Jack Hobbs against South Africa in 1909/10, and then 323 two years later against Australia in Melbourne. His most memorable achievements with the ball at Test level included returns of eight for 68 at Melbourne in 1903/04, and seven for 17 at Edgbaston in 1902 when Australia were dismissed for 36. Recalled at the age of 48, Rhodes played an important part in England's historic victory at The Oval in 1926 when the Ashes were regained, claiming four for 44 in Australia's second innings. Rhodes was the first England cricketer to complete the Test 'double' and the first from any country to extend it to 2,000 runs and 100 wickets. He is forever likely to remain cricket's oldest Test player at 52 years, 165 days.

Three of the four Yorkshiremen selected for Douglas Jardine's 1932/33 MCC tour party to Australia. From left to right: Hedley Verity, Herbert Sutcliffe, and Maurice Leyland. Emerging from The Oval pavilion are Arthur Mitchell and behind Bill Bowes, the fourth Yorkshire player in the party. That 1932/33 Test series in Australia was to become the most controversial in cricket's history, inspired by the tactics that the England captain Jardine employed in an attempt to curb the prolific scoring of Donald Bradman. The 'bodyline' approach, as it was dubbed in Australia, consisted of fast, short pitched bowling at the Australian batsmen who were surrounded by a string of close leg side fielders. These tactics caused unprecedented exchanges between the two countries.

England v Australia, third Test at Old Trafford, July 1934. Maurice Leyland is on his way to 93 not out at the close of the first day's play. Leyland was eventually dismissed by O'Reilly for 153, his second Test hundred in successive innings. The match, blessed with glorious weather from start to finish, ended as a high scoring draw.

Herbert Sutcliffe departs for the pavilion, caught by McCabe off the bowling of Clarrie Grimmett for 28 during England's second innings of the fifth Test at The Oval which Australia won by the comprehensive margin of 562 runs. Sutcliffe's Test career ended in 1935 against South Africa. His tally of 4,555 Test runs was scored at an average of 60.73 per innings to place him amongst the very best at that level. His first-class career effectively ended in 1939 with the outbreak of the Second World War, although he made a brief appearance in 1945. His 38,558 runs for Yorkshire placed him as the county's all time highest run scorer.

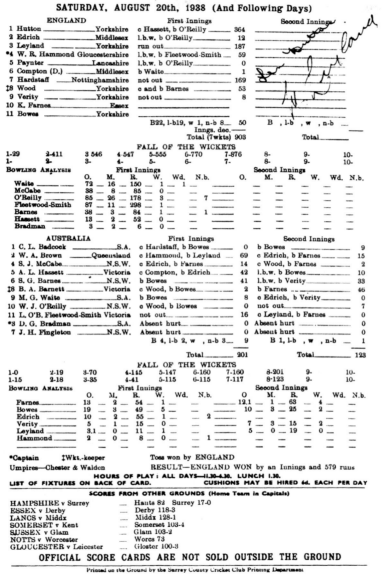

𝔖urrey 𝔆ounty 𝔆ricket 𝔆lub 2ᴰ·

KENNINGTON OVAL

ENGLAND v. AUSTRALIA

SATURDAY, AUGUST 20th, 1938 (And Following Days)

ENGLAND		First Innings		Second Innings
1 Hutton	Yorkshire	c Hassett, b O'Reilly	364	
2 Edrich	Middlesex	l.b.w. b O'Reilly	12	
3 Leyland	Yorkshire	run out	187	
*4 W. R. Hammond	Gloucestershire	l.b.w. b Fleetwood-Smith	59	
5 Paynter	Lancashire	l.b.w. b O'Reilly	0	
6 Compton (D.)	Middlesex	b Waite	1	
7 Hardstaff	Nottinghamshire	not out	169	
‡8 Wood	Yorkshire	c and b Barnes	53	
9 Verity	Yorkshire	not out	8	
10 K. Farnes	Essex			
11 Bowes	Yorkshire			
		B 22, l-b 19, w 1, n-b 8	50	B , l-b , w , n-b
		Inngs. dec.		
		Total (7 wkts)	903	Total

FALL OF THE WICKETS

1-29	2-411	3 546	4-547	5-555	6-770	7-876	8-	9-	10-
1-	2-	3-	4-	5-	6-	7-	8-	9-	10-

BOWLING ANALYSIS

	First Innings					Second Innings					
	O.	M.	R.	W.	Wd.	N.b.	O.	M.	R.	W.	Wd. N.b.
Waite	72	16	150	1	1						
McCabe	38	8	85	0							
O'Reilly	85	26	178	3		7					
Fleetwood-Smith	87	11	298	1							
Barnes	38	3	84	1		1					
Hassett	13	2	52	0							
Bradman	3	2	6	0							

AUSTRALIA		First Innings		Second Innings	
1 C. L. Badcock	S.A.	c Hardstaff, b Bowes	0	b Bowes	9
2 W. A. Brown	Queensland	c Hammond, b Leyland	69	c Edrich, b Farnes	15
4 S. J. McCabe	N.S.W.	c Edrich, b Farnes	14	c Wood, b Farnes	2
5 A. L. Hassett	Victoria	c Compton, b Edrich	42	l.b.w. b Bowes	10
6 S. G. Barnes	N.S.W.	b Bowes	41	l.b.w. b Verity	33
‡8 B. A. Barnett	Victoria	c Wood, b Bowes	2	b Farnes	46
9 M. G. Waite	S.A.	b Bowes	8	c Edrich, b Verity	0
10 W. J. O'Reilly	N.S.W.	c Wood, b Bowes	0	not out	7
11 L. O'B. Fleetwood-Smith	Victoria	not out	16	c Leyland, b Farnes	0
*3 D. G. Bradman	S.A.	Absent hurt	0	Absent hurt	0
7 J. H. Fingleton	N.S.W.	Absent hurt	0	Absent hurt	0
		B 4, l-b 2, w , n-b 3	9	B 1, l-b , w , n-b	1
		Total	201	Total	123

FALL OF THE WICKETS

1-0	2-19	3-70	4-115	5-147	6-160	7-160	8-201	9-	10-
1-15	2-18	3-35	4-41	5-115	6-115	7-117	8-123	9-	10-

BOWLING ANALYSIS

	First Innings					Second Innings					
	O.	M.	R.	W.	Wd.	N.b.	O.	M.	R.	W.	Wd. N.b.
Farnes	13	2	54	1			12.1	1	63	4	
Bowes	19	3	49	5			10	3	25	2	
Edrich	10	2	55	1		2					
Verity	5	1	15	0			7	3	15	2	
Leyland	3.1	0	11	1			5	0	19	0	
Hammond	2	0	8	0		1					

*Captain ‡Wkt.-keeper Toss won by ENGLAND

RESULT—ENGLAND WON by an Innings and 579 runs

Umpires—Chester & Walden

HOURS OF PLAY: ALL DAYS—11.30-6.30. LUNCH 1.30.

LIST OF FIXTURES ON BACK OF CARD. CUSHIONS MAY BE HIRED 6d. EACH PER DAY

SCORES FROM OTHER GROUNDS (Home Team in Capitals)

HAMPSHIRE v Surrey	...	Hants 82 Surrey 17-0
ESSEX v Derby	...	Derby 118-3
LANCS v Middx	...	Middx 128-1
SOMERSET v Kent	...	Somerset 103-4
SUSSEX v Glam	...	Glam 103-2
NOTTS v Worcester	...	Worcs 73
GLOUCESTER v Leicester	...	Gloster 100-3

OFFICIAL SCORE CARDS ARE NOT SOLD OUTSIDE THE GROUND

Printed on the Ground by the Surrey County Cricket Club Printing Department

The name of 22 year old Len Hutton became firmly engraved in the annals of Test cricket at The Oval in August 1938 when the young Yorkshire batsman eclipsed Wally Hammond's record Test score of 336 not out and Don Bradman's previous Test record 334, made back at Headingley in 1930, a match the 14 year old Hutton had witnessed. Eight years later he moved the record up several notches to 364, achieved in 13 hours 17 minutes at the crease.

At Lord's on 25 June 1934, Yorkshire slow left-arm bowler Hedley Verity captured 14 Australian wickets (at a cost of 80 runs) to secure England's first win over Australia at Lord's since 1896. Six of those wickets fell in the last hour of the day, and his match analysis of fifteen for 104 was then the England v Australia record until eclipsed by Jim Laker at Old Trafford in 1956. Verity was a victim of the Second World War. Whilst serving for the Green Howards on a Sicilian battlefield in July 1943, Captain Verity was badly wounded in the chest when leading his company into battle on the plains of Catania on a blazing cornfield below Mount Etna. He was operated on and evacuated to Italy where he died of his wounds in Caserta hospital, south of Naples on 31 July.

Abe Waddington and his bride Doris Garforth are toasted by his former Yorkshire colleagues. Left to right: Herbert Sutcliffe, the bridegroom, the bride, Maurice Leyland, and Brian Sellers. Waddington's left-arm fast medium bowling won him selection for the 1920/21 tour of Australia where he played in two Tests at Sydney and Melbourne without much success – his one Test victim was C.G. Macartney, a worthy scalp nonetheless.

Gerald Smithson, who served as a 'Bevin Boy', played only thirty-nine times for Yorkshire between 1946 and 1950, but despite the shortness of his career, he won two Test caps for England on the 1947/48 tour of the West Indies. He suffered an arm injury on that tour and missed the whole of the 1948 season. Having failed to establish himself in the Yorkshire ranks, Smithson, a left-handed batsman, joined Leicestershire where he played until 1956. He later played for Hertfordshire (1957-1962) before his death at the early age of 43 in 1970.

Norman Yardley (right) captain of Yorkshire and England alongside Lindsay Hassett (who toured England three times in 1938, 1948 and 1953 when he led the Australian party) at Scarborough. Yardley first played for Yorkshire in 1936. A right-handed batsman, he was also a good enough right-arm medium paced bowler to dismiss Don Bradman on three successive occasions. In the immediate pre-war era, his experiences included tours to India (1937/38) and South Africa (1938/39). The latter was where he won the first of his twenty Test caps. In the post-war period, as captain of county and country, he faced two mighty opponents in Don Bradman's 1948 Australians and at domestic level, the powerful Surrey team of the 1950s.

Brian Close made a spectacular entry into the first-class game. A naturally talented left-handed batsman and right-arm medium or off-break bowler, he did the 'double' in 1949, his debut summer in first-class cricket (1,098 runs at 27.45 and 113 wickets at 27.87). At the age of only 18, he thus became the youngest player to attain that landmark as well as being the youngest to gain a Yorkshire cap. He broke more new ground when he made his Test debut at Old Trafford in the third Test against New Zealand, becoming the youngest player at 18 years 149 days to represent England at Test level.

A section of the imposing Headingley crowd enjoying the 1953 England v Australia Test match. Crowd records were a feature of Headingley's post-war history. In 1948, 44,507 spectators watched the Yorkshire v Lancashire match; that same season a record 30,000 poured into the ground to see Don Bradman's Australian side score over 400 on the last day, to win a remarkable game against England.

Three of the 1950/51 MCC tour party to Australia and New Zealand. Left to right: Freddie Brown (tour captain), Cyril Washbrook (who joined the party later having declined the original invitation), and Leonard Hutton (who headed the tour averages). The three are pictured together here in 1957 during the Lancashire v MCC Old Trafford Centenary match.

Three for Trueman in 14-ball feat

By BILL BOWES

HEADINGLEY, Saturday.

SENSATIONAL England bowling to-day rocked India, who lost four second innings wickets for no runs—all in 14 balls. Trueman took three of the wickets and Bedser the other, and the 25,000 crowd cheered wildly — certainly nothing more dramatic has happened in Test cricket for many years.

England v India at Headingley during the first Test in 1952. Forty-one runs behind after the first innings, India made Test history by losing four of their second innings wickets for no runs to the first 14 balls. Three of those four wickets fell to Yorkshire fast bowler Fred Trueman, who was making his Test debut. The *Yorkshire Evening Post* report of Saturday 7 June proclaimed Trueman's feat.

Neil Harvey, caught by Vic Wilson off the bowling of Johnny Wardle for 37, during the Australians match against Yorkshire at Bradford in May 1953. Don Brennan is the Yorkshire wicket-keeper who played twice for England against South Africa in 1951. The 1953 Australians 'outclassed Yorkshire in every phase of the game' *Wisden* commented. Yorkshire were beaten by an innings and 94 runs with Keith Miller scoring 159 not out for the tourists.

John Henry Wardle was Yorkshire's next 'great' slow left-arm bowler after Hedley Verity. He played his first game for the county in 1946, and his Test debut came at Port-of-Spain, West Indies on the 1947/48 tour. The presence of Surrey's Tony Lock and a dispute with the county which brought his career to a premature close in 1958, prevented Wardle from winning more than his eventual twenty-eight Test caps. A fierce competitor with a quick temper, Wardle possessed an abundance of natural talent. He later developed the googly and chinaman deliveries and used his unorthodox skills to best effect at international level in South Africa on the 1956/57 tour, where his 26 Test wickets cost just 13.80 each. In total on that tour he captured 90 first-class wickets at an average of 12.25. His 102 Test victims for England cost 20.39 apiece with a best of seven for 36 against the South Africans at Newlands on that successful 1956/57 trip.

Raymond Illingworth came into first-class cricket in 1951. An off-spin bowler and useful middle order right-handed batsman, he announced his arrival in 1957 passing 1,000 runs and 100 wickets in that summer. The first of his sixty-one Test appearances came the following season against New Zealand at Old Trafford. He first captained England in 1969 against the West Indies after Colin Cowdrey tore his achilles tendon before the series got underway. Originally a temporary appointment, Illingworth showed such astute leadership skills that he remained in the post for a further thirty Tests; under his captaincy the Ashes were regained in Australia in 1970/71 and then retained in 1972. In retirement Illingworth became a much respected BBC cricket commentator, before being appointed Chairman of Selectors in 1994. His eventful, and at times controversial, tenure in the position ended at the close of the 1996 season with a record of six wins out of twenty-eight Tests.

Fred Trueman, who made such a dramatic entry into Test cricket against the Indians at Headingley in 1952, became the first bowler to capture 300 Test wickets. He reached this feat during The Oval Test of 1964 when Neil Hawke of Australia was caught by Cowdrey in the slips to register a historic landmark. Trueman remained the leading wicket taker in Test cricket until 1975/76 and held the England record until 1983/84. His 67 Test appearances harvested a final haul of 307 wickets at 21.57 each.

Geoffrey Boycott acknowledges the applause for the first of his 22 Test hundreds for England. His innings of 114 came in the same match at The Oval in 1964 when Trueman claimed his 300th Test scalp. Boycott's first Test hundred came just two years after his county debut, and ahead lay over two decades of prolific batsmanship from this most single-minded and dedicated of players. At 5.49pm at Headingley on 11 August 1977, Boycott on-drove Australia's Greg Chappell for four to become only the third Yorkshire player (Hutton and Sutcliffe being the other two) to reach the exclusive landmark of 100 hundreds in first-class cricket. He batted for 5 hours 20 minutes before reaching that century, but stayed to add a further 91 runs to his score, enabling England to win the match by an innings and 85 runs and thus regain the Ashes.

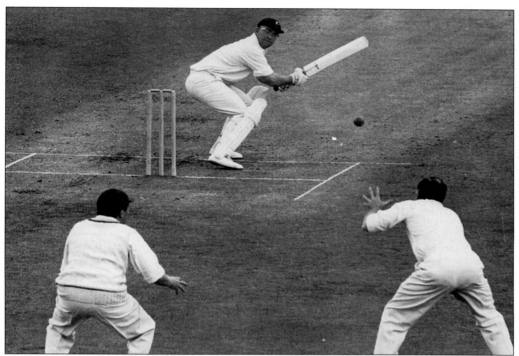

Brian Close about to drop South Africa's Eddie Barlow during the tourists match with Yorkshire at Sheffield in 1965; Phil Sharpe looks on. Close made up for the error by scoring 117 not out for the county as the match finished in a draw.

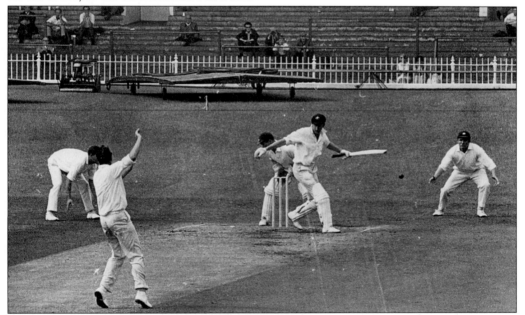

Bill Lawry pads away a delivery from Yorkshire's slow left-arm bowler Don Wilson during the Australian's encounter with the White Rose at Bramall Lane in 1968. Jimmy Binks is behind the wickets, Phil Sharpe at slip, and John Hampshire close in on the left of the picture.

Yorkshire triumph after 66 years

Yorkshire Post Sports Reporter

YORKSHIRE gained their first victory over an Australian touring cricket team since 1902 when they beat them by an innings and 69 runs at Sheffield yesterday.

The Australian team included eight players who appeared in the second Test last week. It was the first defeat of Lawry's team.

The 1964 Australian team were beaten by three counties — Glamorgan, Warwickshire and Essex.

Crowds gathered outside the pavilion to cheer the victorious Yorkshire team after the match.

Freddie Trueman, the Yorkshire captain, said: "It was a great team effort and the boys played splendidly throughout in batting, bowling and fielding. I would not like to single out anybody they all did well.

"The Australians came up to our dressing room immediately after the match to congratulate us. I think they are a great bunch of boys."

'Better cricket'

Freddie Trueman's victory grin yesterday.

Mr. Bob Parrish, the Australian manager, who said that Bill Lawry, agreed with his sentiments said: "Yorkshire outplayed us all the way. They played better cricket than we did and thoroughly deserved to win. We congratulate them."

Yorkshire's last victory over the Australians was at Headingley in 1902 when they won by five wickets o nthe second day.

On the first day, a public holiday, 35,000 saw both sides bat. Yorkshire falling into first innings arrears of 25.

In the Australian second innings G. H. Hirst and F. S. Jackson shared the wickets, Hirst taking 5 for9 and Jackson 5 for 12. The Australians were all out

The newspaper headlines tell the story – Yorkshire victors over the Australians at Bramall Lane, 2 July 1968 – the county's first triumph over the Aussies for 66 years, achieved by an innings and 69 runs. Fred Trueman led Yorkshire in Close's absence and, after declaring the county's first innings closed at 355 for 9, he shared in the glory taking six wickets in the match. It was the Australians' first defeat at the hands of Yorkshire since the days of Lord Hawke and their 1902 batting disgrace (23 all out) at the hands of F.S. Jackson and George Hirst.

Harold Dennis Bird, son of a Barnsley miner, made his county debut for Yorkshire in 1956. Against Glamorgan at Bradford in 1959, he made what proved to be a career best of 181 not out, his one and only century for Yorkshire. Such was the strength of Yorkshire cricket at that time, he was then left out of the side for the next match. At the end of that season he joined Leicestershire in search of a regular first team place and he played there until 1964. Appointed to the first-class umpires list in 1970, 'Dickie' as he is known universally, was promoted to the Test panel in 1973. Since then he has stood in sixty-six Test matches, a world record tally, as well as three World Cup finals. His final Test at Lord's, England v India, June 1996, proved an emotional occasion for Dickie and many thousands of cricket followers alike. Over the years, Dickie has established a reputation as one of the finest umpires in the history of the game. A much loved character, known for his eccentricities and gestures, he is held in very high regard by the players of all the cricket playing nations for his fairness, good humour, honesty, and above all his consistency of decision.

Five

The Era of Hutton

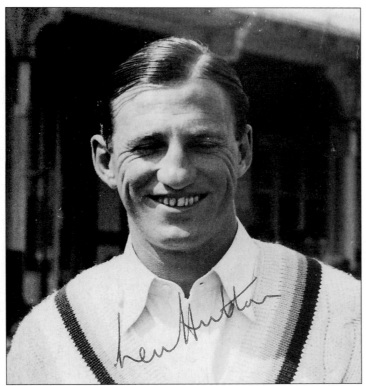

Leonard Hutton – one of Yorkshire and England's greatest batsmen. A boyhood hero to a generation, Hutton was the rock upon which many county and Test bowlers floundered in the era immediately before and after the Second World War.

Fourteen year old Len Hutton bowling at Headingley back in 1931 during a trial for the county. At that time, Hutton, born in Fulneck near Pudsey on 23 June 1916, was playing for Pudsey St Lawrence CC. Herbert Sutcliffe, having watched the Pudsey boy in the Headingley practice nets, concluded that Hutton, 'was a marvel – the discovery of a generation': an extravagant tribute that was destined to prove an inspired observation.

Middlesex v Yorkshire at Lord's, June 1939. Herbert Sutcliffe loses his bat in playing a delivery from Middlesex fast/medium bowler L.H. Gray. Sutcliffe and Len Hutton shared a modest opening partnership of 56 in Yorkshire's first and only innings. Hutton was dismissed for 29, but veteran Sutcliffe, still the supreme craftsman, stayed to make 175, his fourth consecutive innings of 100 or more. Together Sutcliffe and Hutton compiled 15 century opening stands for Yorkshire including two of 315, one against Leicestershire in 1937 and then again in that last pre-war summer of 1939 against Hampshire, at Sheffield, when Hutton made an unbeaten 280, his career best for Yorkshire.

The youthful batting prodigy from Pudsey St Lawrence Cricket Club. Leonard Hutton first played at Tofts Road in the late 1920s. In 1933 he registered his first century for the club in a Priestley Cup match against Bradford and just a year later he made his debut for Yorkshire. In 1936 he registered his first tally of over 1,000 runs in a season (1,282 at an average of 29.81) to confirm his potential. The summer of 1937 silenced any remaining sceptics who doubted Hutton's ability and temperament. For Yorkshire that season, he scored 2,448 runs at an average of 62.76, including 8 centuries. He also made his first Test appearance at Lord's against New Zealand and he bounced back from scores of 0 and 1 on debut to hit the first of his eventual 19 centuries for England in the next match at Old Trafford.

The 22 year old Len Hutton pulls his batting gloves back on and prepares to continue his record breaking innings of 364 against Australia at The Oval in 1938. Hutton's innings established the substantial platform for England's eventual crushing victory by an innings and 579 runs. *Wisden Cricketers' Almanack* 1939 wrote, 'No more remarkable exhibition of concentration and endurance has been seen on the cricket field than that of Leonard Hutton…This Test, which enabled England to share the series, will always be remembered as 'Hutton's Match'.'

Five members of Yorkshire's all-conquering 1930s side pose for a wartime reunion picture. From left to right: Captain Hedley Verity, Sergeant-Major Frank Smailes, Captain Herbert Sutcliffe, Sergeant Maurice Leyland and Sergeant Instructor Len Hutton. Sutcliffe served in the Royal Army Ordnance Corps until November 1942, when a shoulder injury and sinus trouble led to his discharge from the army at the age of 48. Len Hutton joined the Army Physical Training Corps. During a gymnastics demonstration at York in the spring of 1941, he sustained an injury which threatened to end his cricket career in its prime when he suffered a complicated fracture of the left fore-arm. The injury left him with a left arm almost 2 inches shorter than the right making his vast achievements in the game after the war all the more remarkable.

Brian Sellers leads Yorkshire out at Scarborough in the immediate post-war era, with Frank Smailes (left) and Ellis Robinson (right). Behind them Norman Yardley chats to Bill Bowes, and Willie Watson marches out eagerly in the distance. At the age of nearly 40, Sellers led the county to its sixth title under his leadership in 1946, blending the experience of Bowes, Smailes, Leyland and Hutton with the youthful talent of Wardle, Lester and Smithson, amongst others.

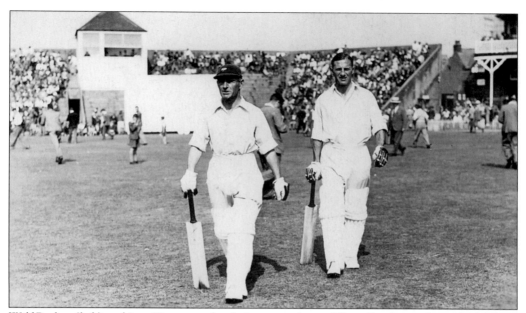

Wilf Barber (left) and Len Hutton make their way to the middle at Scarborough in 1946. These two players were the only members of the Yorkshire side to exceed 1,000 runs that summer (Barber 1,170 and Hutton 1,322). Barber was in his last full season for the county, although he made one appearance in 1947. Hutton's average of 52.88 in 1946 was over 20 runs per innings higher than his nearest rival Paul Gibb. Any fears concerning the 'master' batsman's arm injury were quickly dispelled with centuries against Leicestershire (111), Surrey (101), Northamptonshire (171 not out), and the Indian tourists (183 not out).

August 1946 and Len Hutton selects the bats that later accompanied him during the 1946/47 tour of Australia under Wally Hammond. Hutton topped the tour batting averages with 1,267 runs at 76.38 per innings but could do little to prevent England losing the Test series 3-0 as Bradman, after a shaky and controversial start to the series, reasserted his dominance.

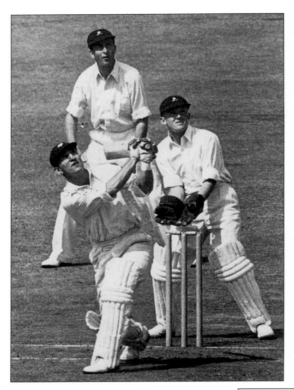

Hutton hits out against the 1947 South Africans. In the match against the tourists at Sheffield, Hutton made 137 for Yorkshire although the match ended as a draw. His other century against the South Africans that summer came in the fourth Test at Headingley which England won by ten wickets.

Ronald Aspinall, from Almondberry near Huddersfield, was a strongly built right-arm fast medium bowler who first played for Yorkshire in 1946. After several unsuccessful first team appearances, he had a dramatic impact on the fixture against Northamptonshire in August 1947. Bowling with a combination of pace and accuracy, Aspinall had match figures of fourteen for 65 (eight for 42 and six for 23 in the second innings). Unfortunately injury prevented Aspinall's progress and he played his final game for Yorkshire in 1950, after which he played seven seasons for Durham before becoming a first-class umpire.

Harry Halliday (left) and Len Hutton about to open the innings for Yorkshire at Swansea, against Glamorgan, in May 1947. They shared an opening stand of 91 in that match. Halliday, a dependable right-handed batsman, made 32 whilst Hutton went on to make 197 in Yorkshire's 320 all out. Halliday played for Yorkshire between 1938 and 1953 and scored over 8,500 runs at 31.80 in his career.

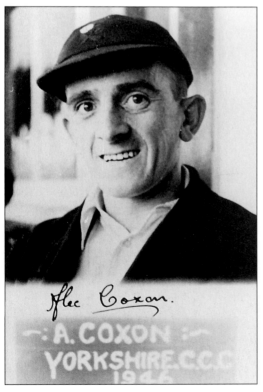

Alec Coxon, a right-arm aggressive new ball bowler from Huddersfield, served the county well for five years after the war and captured 473 first-class wickets at 20.91. Coxon won one Test cap for England at Lord's against Australia in 1948. He stayed with Yorkshire until 1950 when he left to play for Durham at the age of only 34, when many felt he still had several good years of service left to offer.

LEN HUTTON BEATS RECORD SET BY HAMMOND

The newspaper headline of 1949 declares Hutton's achievement of scoring 1,294 runs during June that year to surpass Walter Hammond's previous tally back in 1936. Hutton was in majestic form throughout the summer. For Yorkshire he scored 2,640 runs at 69.47 and in all first-class matches his final run tally was 3,429, the highest ever run aggregate in one season by a Yorkshireman. Only Compton, Edrich, and Hayward have scored more. *Wisden Cricketers' Almanack* paid this tribute to Hutton in its 1950 edition, 'For Hutton's art is of a garden, tended through the years by fond Yorkshire hands, a pure white rose, all satin and sheen, the beholder's joy, the possessor's pride.'

There were three major debutants in 1949, each destined to reach high levels in the game: F.S. Trueman, D.B. Close and F.A. Lowson all made their Yorkshire debuts in the game at Fenner's against Cambridge University. Frederick Sewards Trueman, born at Scot Springs, Stainton near Maltby in 1931, was a young, raw, but still erratic quick bowler. Capable of genuine speed, he took 31 wickets that summer at 23.19. In the seasons ahead greater maturity brought with it a control of pace which made him one of the most feared bowlers in the world during the 1950s and early '60s.

Yorkshire team 1949. Back row, left to right: B. Heyhirst (masseur), H. Halliday, F.P. McHugh, D.B. Close, E.I. Lester, J.H. Wardle, F.A. Lowson. Front row, left to right: W. Watson, D.V. Brennan, N.W.D. Yardley (captain), L. Hutton, E.P. Robinson and A. Coxon. Yorkshire shared the Championship title with Middlesex, even though Yardley's men were beaten only twice to Middlesex's three defeats. Needing to win all of their last six matches to secure a share of the title, Yorkshire, against the odds, accomplished the feat.

Ted Lester, an unorthodox forcing, right-handed batsman from Scarborough, drives Surrey's Tony Lock during a Yorkshire v Surrey match in 1954. Lester first played for the county in 1945 and enjoyed his best season in 1949, scoring 1,801 runs at 37.52 including a career highest score of 186 against Warwickshire. He hit 1,000 runs in a season six times and his last good summer was 1954. Thereafter a loss of form, explained to some extent by a foot problem, saw him displaced in the first XI. He took over the captaincy of the second XI and led them from 1958 to 1961. Appointed Yorkshire scorer in 1962, he held the position until 1992 and was always on hand to offer guidance and assistance to any of the Yorkshire players and captains who sought his advice. A loyal servant to the Club, he is also an honorary life member.

Talking Yorkshire and Test matters with the weighty expressions that such subjects deserve, Len Hutton chats to Bill Bowes in Melbourne, Australia in February 1951. England, already 4-0 down in the series, salvaged some consolation in that fifth Test winning by eight wickets. Hutton contributed scores of 79 and 60 not out, to end the rubber with an average of 88.83. Bill Bowes had played his final match for Yorkshire in 1947, having captured 1,639 wickets and thereafter embarked upon a successful career as a cricket writer and reporter with the *Yorkshire Evening News* and *Yorkshire Evening Post*. This genial giant of Yorkshire cricket passed away in September 1987 at the age of 79.

Bob Appleyard, in his first full season for Yorkshire, grabbed all the headlines in 1951 by becoming only the fourth bowler to take 200 wickets in a season for the county and the first since George Macaulay in 1925. Appleyard, with a mixture of medium pace and off-break bowling, topped the first-class averages that summer. His 200 wickets cost him 14.14 each including 12 wicket match returns against Somerset, Leicestershire, and Essex. Injury plagued him in 1952 and 1953, but he made a comeback in 1954 and finished second in the national bowling averages with 154 wickets. He made his Test debut that summer against Pakistan and won selection for the 1954/55 tour of Australia. In all he was capped nine times for England before he finally ended his career in 1958 with 708 first-class wickets at the exceptional average of 15.44. Most judges, including no less a bowling expert than Yorkshire's own Bill Bowes, considered Appleyard one of the best bowlers of all time. A danger on all types of wickets, he was destructive on a sticky wicket. Even on good pitches, no batsman was safe from his craft and guile.

Len Hutton leads England out at Headingley, June 5 1952, in the first Test against India that summer. Hutton's appointment as England's first professional captain since Arthur Shrewsbury in 1886/87, broke one of cricket's most jealously guarded traditions of the amateur captain and was not met with universal approval. The die-hard traditionalists echoed the words of Yorkshire's own Lord Hawke who proclaimed in 1925, 'Pray God no professional shall ever captain England.' Hutton though, was to prove all the cynics wrong, as he developed into a canny and effective skipper. He enjoyed a highly successful start, winning three of the four Tests against India. The Ashes were regained from Australia in 1953 (Coronation Year), after almost 19 years 'down under' and retained in 1954/55. In all, under Hutton's leadership England won 11 Tests, drew 8, and were beaten on only 4 occasions. The players pictured at Headingley in 1952 are from left to right: A.V. Bedser, P.B.H. May, D.C.S. Compton, R.T. Simpson, A.J. Watkins, J.C. Laker, L. Hutton (captain), T.G. Evans, and T.W. Graveney. The two players obscured from view are R.O. Jenkins and F.S. Trueman.

Michael Joseph Cowan, a left-arm medium quick bowler, played for the county ninety-one times between 1953 and 1962. Plagued by injury and illness, much of Mike Cowan's career was interrupted by such problems. His best season was 1960 when he captured 66 wickets for the county including career best figures of nine for 43 against Warwickshire at Birmingham. After retiring he completed engagements at Rochdale and Littleborough CC before returning to Yorkshire with spells at Wakefield, Brodsworth, and Doncaster Town. He also became a noted after dinner speaker.

The stylish left-handed batsman Willie Watson, a product of the late Sellers era, batting for the Players against the Gentlemen at Lord's in 1955. A double international, Watson won four soccer caps for England and played twenty-three times for his country at cricket, being best remembered for his stand with Trevor Bailey at Lord's in 1953 when the pair batted for 257 minutes in a partnership of 163 to deny the Australians what had seemed an almost certain victory. Watson left Yorkshire at the end on the 1957 season and led Leicestershire from 1958 until 1961, before returning in 1964. In 1966 he emigrated to South Africa to take up a position as coach and administrator of the Wanderers Club in Johannesburg.

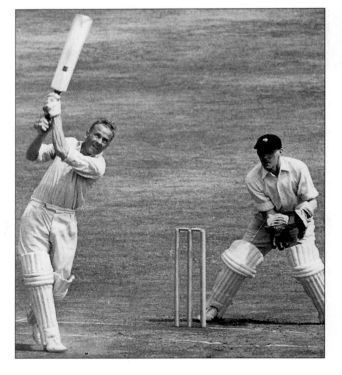

Len Hutton and Frank Lowson (right) go out to bat for Yorkshire in 1954. Lowson, a sound right-handed opening batsman was very much in the mould of Hutton as a player. In a career which lasted until 1958, he played seven times for England and scored 15,321 first-class runs at 37.18 with 2,152 runs in 1950 being his best return.

Yorkshire take the field at Bournemouth against Hampshire in late June 1955. From left to right: J.V. Wilson, D.B. Close, J.H. Wardle, N.W.D. Yardley (captain), L. Hutton, F.A. Lowson, W. Watson, J.G. Binks (wicket-keeper), and R. Appleyard. Yorkshire won the match by 96 runs on the second day, but the White Rose ended the season in the runners-up position for the second consecutive year as Surrey claimed their fourth successive Championship title.

Len Hutton walking out to net practice at Headingley with Fred Trueman in 1955. After successfully retaining the Ashes in Australia during the winter of 1954/55, the selectors appointed Hutton to lead England in the home series against South Africa, but he was forced to decline the invitation. The back pain which had tormented him even before the war, and a general weariness of spirit, meant that the summer of 1955 was to be Hutton's last. He missed the entire South African Test series and in fact managed only ten outings for Yorkshire before taking the inevitable step of announcing his retirement from the game he had graced with his stylish batsmanship in January 1956.

Present meets future – Yorkshire's captain since 1948, Norman Yardley, (left), talks with his successor Billy Sutcliffe, son of Herbert, who took on the honour his father had once declined and led the county for two seasons – 1956 and 1957, finishing seventh and third respectively in the Championship. Sutcliffe's time in charge coincided with the loss of both Hutton and Yardley. Difficulties within the county dressing room made his task a good deal more difficult.

Eminent Yorkshire artist Henry Carr captures Len Hutton on canvas back in 1951, following his achievements on the 1950/51 MCC tour of Australia. The portrait in oils was the result of subscriptions to the *Yorkshire Evening News* who arranged the tribute. Contributions came not only from Yorkshire but also from all over England and Australia. Hutton's final career statistics, following his inevitable but sadly premature retirement in 1955, underlined the claims that he was one of England's finest ever batsmen – 40,140 first-class runs at an average of 55.51 including 129 centuries. For his county, Hutton made 24,807 runs and for England 6,971 Test runs, with his innings of 364 in 1938 remaining the outstanding achievement of his many batting feats.

171. Yorkshire team 1956: Back row, left to right: F.A. Lowson, R. Illingworth, M.J. Cowan, R. Appleyard, D.B. Close, F.S. Trueman, D.E.V. Padgett, J.G. Binks. Front row, left to right: J.V. Wilson, J.H. Wardle, W.H.H. Sutcliffe (captain), W. Watson and E.I. Lester. The first season without the presence of Leonard Hutton saw Yorkshire finish seventh in the County Championship. They won only 8 of their 28 fixtures. Surrey claimed their fifth successive title.

Len Hutton became Sir Leonard Hutton when he received a knighthood in the Queen's Birthday Honours list of 1956 for 'services to cricket', the first Yorkshire cricketer to be so honoured and only the second professional cricketer after Sir Jack Hobbs to receive the accolade. Sir Leonard, having moved south to Kingston in Surrey, thereafter concentrated on business for J.H. Fenner Ltd, a Hull based engineering company. He served briefly as a Test selector in the mid 1970s and in later years he wrote perceptively for *The Observer*. He died in Kingston Hospital on 6 September 1990, just over six months after he had accepted the Presidency of Yorkshire CCC. He left behind his widow Dorothy and two sons John and Richard, who himself played for Yorkshire and England. At a service of thanksgiving at York Minster in November 1990, the Dean of York summed up Sir Leonard Hutton's rich life, 'We give thanks for his devotion to his family, his modesty and humility, his bravery in adversity, his honour and integrity, and his own special sense of humour.'

Six

White Rose Revival and Sixties Success

The Yorkshire team, 1966. Back row, left to right: J.S. Waring, P.J. Sharpe, J.G. Binks, D. Wilson, R.A. Hutton, J.H. Hampshire, D.E.V. Padgett, G. Boycott. Front row, left to right: R. Illingworth, D.B. Close (captain), F.S. Trueman and K. Taylor. Yorkshire reclaimed the Championship that summer from Worcestershire, who had won the title in successive seasons (1964 and 1965).

Yorkshire's Willie Watson and Surrey captain Stuart Surridge (right) share a joke together in 1956. Surrey dominated the Championship during the 1950s as Surridge and then Peter May led them to seven consecutive Championship titles between 1952 and 1958. Yorkshire had to settle for the runners-up position in 1952, 1954, and 1955, but it was they who brought an end to Surrey's monopoly in 1959. The dawning of a new decade brought with it a return to White Rose supremacy.

Jimmy Binks was Yorkshire's regular wicket-keeper from 1955 until 1969. In his career he made 412 consecutive appearances for the county (a club record). He followed in the great line of White Rose keepers from Pinder, Hunter, Dolphin to Arthur Wood, and onwards to his successor David Bairstow. A quiet, unruffled wicket-keeper, he was at his best in 1960 with his haul of 107 victims standing clear as yet another county record. His batting alone perhaps prevented him from making more than two appearances for England.

Two years after retiring from the game, Sir Leonard Hutton was briefly pursuaded back into the first-class arena for the Old Trafford Centenary match in June 1957. Opening the batting for the MCC with Sussex's Don Smith (left), Sir Leonard stroked his way to 76, including ten 4s.

Yorkshire team, 1958. Back row, left to right: M. Ryan, R. Illingworth, R.K. Platt, M.J. Cowan, D. Pickles, D.E.V. Padgett, J.G. Binks. Middle row, left to right: F.S. Trueman, J.H. Wardle, J.R. Burnet (captain), J.V. Wilson, D.B. Close. Front row, left to right: W.B. Stott and K. Taylor. Yorkshire's descent to eleventh position in the Championship table, under new captain Ronnie Burnet, had much to do with events off the field.

John Henry Nash was appointed Assistant Secretary of Yorkshire CCC in 1922 and succeeded Frederick Toone as Secretary in 1931, at the age of only 25. He held the position until 1971. A somewhat distant and aloof personality, Nash was a shrewd man and he exerted a gentle control of the Club during two of the county's finest eras – the 1930s and the '60s. In 1958 it was he who announced the dismissal of Johnny Wardle, perhaps the saddest of all his duties during his forty years as Club Secretary.

The downfall of Yorkshire's Johnny Wardle was as swift as it was tragic, but it had been a likelihood for several seasons. Wardle was very much his own man, but unrest in the dressing room stemmed somewhat from his attitude. His dismissal seemed the only way to regain discipline within the Club. Wardle's name was linked with a series of newspaper articles published by the *Daily Mail* in which he criticised Yorkshire's captain and his colleagues. His invitation to tour Australia in the winter of 1958/59 was withdrawn by the MCC, and the game effectively lost a bowling genius. He left the first-class game with an incomplete career record – 1,539 wickets for Yorkshire at 18.13. In later years the rift with Yorkshire was healed and he helped to remodel Geoff Cope's bowling action in the early 1970s thus repairing the bowler's confidence in the process. In 1985 the county welcomed Wardle as their bowling consultant, but before he took up his post he died on 23 July 1985 at the age of 62, having never fully recovered from an operation to remove a brain tumour earlier in the year. For a second time Yorkshire had lost Wardle, his vast bowling knowledge wasted, just as his skills on the field had been in the late 1950s.

Ronnie Burnet led the Yorkshire second XI to the Minor Counties Championship in 1957 and in 1958 was appointed the county's first team captain at the age of 39. A useful middle-order batsman, Burnet was a firm disciplinarian and, following the sacking of Johnny Wardle, harmony within the dressing room brought its reward in 1959. He led the county, in his second and final season as skipper, to the Championship title for the first time outright since 1946, all this without the Test players Watson, Lowson, Appleyard, and of course Wardle. His job done, Burnet returned to cricket in the Bradford League and in later years served on the Yorkshire CCC Committee.

Below: Surrey v Yorkshire at The Oval in 1959. Surrey's Micky Stewart fails to hang on to a chance from Yorkshire's Jimmy Binks off the bowling of Lock. Surrey fought Yorkshire all the way to hang on to their unbeaten Championship sequence, but despite winning at The Oval by 86 runs at the end of the season they had to be content with joint second position behind the new northern Champions.

The smiles in the Yorkshire dressing room at the County Ground, Hove, on 1 September 1959, as the Championship returns to the White Rose for the first time outright since 1946. Burnet and his men savour the moment. Requiring 215 to win the match with Sussex, Yorkshire raced to their target in only 98 minutes. Victory, in what was the final Championship match of the season, was achieved with a display of breathtaking stroke play.

Roy Ullyett's interpretation of a typical Surrey supporters reaction to Yorkshire's 1959 Championship success.

Surrey County Cricket Club
KENNINGTON OVAL

4D.

CHAMPION COUNTY v. REST OF ENGLAND
Saturday, September 12th, 1959 (3 Day Match)

REST OF ENGLAND

		First Innings		Second Innings	
1	Pullar, G. ...... Lancashire	b Trueman	103	c Stott, b Close	4
2	Gale, R. A. ...... Middlesex	c & b Wilson, D.	40	c Padgett, b Platt	11
3	Barrington, K. ...... Surrey	st Binks, b Illingworth	15	c Bolus, b Illingworth	18
4	M. J. K. Smith .... Warwickshire	c Padgett, b Illingworth	77	c Padgett, b Close	25
*5	D. B. Carr ...... Derbyshire	c Close, b Platt	13	c Wilson J., b Illingworth	7
6	T. E. Bailey ...... Essex	c & b Wilson, D.	59	st Binks, b Illingworth	32
‡7	Evans, T. G. ...... Kent	c Close, b Platt	10	c Trueman, b Close	27
8	Allen, D. A. ...... Gloucestershire	b Close	6	c Illingworth, b Close	2
9	Lock, G. A. R. ...... Surrey	not out	44	c Padgett, b Illingworth	2
10	Rhodes, H. J. ...... Derbyshire	not out	10	not out	0
11	Moss, A. E. ...... Middlesex			c Wilson J., b Close	0
		B , l-b7 , w , n-b	7	B2 , l-b5 , w , n-b	7
		Innings dec.——		Total	135
		Total (8 wkts)	384		

FALL OF THE WICKETS

1—130 2—146 3—196 4—249 5—250 6—264 7—288 8—359 9— 10—
1—41 2—49 3—53 4—96 5—96 6—120 7—132 8—134 9—135 10—135

BOWLING ANALYSIS	First Innings						Second Innings					
	O.	M.	R.	W.	Wd.	N.b.	O.	M.	R.	W.	Wd.	N.b.
Trueman	27	8	61	1			8	2	18	0		
Platt	17	6	40	2			8	2	23	1		
Illingworth	28	4	109	2			13	2	40	4		
Close	15	1	92	1			12.4	1	47	5		
Wilson, D.	16	3	75	2								

NEW BALL may be taken at the discretion of the fielding captain either (a) after 200 runs have been scored or (b) after 75 overs have been bowled. In the latter case a WHITE disc will be shown on the main score board at the end of the 65th over and will be replaced by a YELLOW disc after the 70th over. At the commencement of the 75th over both discs will be exposed and remain until the new ball has been taken.

CORINTHIAN CASUALS FOOTBALL SEASON — SAT. OCT. 3rd. — OVAL

YORKSHIRE

		First Innings		Second Innings	
1	Stott, W. B.	b Moss	5	c Lock, b Rhodes	61
2	Bolus, J. B.	b Moss	1	lbw b Lock	44
‡10	Binks, J. G.	c Smith, b Rhodes	3	not out	21
3	Padgett, D. E. V.	b Rhodes	2	c Lock, b Allen	18
4	Close, D. B.	c Bailey, b Lock	34	b Bailey	86
5	Wilson, J. V.	b Allen	41	c Pullar, b Allen	105
6	Illingworth, R.	c Carr, b Barrington	37	hit wkt., b Allen	32
7	Wilson, D.	c Gale, b Lock	7	b Barrington	0
*8	J. R. Burnet	not out	17	b Barrington	0
9	Trueman, F. S.	b Barrington	5	c Gale, b Lock	45
11	Platt, R. K.	b Barrington	4	b Lock	3
		B , l-b2 , w , n-b	2	B 4 , l-b5 , w , n-b1	10
		Total	160	Total	425

FALL OF THE WICKETS

1—2 2—9 3—9 4—16 5—70 6—96 7—111 8—142 9—150 10—160
1—78 2—131 3—132 4—256 5—318 6—319 7—323 8—382 9—410 10—425

BOWLING ANALYSIS	First Innings						Second Innings					
	O.	M.	R.	W.	Wd.	N.b.	O.	M.	R.	W.	Wd.	N.b.
Rhodes	8	2	31	2			15	4	66	1		1
Moss	6	2	16	2			13	1	46	0		
Lock	12	3	36	2			27.5	7	107	3		
Bailey	6	1	22	0			12	1	31	1		
Allen	8	1	35	1			24	6	85	3		
Barrington	5	0	18	3			22	4	72	2		
Carr							2	0	8	0		

*Captain ‡Wkt.-keeper

Umpires—Crapp & Elliott, H.

Toss won by—Rest

RESULT—Yorkshire won by 66 runs

HOURS OF PLAY—ALL DAYS—11.30—6.30   LUNCH 1.30

Printed on the ground by the Surrey County Cricket Club Printing Department

Scorecard of Champion County v Rest of England in 1959. Yorkshire set the seal on their successful season by beating the Rest of England by 66 runs at The Oval in mid September. The match was memorable for centuries from Lancashire's Pullar and Yorkshire's J.V. Wilson, who batted for over 4 hours.

Yorkshire team, 1959, at Scarborough. From left to right: D. Wilson, F.S. Trueman, J.R. Burnet (captain), D.B. Close, R. Illingworth, J.G. Binks, D.E.V. Padgett, W.B. Stott, J.B. Bolus, H.D. Bird and J. Birkenshaw. After the tragedy of Wardle's dismissal and seven seasons spent chasing Surrey in the Championship race, Yorkshire with a young and raw side registered the county's 23rd Championship title.

Brian Bolus, an aggressive right-handed opening batsman, played 107 matches for Yorkshire between 1956 and 1962 before going on to play for, and captain, Nottinghamshire and Derbyshire. He made his highest score for Yorkshire (146 not out) against Hampshire in 1960. In a career which extended until 1975, Bolus scored over 25,000 first-class runs and made seven appearances for England in 1963 and 1964.

Douglas Padgett turns a ball to leg in a Championship match against Surrey. He was a technically correct opening and middle order batsman who never quite realised his boyhood promise, having made his debut for Yorkshire in 1951 at the age of 16 years, 321 days. A stalwart of Brian Close's team of the '60s, Padgett ended his career in 1971 with over 21,000 runs to his name in first-class cricket. He was later appointed Yorkshire's chief coach in succession to Arthur Mitchell.

Ken Taylor, a dashing right-handed opening batsman from Huddersfield, formed an attractive opening partnership with Bryan Stott in the late '50s and early '60s. Taylor passed 1,000 runs in a season on six occasions. His best batting effort came in 1961 when he made 1,494 runs at 34.74, including 203 not out against Warwickshire. One of the best cover points to have patrolled that area of the field for Yorkshire, Taylor played for the Club until 1968. A man of varied talents, he moved into teaching after his retirement.

Vic Wilson, accompanied by Fred Trueman, about to embark on the first full practice at the Headingley winter sheds in April 1962. Wilson became Yorkshire's fifth captain since the Second World War in 1960 and the first professional skipper of the county since Tom Emmett way back in 1882. The powerfully built left-hander led the side with a natural ability, strength, and authority. His three year reign as Yorkshire captain (he retired at the age of 41 after the 1962 season) brought two Championship titles and, in a distinguished career stretching back to 1946, he scored over 20,000 runs. He left his successor, Brian Close, the nucleus of a very powerful and talented side.

The successor to Johnny Wardle as Yorkshire's slow left-arm bowler was the adventurous young Don Wilson from Settle. Tall and lean, he developed steadily from his county debut in 1957. Ever enthusiastic, he quickly became a favourite with spectators in much the same way as Roy Kilner had in the 1920s. He took 100 wickets in a season five times and in 1966 became the third Yorkshire bowler to capture two hat-tricks in the same season after George Macaulay in 1933 and George Freeman in 1868. After leaving Yorkshire, Wilson became chief coach at Lord's until 1991, when he returned to his native county to take up a coaching role at Ampleforth College in North Yorkshire.

Brian Close (right), and Bryan Stott (left), absorb the advice offered by mentor and fellow left-hander Maurice Leyland at Headingley in 1960. The young colts, and many within the game, held Leyland in high regard as a man and a cricketer. His last years were blighted by Parkinson's disease and he passed away in Knaresborough on 1 January 1967. Bryan Stott was an aggressive opening batsman from Yeadon. He scored 1,000 runs in a season five times, his best being 2,034 runs at 37.66 in 1959. His career ended prematurely in 1963 when, at the age of only 29, he left the game to concentrate on the family business.

John Christopher Balderstone was a right-handed batsman and slow left-arm bowler from Longwood, Huddersfield. He made his first-class debut for Yorkshire against Glamorgan at Headingley in 1961 and stayed with the county until 1969 before moving to play at Leicestershire where he stayed until 1986. An attractive opening batsman, he played twice for England against the formidable 1976 West Indian side. As well as cricket he also played soccer for Huddersfield Town, Doncaster Rovers, Carlisle United, and Queen of the South.

Yorkshire team, 1962. Back row, left to right: E.I. Lester (scorer), P.J. Sharpe, D.E.V. Padgett, M. Ryan, M.J. Cowan, R.K. Platt, D. Wilson, J.B. Bolus, K. Gillhouley, G. Alcock (masseur). Front row, left to right: K. Taylor, R. Illingworth, D.B. Close, J.V. Wilson (captain), F.S. Trueman, J.G. Binks and W.B. Stott. Yorkshire won 14 of their 32 Championship fixtures, claiming the title ahead of Worcestershire.

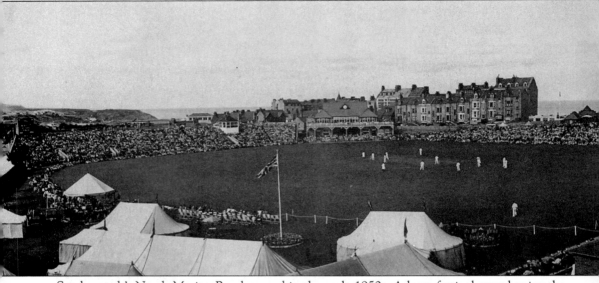

Scarborough's North Marine Road ground in the early 1950s. A large festival crowd enjoy the cricket and during the break for lunch and tea they could listen to the band play from their stand on the left of the picture, close to the festival marquees in the foreground. Sometimes they would play whilst the game was in progress, and the national anthem was always played at the end of the day's cricket.

Richard Hutton, elder son of Sir Leonard Hutton, made his Yorkshire debut in 1962. An all-round cricketer, he bowled right-arm medium quick and was a powerful right-handed middle order batsman. Strong of frame, he took just nine wickets at 21.88 and scored 123 runs at 15.37 in his first season. He failed to establish himself as a regular member of the Yorkshire team until 1965, but thereafter became a valuable part of the county XI until his retirement in 1974.

Fred Trueman opens his broad shoulders during a typical hard-hitting innings of 63 for the Players against the Gentlemen at Lord's in 1962. Trueman was far more than a high class quick bowler; with the bat he was a prolific hitter, possessing a fine array of orthodox strokes and having a sound enough defence to score three first-class hundreds. An exceptional short-leg fielder, Trueman caught most things that went his way.

John Hampshire, a powerful right-handed batsman from Thurnscoe in South Yorkshire, made his debut in 1961 and passed the 1,000 run mark for the first time in 1963 scoring 1,236 runs at 26.86 with a mixture of sound defence and aggressive driving. His eight Test caps for England fell sadly short of expectations, but still he ended his career with over 28,000 runs and 43 first-class centuries to his name. He succeeded Geoff Boycott as Yorkshire captain in 1979 but outside pressures forced his resignation after two difficult seasons in charge. A first-class umpire since 1985, he was appointed to the Test match panel in 1989.

Philip Sharpe, a short, stocky, middle order hard hitting batsman, scored 22,530 first-class runs at 30.73 per innings in a career which began for Yorkshire in 1958 and ended in 1976 at Derbyshire where he played for two seasons. As a slip fielder, Sharpe was amongst the best in Yorkshire's and indeed the game's, long history. Capable of hanging onto catches that few others would have, he was able to make the most difficult of chances appear straightforward. In 1962 he equalled 'Long John' Tunnicliffe's county record set in 1901, of seventy catches in a season. For England in his twenty Test matches he averaged 46.23. Outside the game, he played hockey for his county and maintained an interest in amateur operatic productions.

Yorkshire v Essex at Hull in May 1964. M.J. Bear is given out lbw off the bowling of Tony Nicholson for 21. Yorkshire wicket-keeper Jimmy Binks appeals and Brian Close offers vocal support in the background. Yorkshire won the match by a comfortable seven wicket margin.

The loss of the County
Championship to Worcestershire
in 1964 and 1965 was compensated
for somewhat by Yorkshire when
they won the new, one-day Gillette
Cup competition in 1965. Man of
the match Geoff Boycott produced
a devastating batting display.
Yorkshire's 317 for 4 (the highest
total in the 60 over a-side
competition until eclipsed by both
Sussex and Warwickshire in 1993)
was due in large part to a second-
wicket stand of 192 between Brian
Close, who made a swashbuckling
79 and Boycott, who cast off his
normal cautious approach in
making 146, which included three
6s and fifteen 4s. Surrey were out
played and crumbled to 142 all out,
losing the match by an
overwhelming 175 runs.

A young Tony Nicholson (left)
chats with fellow Yorkshire bowler
Mike Cowan. Nicholson, a right-
arm fast, medium pace bowler from
Dewsbury, made his county debut
in 1962 and in 1966 took his first
haul of 100 wickets in a season. A
perfect foil in many respects to his
bowling partner Trueman,
Nicholson picked up many of his
wickets with variation of pace and
movement. He was a popular
player with spectators and
colleagues alike. His career for the
county ended in 1975; his 876
wickets were taken at a cost of
19.74 runs apiece. His early death
in November 1985 came as a tragic
loss to Yorkshire cricket.

121

Chris Old, a right-arm, medium fast bowler from Middlesbrough, was one of the three Yorkshire debutants in 1966 along with batsman Barrie Leadbeater and off spinner Geoff Cope. Old played only two matches that season, but following Trueman's retirement he became a regular member of the side in 1969. His control of line and length won him 46 Test caps and, following a troubled spell as Yorkshire captain, he departed for Warwickshire where he finished his career in 1985, having taken 1,070 first-class wickets.

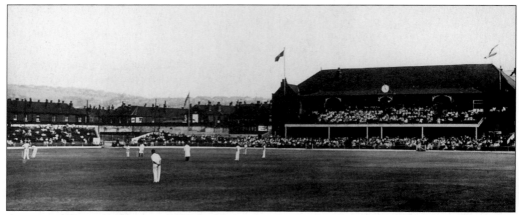

A view of Bramall Lane in 1959 looking towards the South East stand and pavilion. The ground's days as a venue of first-class cricket were numbered. On 7 August 1973, Yorkshire and Lancashire concluded their drawn Roses match there, the last county fixture to be played on the famous Sheffield ground. A new football stand was built on the site. A 118 year association with Yorkshire cricket was over, and with Bramall Lane's demise went part of the county's cricketing heritage.

A somewhat sarcastic newspaper cartoon from 1967 hints at the problems encountered by Yorkshire skipper Brian Close. In the Championship game against Warwickshire in mid-August, Close's tactics attracted national criticism. Needing only 142 to win the match in an hour and a half, Warwickshire were left frustrated on 133 for five after Yorkshire's bowlers, under Close's instructions, had sent down only 24 overs in the allocated time. His deliberate time-wasting ploy eventually cost him the captaincy of England.

Veteran Kent and England wicket-keeper Godfrey Evans, at the age of 46 and in his final season of first-class cricket, turns a ball down the leg side during his county's match against Yorkshire at Canterbury in August 1967. Jimmy Binks is the Yorkshire wicket-keeper and John Hampshire turns to chase the ball. Yorkshire won the match by seven wickets and by the end of the season were County Champions again for the 28th time.

Yorkshire v Glamorgan at Bramall Lane, 1968. Jimmy Binks is caught by Glamorgan's Peter Walker off the bowling of Don Shepherd for no score as Yorkshire tumbled to defeat by 103 runs. Despite that defeat, one of four losses that summer, Yorkshire won their third consecutive Championship and, to date, the last of their twenty-nine county titles.

The breaking up of a truly great sporting side is always a time of sadness and regret. That was certainly the case for Yorkshire in 1968, with the departure of three of the county's best post-war players: Ken Taylor, Fred Trueman, and Raymond Illingworth. Illingworth's departure was perhaps the most damaging loss to Yorkshire. Unable to finalise terms for a new contract with the Club, he departed to join Leicestershire as captain at the start of the 1969 season. In his eighteen years at Yorkshire, Illingworth took almost 1,400 wickets and scored in excess of 14,000 runs, accomplishing the double six times. Illingworth's departure in 1968 in many ways affected Yorkshire's subsequent history. He was the obvious successor to Brian Close as county captain and, had he stayed, might have held together what later became the divided factions within the Club.

Fred Trueman, alongside Geoffrey Boycott, finally hung up his boots after the summer of 1968. His belligerent quick bowling brought him 1,745 wickets for Yorkshire and 2,304 in all first-class cricket. The batsmen of England breathed a sigh of relief at Trueman's departure; for Yorkshire followers came the stark realisation that it would be a long while before the county saw his like again. In retirement, Fred Trueman became a well known TV personality and a highly respected member of radio's *Test Match Special* team. Forthright with his views of the modern game and players, his vast cricket knowledge, like that of Johnny Wardle, has sadly been lost by Yorkshire.

MCC v Yorkshire at Lord's in April 1969. Yorkshire's Phil Sharpe cuts Pat Pocock for two runs during his innings of 101. Derbyshire's Bob Taylor is the wicket-keeper and Dennis Amiss and Colin Milburn are the close fielders. MCC won the match by seven wickets.

Brian Close and his Yorkshire team-mates celebrate their Gillette Cup final victory over Derbyshire on 6 September 1969. From left to right: A.G. Nicholson, R.A. Hutton, D.B. Close (captain), J.G. Binks, P.J. Sharpe, D. Wilson and J.H. Hampshire. One of the Yorkshire players not pictured, Barrie Leadbeater, playing with a broken bone in his left hand, played a vital

innings of 76 which was sufficient to take his county to a 69 run win and also secured him the Man of the Match award. This was Yorkshire's second Gillette Cup title and sadly, the county's last major domestic honour for fourteen barren years.

Brian Close's successful reign as Yorkshire captain came to an abrupt and controversial end in 1970, when the committee announced that he was not to be reappointed for the 1971 season. Close, sacked by Yorkshire, left to play with Somerset which he captained until his retirement from the game in 1977 when he also received the CBE for services to cricket. One of the aspiring young talents who blossomed under Close's leadership at Somerset was a certain I.T. Botham.

Yorkshire team, 1971. Back row, left to right: A.J. Dalton, M.K. Bore, N. Smith, B. Leadbeater, C.M. Old, R.G. Lumb, G.A. Cope, J.D. Woodford, D.L. Bairstow. Front row, left to right: P. Carrick, J.H. Hampshire, P.J. Sharpe, D. Wilson, G. Boycott (captain), D.E.V. Padgett, A.G. Nicholson and P.D. Borrill. The next generation of White Rose cricketing talent is on show at the start of a new decade. Why should the 1970s have been any different from that of previous eras? The years of internal strife and despair that bedevilled the Club during the 1970s and 1980s are thankfully now confined to history, and those who cherish Yorkshire cricket will hope that the likes of Gough, Silverwood, Vaughan and McGrath, amongst others, can revive the glorious past triumphs that brought the White Rose county both honour and respect throughout the cricketing world.

WHISKY

A TASTING COURSE

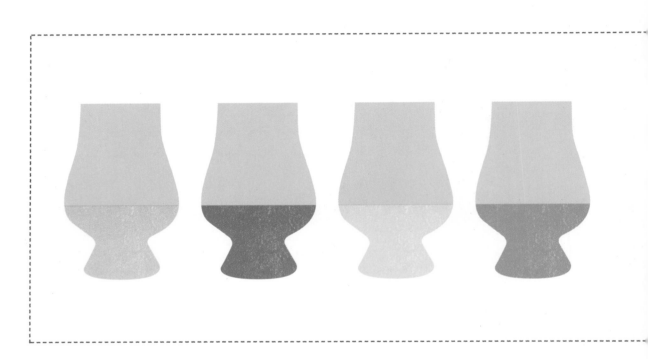

WHISKY
A TASTING COURSE

A NEW WAY TO **THINK** – AND **DRINK** – WHISKY

EDDIE LUDLOW

DK | Penguin Random House

Senior editor Ian Fitzgerald
Senior designer Saffron Stocker
Designers Simon Murrell, David Ball
Design Assistant Sophie State
Map Illustrator Arunas Kacinskas
Picture researchers Nic Dean, Sarah Hopper
Editorial assistant Kiron Gill
Senior Jacket Creative Nicola Powling
Jackets co-ordinator Lucy Philpott
Managing editor Dawn Henderson
Managing art editor Marianne Markham
Senior producer, pre-production Tony Phipps
Producer Luca Bazzoli
Art director Maxine Pedliham
Publishing director Mary-Clare Jerram

First published in Great Britain in 2019 by
Dorling Kindersley Limited
One Embassy Gardens, 8 Viaduct Gardens,
London, SW11 7AY

The authorised representative in the EEA is
Dorling Kindersley Verlag GmbH. Arnulfstr. 124,
80636 Munich, Germany

A CIP catalogue record for this book is available
from the British Library.
ISBN: 978-0-2413-4521-4

Printed in the UAE

For the curious
www.dk.com

MIX
Paper | Supporting
responsible forestry
FSC™ C018179

This book was made with Forest
Stewardship Council™ certified
paper – one small step in DK's
commitment to a sustainable future.
For more information go to
www.dk.com/our-green-pledge

CONTENTS

FOREWORD

LIKE A LOT OF PEOPLE, I was far too young the first time I tasted whisky. Not surprisingly, I didn't like it.

In fact, I only began to revisit the spirit when I started my first job in the drinks industry, as a sales assistant at Oddbins, in Newcastle upon Tyne. I had walked into the shop because I needed a job and had no real background in the drinks industry, apart from a stint working in a real ale pub a year previously. So this is where it all began for me. What I found in that wondrous place were people with a genuine passion about the things they sold. And they knew about it, too. They soon started to infect me with their enthusiasm, and, before I knew it, I was conducting customer tastings for both wine and whisky. But it was the latter that quickly took up most of my heart- and head-space. A few trips to Scotland later I was all in. My love was cemented.

A brief foray into brand ambassadorial duties at Ardbeg and Glenmorangie put me in direct contact with some of the industry's key whisky makers for the first time. Life-long friendships were forged. Usually over a few drams…

However, this only made me realize that I needed to talk to people about *all* good whisky, not just a handful of brands. That's why my wife Amanda and I set up The Whisky Lounge in 2008 after taking the scary step of leaving full-time employment.

To begin with, The Whisky Lounge was just me, driving my battered old car around the country, preaching the good word to the whisky-curious. At first it was just to ten people in London, or twelve souls in Brighton. It didn't matter. I was doing what I loved. It took a seeming age to get the business established, to the point where Amanda could join me, but we did it. There was – and is – a need for whisky knowledge out there, and we were doing our bit to share what we knew.

This book hopefully helps other people to scratch their whisky itch. I am not a scientist or a boffin that knows the hidden secrets of how to create magical whiskies. I have picked up a thing or two on my travels around the whisky world, but that's not the job of this book. Its function is more about what I do day to day, and what whisky really is all about: tasting. Everything else flows from that, and it's what forms the heart and soul of this book. I hope you like it.

CHAPTER 1

WHAT IS WHISKY?

IT'S A BIG QUESTION, and attempting to answer it reveals the rich variety and almost infinite complexity of this most characterful of drinks. In this chapter, the focus is on some of the most important issues: why drink whisky, what is whisky's "story", why is it held in such high regard around the world, and, importantly, how it is made. In a book dedicated to getting the most out of such a fascinating spirit, knowing beforehand what whisky actually is forms an essential part of your whisky-tasting journey.

▲ **Spoilt for choice.** There are hundreds of whisky brands and a variety of styles. Finding "your" whisky or whiskies will take time.

WHY TASTE WHISKY?

It sounds obvious, but the best way to discover whisky is to taste it. Not drink it. *Taste* it. There is a difference, as you will discover for yourself, hopefully with a little help from this book.

Whisky is one of the world's most popular spirits but, like its flavour, it can appear too complex – even confusing – to get to know.

The sheer number of distilleries in traditional whisky-making areas such as Scotland, Ireland, the US, and Canada is bewildering enough. Add in relative newcomers such as Japan, Sweden, Taiwan, and Australia, and the world of whisky can seem too big. Where do you even start getting to grips with this huge subject? What are the most important things to look out for?

MASTERING THE BASICS

The key, as far as this book is concerned, is mastering how to taste whisky. There is more to it than pouring a measure and drinking it. You will certainly be doing that, but along the way you will learn the best ways to identify and interpret whisky's many tastes and styles. By mastering taste, you should be able to answer questions such as:

- why does this whisky taste the way it does?
- what other whiskies would I enjoy if I like this whisky?
- how do I get the most out of the whiskies I buy?
- how do I describe taste?

NO TWO TASTE THE SAME

Taste is ultimately a personal experience, but that is what makes discovering whisky a potentially enlightening undertaking.

The flavours you get from a whisky may not be the same as those for the person drinking it next to you. That is where learning the "language" of tasting comes in, so that, as you grow in confidence, your palate develops, and your whisky vocabulary increases, you will be able to share your whisky-tasting judgements with others.

Enjoying whisky starts with knowing how to taste it. Bear that in mind and you won't go far wrong.

▶ **One to savour.** You can add water, ice, or mixers to whisky, or enjoy it neat. But remember, it is meant to be taken in moderation.

20 TASTINGS TO GET YOU STARTED

▲ **By the end of this book** you should be something of a whisky devotee – or at least an assured whisky taster making informed choices.

The core of this book is a series of 20 whisky tastings, carefully created to show the range and the variety of world whiskies.

In each tasting you'll find:

- a guided exploration of four whiskies
- details of the whiskies involved and pointers on what to look for
- a "debrief" explaining what you should have learned from the tasting
- style guides to help you choose other whiskies you may enjoy
- Flavour maps to help you identify the characteristics of the four whiskies
- suggestions for alternative whiskies

The focus is always on flavour: what it is, how to identify it, and why mastering taste means mastering whisky.

THE STORY OF WHISKY

We take whisky for granted today, as though it has always been around. It hasn't, and the history of where it came from goes beyond the mists of Scotland and way back into the mists of time.

Many believe that whisky was "invented" in Scotland or Ireland. But its true origins lie elsewhere.

EASTERN ROOTS?

It all began with the Muslim alchemist Abu Musa Jabir ibn Hayyan, who first produced a liquid later dubbed *aqua vitae*: "the water of life".

Arabic works such as Jabir's were translated into Latin by European monks. The first mention of a whisky-like liquid in Scotland dates from 1494, where King James IV's exchequer rolls record a Brother John Cor receiving "eight bolls of malt to make *aqua vitae*" at Lindores Abbey, northwest Fife.

EVOLUTION OF SPECIES

"Whisky" then was very different to what we'd expect now. It probably bore a greater resemblance to a whisky liqueur, adding local ingredients such as heather, lavender and honey to make it more palatable. This style held sway until the rise of commercial distillation at the end of the 18th century in Scotland and Ireland.

WHISKY GOES WEST

A few thousand miles away, settlers in America and Canada – immigrants from Ireland, Scotland, Germany, and Holland, among others – were developing different distillation techniques in their new homelands. The result? Bourbon was being made from corn in Kentucky by the late 1700s, while rye was the preferred grain for distilling spirits further north.

The history of whisky's spread around the world has many twists and turns – and ups and downs – all resulting in the globally dominant spirit of today.

THE FIRST MENTION OF A WHISKY-LIKE LIQUID IN SCOTLAND DATES FROM 1494

WHISKY – A TIMELINE

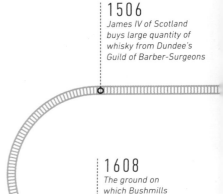

1506
James IV of Scotland buys large quantity of whisky from Dundee's Guild of Barber-Surgeons

1608
The ground on which Bushmills distillery was built is granted a licence

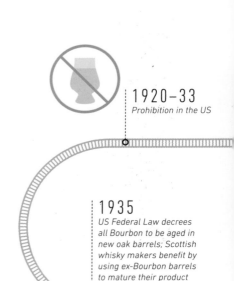

1920–33
Prohibition in the US

1935
US Federal Law decrees all Bourbon to be aged in new oak barrels; Scottish whisky makers benefit by using ex-Bourbon barrels to mature their product

C. 2000 BC
Art of distillation begins in ancient Mesopotamia

C. 200 AD
First written record of distillation, by Alexander of Aphrodisias

C. 750 AD
Abu Musa Jabir perfects the alembic still

1494
First mention of whisky-type spirit in Scottish records

1000–1200
Distillation begins in Scotland and Ireland

1725
The Malt Tax almost ends Scottish whisky industry. Many distillers open illicitly at night, making "moonshine"

LATE 1700s
Bourbon production begins in Kentucky, USA

1820
Johnnie Walker whisky launched

1823
Excise Act legalizes distilling in Scotland

1880
World wine production decimated by phylloxera outbreak; whisky sales soar

1850
First blended whisky released by Andrew Usher

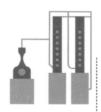

1831
Aeneas Coffey patents the "Coffey still"

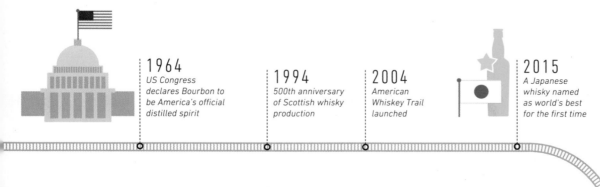

1964
US Congress declares Bourbon to be America's official distilled spirit

1994
500th anniversary of Scottish whisky production

2004
American Whiskey Trail launched

2015
A Japanese whisky named as world's best for the first time

WHAT'S SPECIAL ABOUT WHISKY?

Whisky's place at the top of the spirits league table is constantly being challenged. So, what is it doing to stay ahead of the pack? And where could whisky-making go in the future?

PROVENANCE

All of the dark spirits – Cognac, rum and Armagnac – have long histories, but whisky pre-dates them all. Whilst Cognac and Armagnac are made only in the regions that give them their names, whisky is made worldwide. It is produced by an infinite combination of processes to create a huge number of flavours.

It has also had its fair share of luck, which took whisky from being a popular national and regional drink to a global phenomenon.

INTERNATIONAL APPEAL

Scotch whisky outsells every other dark spirit, and has done for decades. Its export sales are

**10
CANADA**
*1.19 litres.
Exports 70 per
cent of its
whisky to the US*

**07
UK**
*1.25 litres.
US whiskey
sales now rival
those of Scotch*

**08
IRELAND**
*1.24 litres.
Irish whiskey is
the world's
fastest growing
spirit category*

**03
USA**
*1.41 litres.
Jack Daniel's is
America's most
popular whiskey*

**NO.7
TENNESSEE
WHISKEY**

**01
FRANCE**
*2.15 litres.
Buys 200 million
bottles annually*

**02
URUGUAY**
*1.77 litres.
Best-selling
whisky is locally
produced blend
Dunbar*

**05
SPAIN**
*1.29 litres.
Almost 75 per
cent of sales are
Scotch whisky*

steady, and valuable, at more than £4 billion annually. Add to that the yearly American whiskey sales of around $3.5 billion (£2.7 billion) and you see the monster that has been created. Scotch whisky outsells its nearest rival, brandy (including Cognac and Armagnac), by 2-to-1.

EVER POPULAR

Plus, more countries than ever are making whisky now, much of it really good.

Whisky transcends fashions and trends. Despite ups and downs in its history, whisky has maintained its deserved star status. It is adaptable, too. In Spain it is commonly drunk with cola, in Japan with soda water and ice, as a Highball, and in the UK on its own or with water.

It also works in cocktails, seen as one of the biggest challenges to top mixologists due to the complex knit of flavours present in the liquid.

INNOVATION

Many distillers and blenders of whisky, whilst respectful of tradition, history, and regulations, are pushing the boundaries of what can be done. As whisky draws much of its flavour from the cask, that's an area distillers have been especially interested in.

They will commonly use ex-wine, sherry, and port casks to mature their whisky, but some are going even further. One prominent whisky maker, for instance, has used ex-India Pale Ale (IPA) casks to age its spirit in.

Elsewhere, craft whisky-makers and micro distilleries are innovating further, experimenting with grains, such as rice and buckwheat, for instance, helping to ensure that whisky remains at the forefront of the spirit world.

◀ **WORLD SPIRIT**
This map shows the top ten whisky drinking nations, with annual consumption shown in litres per person.

09
INDIA
1.24 litres.
Consumes half the world's whisky

BRILLIANCE SINGLE MALT

06
UAE
1.27 litres.
Muslim state, with 80 per cent expat population

04
AUSTRALIA
1.3 litres.
Single malt and Bourbon are the nation's favourites

GO WITH THE GRAIN

Practically any grain can be fermented into alcohol, but barley, corn, rye, and wheat are the main players for whisky, comprising the majority of the grains used.

ANATOMY OF A GRAIN

All cereal grains are seeds, with a hard outer skin. The job of whisky makers is to penetrate this shell to reach the endosperm, which is full of starchy carbohydrates that are converted to sugar, and then alcohol. The process of converting grains into alcohol was developed across millennia, the result being an enormous variety of beers, ales, and spirits – of which whisky, for many, is the pinnacle. It is accepted that the craft of turning malted barley in particular into whisky was perfected in Scotland.

BARLEY

Barley features in most whiskies. This is due to its high levels of starch and – critically – enzymes that facilitate the fermentation process.

MALTED BARLEY

This is the "malt" element of malt whiskies. Barley is steeped in water, spread out and left to germinate. This breaks down the grain's cell walls, allowing enzymes to access starches.

UNMALTED

Unmalted, or green, barley has not been germinated, so has lower sugar levels. It is used for all single pot still whiskies to produce lighter flavours.

RANK IN WORLD CROP PRODUCTION 4

PREFERRED CLIMATE Most conditions except cold

PREPARATION Germinated, then dried at 55–60°C (131–140°F)

FLAVOUR PROFILE
Unmalted cereal, spice, toasted toffee

BITTER...SWEET

UNMALTED   MALT

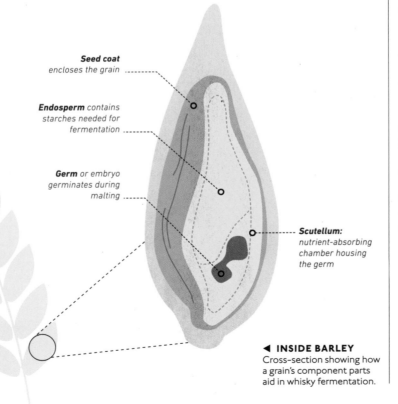

Seed coat encloses the grain

Endosperm contains starches needed for fermentation

Germ or embryo germinates during malting

Scutellum: nutrient-absorbing chamber housing the germ

◀ **INSIDE BARLEY**
Cross-section showing how a grain's component parts aid in whisky fermentation.

CORN

Also called maize, it is the world's most widely produced crop.

Corn is a main ingredient in many American whiskeys. Unlike barley, it has no enzymes, so the kernels are heated at high temperatures to break them down.

RANK IN WORLD CROP PRODUCTION 1

PREFERRED CLIMATE Warm; vulnerable to frost

PREPARATION Heated to 80–90°C (176–194°F) before mashing

FLAVOUR PROFILE
Vanilla and maple-syrup

BITTER..SWEET
▲

RYE

This grass crop is closely related to wheat and barley.

Rye whiskies hail mainly from North America, but are growing in popularity globally. Rye grows fast, and matures more quickly than barley. It is hardy and needs little weeding.

RANK IN WORLD CROP PRODUCTION 6

PREFERRED CLIMATE Thrives in most conditions, including cold

PREPARATION Heated to 65–70°C (149–158°F) before mashing

FLAVOUR PROFILE
Dry, with a spicy, peppery bite

BITTER..SWEET
▲

WHEAT

A worldwide staple, wheat belongs to the genus *Triticum*.

In Canada, immigrant millers used grain left over from bread baking to make whisky. Wheat is increasingly popular with US craft producers. Its low-key, light character is perfect for blending.

RANK IN WORLD CROP PRODUCTION 2

CLIMATE Most conditions, except extreme heat or cold

PREPARATION Heated to 65–70°C (149–158°F) before mashing

FLAVOUR PROFILE
Wholemeal bread with honey

BITTER..SWEET
▲

THE RISE OF CRAFT GRAINS

Some makers are turning to less mainstream grains, with different flavour profiles, to produce distinctive whiskies.

OATS

Once common in Irish whiskeys, oats are low in starch. The grains can stick together in the still, but for some producers the creamy texture and nutty aroma make oats worth the effort.

SORGHUM

Sorghum is becoming popular with makers, particularly in America, for its easy-drinking qualities. Some makers create this whisky using sorghum syrup, extracted from the stalk.

MILLET

Millet is gaining popularity as a component of craft Bourbons, and at least one US distillery produces a 100 per cent-millet whiskey. It is hardy, needing little watering to thrive.

RICE

Found in new whiskies from Japan and America, rice's light, subtle taste is popular with younger drinkers and cocktail-lovers. Rice whisky derives from the Japanese spirit shochu.

HOW WHISKY IS MADE

All whisky is made in essentially the same way, by distilling spirit from grains. This simplified explanation shows how malted barley and other whiskies are produced.

GRAIN PREPARATION

- For barley-based whisky, grains are "malted": steeped in cold water for several days to hydrate the endosperm, the source of their starch.
- The barley is germinated for up to a week on a malting floor or in a germination box.
- The seeds' cell walls begin breaking down. Enzymes and starches develop for conversion into fermentable sugars.

Barley grains are raked out on the malting floor

▲ **THE MALTING FLOOR**
These are only used for barley. Corn, rye, and wheat don't contain enzymes that are activated by steeping. They are cooked at high temperatures to soften the hard cell walls, ready for milling.

MAKING THE GRIST

- Barley's germination is halted by air-drying or kilning it.
- Once dried, all grains – barley, rye, corn, and wheat – are ground into "grist" to make their starches accessible.

Grains are ground into fine flour

▲ **GRIST TO THE MILL**
The grist is the useful part of the ground grains. The unusable part is called chaff. For "harder" grains such as corn, rye, and wheat, a portion of malted barley is added to the grist to aid fermentation.

MASHING

- Increasingly hot water is flushed through the grist, normally three times, to extract its sugars. Water allows the enzymes to complete the conversion of starch into fermentable sugars.
- The warm, sweet liquid produced is called "wort".

As the wort heats enzymes are released

▲ **CHEMICAL REACTION**
The mixture of grist and water is added to a receptacle known as a mash tun. This vessel is insulated, so that it maintains the liquid within at a constantly maintained and regulated temperature.

FERMENTATION

- Yeast, normally in liquid form, is added to the wort.
- The yeast converts the wort's fermentable sugars into heat, carbon dioxide (CO_2), and alcohol.
- No hops or other flavourings are added.
- Fermentation takes place over 48–100+ hours, depending on the distillery.
- The resultant beer, or "wash", is normally 7–9% alcohol by volume (ABV).

Fermentation begins when yeast is added to the wort

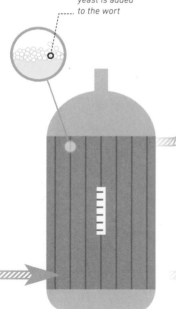

▲ THE WASHBACK
This is the container where fermentation occurs. The wort and yeast combine and react in a volatile, frothing manner that results in a beer-like foaming head that must be skimmed off.

DISTILLATION

- For malt whisky, the wash is pumped into the wash still and heated until it boils.
- Alcohol vaporizes from the liquid, rising into a condenser to become liquid "low wines" at around 25% ABV.
- The low wines go into a second still to repeat the process. The "middle cut" of this distillate becomes the final spirit.

Liquid vaporizes and condenses

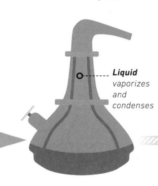

▲ POT STILL
Used for Scotch and Scotch-style whiskies, pot stills make whisky in batches: each filling and emptying of the still equates to one "batch". In column stills, the liquid flows through continuously.

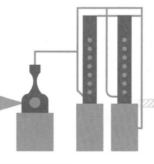

▲ COLUMN STILL
Grain whiskies, made from corn, rye, or wheat, are distilled in a column, or Coffey, still. Bourbon and Bourbon-style whiskies use both standard column stills and a type of column still called a doubler.

MATURATION

- Almost all whiskies from around the world are matured in oak barrels.
- Maturation length depends on several factors, including local whisky regulations and regional climates.

Whisky casks are almost always oak

▲ OLD CASKS
Scotch and Scotch-style whiskies are matured in used casks. These include ex-wine, ex-Sherry, and ex-Port barrels. Former Bourbon casks are also particularly popular.

▲ NEW CASKS
Bourbon and Bourbon-style whiskeys, by US law, must be matured in new, charred oak barrels. There is no minimum maturation period. Other styles of US whiskey can be aged in used casks.

HOW WHISKY AGES

Aside from a few rare cases, whisky isn't whisky if it has not been matured in oak casks. But why mature it at all, and for how long? There's much more to keeping whisky in barrels than meets the eye.

Once whisky has been distilled it is not ready to drink. Called "new-make" or "white-dog", it contains less-than-palatable flavours that need to be removed.

The maturation process dissipates these unwanted elements whilst helping develop more enticing flavours.

PURE AND SIMPLE

As it matures, usually in oak casks, whisky is also "filtered". Oak's grain and chemical composition, and its lack of unpleasant-tasting sap, allow it to remove impurities and sour notes from newly distilled whisky, whilst imbuing it with favourable aromas and flavours. The time this takes depends on the freshness of the cask.

WHISKY GROWS UP

Each year whisky spends in an oak cask deepens and develops its flavour. As most Scottish single malts, for example, are kept in barrels for 5–10 years before bottling, that is a lot of taste being developed. Climate plays its part, too. In warmer regions, whisky interacts rapidly with the wood and matures fast.

In humid areas, such as Scotland, more alcohol is lost during maturation; in low-humidity regions, such as Kentucky, water evaporates at a faster rate, meaning the alcoholic strength of the spirit actually increases.

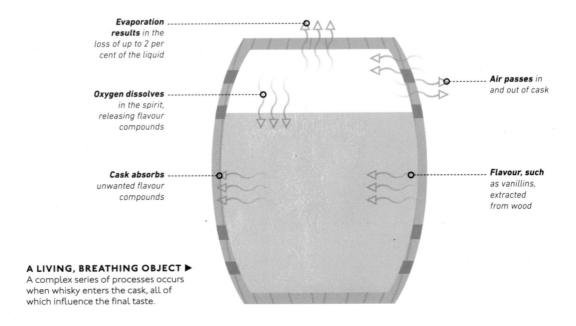

Evaporation results in the loss of up to 2 per cent of the liquid

Oxygen dissolves in the spirit, releasing flavour compounds

Cask absorbs unwanted flavour compounds

Air passes in and out of cask

Flavour, such as vanillins, extracted from wood

A LIVING, BREATHING OBJECT ▶
A complex series of processes occurs when whisky enters the cask, all of which influence the final taste.

Whisky lost through evaporation is known as "the angels' share", and accounts for around 2 per cent of the product in volume and alcohol content.

THE OAK EFFECT

Other woods such as maple or hickory are sometimes, though rarely, used for maturing whisky. But it is also the case that almost all forms of whisky production worldwide specify the use of oak as a legal requirement.

Oak is abundant, waterproof, strong, flexible, and hard-wearing. Plus, it has the right quantities of bitter tannins and acidic vanillins to ensure a balanced flavour profile. The vanillins, in particular, help to give many whiskies a vanilla-like flavour. But oak on its own is not enough. It needs a cooper to bring out its best qualities. The cooper is the skilled artisan who makes oak barrels. Part of this process involves toasting or charring the inside of the cask. This destroys distasteful compounds, helps activate flavour-enhancing wood polymers, and creates a carbon layer that filters out sulphur.

Not all oak species are suitable for whisky-making, though. The most common varieties are:

▲ **In the UK**, it takes around four years to train as a cooper – but it's a life-long commitment in reality.

Quercus alba, or American white oak; *Quercus robur*, the European oak, often from France and northern Spain; and *Quercus mongolica*, or Japanese mizunara oak. Each imparts different characteristics to the whiskies matured in them.

EACH YEAR WHISKY SPENDS IN AN OAK BARREL DEEPENS AND DEVELOPS ITS FLAVOUR

CHAPTER 2

HOW ----- TO ----- TASTE

AS TEMPTING AS IT IS to dive in and start tasting, you will get much more from your whiskies by discovering *how* to taste them. It is a skill that is instantly rewarding. Who would have thought, for example, that the road to enjoying whisky begins by simply *looking* at it? There is of course more to it than that, and the following pages take you, step by step, along the right path. It will help you assemble your whisky-tasting "toolkit" and show you the way to whisky Nirvana. Better still, you will actually begin tasting.

WHISKY-TASTING CHECKLIST

To get the most from this book, some basic tools will enhance your whisky-tasting experiences. This is what you will need, and need to know, in order to have productive tastings. You may in time develop your own checklist, but this one is a good start.

01

GLASSWARE

This should be comfortable to hold but narrow at the opening. Tumblers are too wide and allow aromas to escape.

Glencairn tasting glasses are ideal, but a conical, small wine glass will also work. Try to use a clean glass for each "flight" (whisky tasted): whisky sticks to the glass and the residue can affect subsequent tastings. The fewer opportunities you encounter to interfere with the whisky's taste the better.

02

A WORKSPACE

Ensure there is enough space to hold your glasses and bottles. This may sound obvious, but once you have laid out all of your other tasting equipment alongside your whiskies, you will be surprised how much room you will need.

03

WHEN TO EAT

Never taste whisky on an empty stomach. Ideally, eat something an hour before tasting. Be sure not to eat too much.

04

NIBBLES

Go for neutral, palate-cleansing snacks such as unsalted (or low-salt) oatcakes. Bread can also work, but should be free from, or low in, salt. Ensure you don't over-eat, though. The whisky should always be your focus.

05

WATER

Use still water to add to the whisky and sparkling water to hydrate yourself and to cleanse your palate. Choose spring water over mineral water as it is pure, with fewer taste-affecting additives, natural or otherwise.

06

GO SOLO?

Tasting with friends can work well, if they appreciate what you are trying to achieve. Two to four people is a good number. After all, whisky is precious and doesn't grow on trees!

07

PEN AND PADS

Something to make notes with, including a tablet or phone with note-taking apps – but keep any electronic equipment away from the liquids.

08

THE TASTING ORDER

Always taste from left to right, just like in this book. Ideally, taste whiskies "blind" – with the bottles covered – as the colour, shape, and design of a bottle can influence you before you have taken your first sip.

A numbered tasting mat will help you keep track of which whisky is which until the big reveal at the end.

09

SAMPLE SIZE

For tasting purposes, 15ml (½fl oz) is fine. If you have the glassware, pre-pour all of the samples, ready to taste.

Whisky is strong, remember, so drink it responsibly.

10

BE HEALTHY

Don't embark on a tasting if you have a cold or any other illness. You will need your taste buds to be unimpaired. Similarly, try not to smoke at least an hour beforehand. This also suppresses taste.

11

FINAL CHECK

Once you are ready to begin, double-check your equipment. Nothing ruins the flow of tasting more than having to stop because your pen has run out of ink or you don't have enough snacks to hand!

12

TAKE YOUR TIME

Now taste, slowly and carefully. Look at the whisky first and nose it. Then savour each drop, extracting every element of flavour and aroma. Only move from one drink to the next when you're ready.

START TASTING

Take a tasting glass and pour around 2cm (1in) of whisky. Use the same techniques for every drink you try. It provides a great benchmark from which to assess each whisky's characteristics.

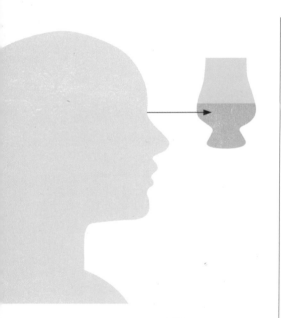

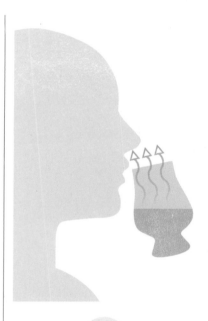

1

LOOK AT THE COLOUR

Hold the glass up against a white background. Colour can provide a clue as to what type of cask the whisky has been aged in and for how long. The spirit will normally be clear, but if it is not this may be because it has not been chill-filtered to remove any fatty acids.

2

SWIRL THE WHISKY

Gently swirl the whisky in the glass. Higher-alcohol, or cask-strength, whiskies may throw slower "tears" – those oily trails that cling to the side of the glass. This process also agitates the whisky, forcing the aromas up to the top of the glass.

3

TAKE A SNIFF

Bring the glass to your nose and sniff gently: remember, whisky is high in alcohol and is absorbed by your nasal membranes. Once you are comfortable with the alcohol in your olfactory organs, breathe in more deeply, taking note of any specific aromas you detect.

COLOUR CAN PROVIDE
A CLUE AS TO WHAT
TYPE OF CASK THE
WHISKY HAS BEEN
AGED IN AND FOR
HOW LONG

TO PIPETTE OR NOT?

A pipette is a useful tool for adding precise amounts of water. Start small and add more until it feels right. You can go "freehand", and not use a pipette, but this gives you less control.

4

TAKE A SIP

Take enough whisky into your mouth to cover your tongue. Roll it around in your mouth, coating as many sensory areas as possible. Does it taste the same as it smelled? What additional flavours have you stumbled across? Do you like what you are tasting?

5

ADD A LITTLE WATER

Try adding a little spring or filtered water, gradually and preferably using a pipette. Add just a few drops to begin with, so as not to over-dilute your whisky. The introduction of water releases the aromas and flavours otherwise locked in by the alcohol.

6

FINISH UP!

When you swallow the whisky, with and without water, take note of the flavour and the texture in your mouth and on your tongue. Is it oily, velvety or waxy? You are looking for a finish that rounds off the experience beautifully, leaving you wanting more.

THE LANGUAGE OF WHISKY

Whisky is arguably the world's most complex spirit. Articulating its flavours can be a challenge, particularly when you're tasting for the first time. Once you master whisky's "language" you will find your tasting voice.

ZESTY **PEATY**

SWEET SOFT

SPICY CHEWY

MEDIUM-LENGTH

▲ **WHISKY WORDS**
These words crop up often in whisky tastings. Use them, but add your own terminology, too.

LEARN THE LINGO

Before you start, remember: what you are doing in this book is *tasting*, not drinking. You'll be looking for words to describe flavours, aromas, and more, in order to understand and enjoy your whiskies better.

You may struggle at first, or you may feel self-conscious uttering words and phrases that at first seem a bit silly or over-the-top. But this is how you'll learn how to identify the spirits' flavour elements. Just let yourself go. Express yourself!

A PERSONAL TASTE

There is no right or wrong when it comes to the words you use. You will taste things your friends don't, and vice versa, because people's palates and experiences are all different. So don't worry if your notes aren't the same as those of the taster standing next to you; they're bound to be different – and that's the whole point. Tasting whisky is a personal experience.

CHOOSE YOUR WORDS

The best tasting notes are those that have clearly been extracted from tasters' imaginations and show that a whisky has really "spoken" to them.

They're not just a shopping list of flavours, but a window into what that whisky has meant to a person and why.

The important thing is to make your description personal and something that you can relate to.

So, how to begin? Start by using simple, broad terms, such as:
• Fresh
• Fruity
• Malty
• Spicy
• Smoky

THE BEST TASTING NOTES ARE THOSE THAT HAVE BEEN CLEARLY EXTRACTED FROM THE TASTERS' IMAGINATIONS

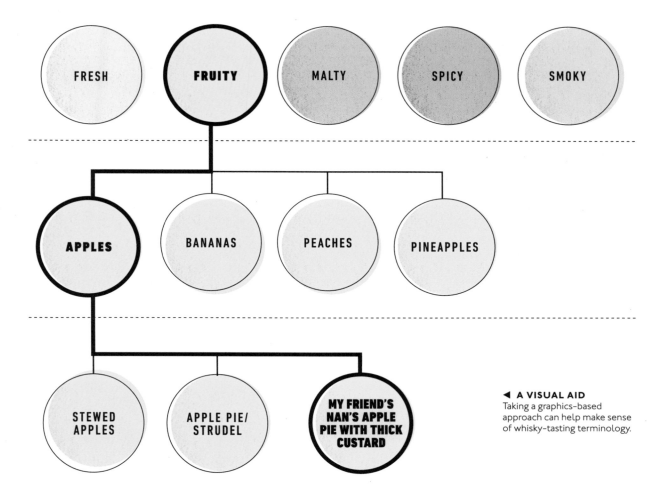

FRESH	FRUITY	MALTY	SPICY	SMOKY

APPLES   BANANAS   PEACHES   PINEAPPLES

STEWED APPLES   APPLE PIE/ STRUDEL   MY FRIEND'S NAN'S APPLE PIE WITH THICK CUSTARD

◄ **A VISUAL AID**
Taking a graphics-based approach can help make sense of whisky-tasting terminology.

BEYOND THE BASICS

Some, but not necessarily all, of these basic flavours will be found in any whiskies you taste. Once you have identified a whisky's flavour category (or "camp"), try exploring that category further.

For example, if you've detected a fruity flavour in your glass, which fruit does it most resemble? What is the dominant fruit flavour? Try thinking:

• Apples
• Bananas
• Peaches
• Pineapples

If it is apples, what kind? Fresh, candied, cooked, spiced? Your notes should now begin to look something like this:

• Fruity
  • Apples
    • Stewed apples
      • Apple pie/strudel
        • My friend's nan's apple pie with thick custard

DO IT YOUR WAY

You will in time evolve your own "language", but basing it on a system of categories and sub-categories like this is a good start.

KEEPING A RECORD

There is no "official" way to make tasting notes.

However, a good basic structure would be to first write down the name of the whisky you taste, and when you tasted it. Then describe, in your own words: how the whisky looks; its aroma, or "nose"; its taste, or palate; the length or otherwise of its finish; and then any general comments you have.

WHISKY AND WATER

To add or not to add water: that is the question. Let's look at what the addition of H_2O does to your precious dram, and when, or even why, you should add it.

IN ORDER TO NOT "COLOUR" THE WHISKY WITH EXTERNAL FLAVOURS, THE WATER SHOULD BE AS PURE AS POSSIBLE

UNLOCKING FLAVOUR

Alcohol dulls and inhibits your taste receptors. As whisky typically has a high level of alcohol, usually above 40% ABV, it can be worth lowering that level to get the best out of it.

Add a drop of water to most whiskies and something magical happens. The alcohol molecules agitate, unlocking access to the full range of the spirit's flavours. You can see it happening, as oil tendrils in the liquid swirl and separate as you add the water.

Diluting whisky also aids the senses, opening the flood-gates to a tidal wave of new and intensified aromas.

It is not the same for all whiskies, though. Older or lighter whiskies with delicate flavour sets may actually "fall apart" if water is added. The only rule is to try for yourself. Nose your whisky and taste it without water. If you like it as is, you may be inclined to leave it alone. But try it with water anyway. It may taste even better for you.

HOW MUCH TO ADD?

It is all about trial and error. Get yourself a small pipette, so that you can gradually add water to your whisky, taking written notes each time. After each addition, nose and taste your whisky, repeating until you find your whisky–water Nirvana!

WHAT TYPE OF WATER?

In order to not "colour" the whisky with external flavours, the water should be as pure as possible. A good-quality bottled spring water or even filtered tap water both work well. Water from the distillery that made the whisky would be ideal, but

is not often possible! Try to avoid mineral waters, as the compounds in the water can be quite noticeable and may affect how you taste the whisky.

WHAT ABOUT ICE?

In some countries and cultures, such as Japan, good single malts are mixed with ice and soda water to create a Highball, a refreshing and delicious long drink. Intense whiskies enjoyed in warmer climates often benefit from a cube or two of ice.

For tasting, however, be more cautious. Ice has a double-block effect: it both numbs the palate and "locks in" the flavours of the whisky, making them harder to detect.

▲ **Always look** before you taste whisky. Every professional taster will begin their appreciation of a whisky by checking its appearance.

HOW WHISKY LOOKS

How important is the colour and appearance of a whisky? What can it tell us before we even pick up a glass? Looking at whisky is a vital part of the "tasting" process and should not be neglected.

THE HERBAL REMEDY

Whisky was not always whisky-coloured. Before it was the spirit we know today, and before wooden casks were used for storage, whisky was various shades of clear. "Various" because, before distilling

became a formal process, colour-giving herbs and spices were added to the spirit, in order to flavour it. In addition, early distilling equipment was usually pretty rudimentary (and not entirely clean) and filtering techniques probably quite minimal. AN

ACCIDENT OF HISTORY

All that changed when wooden barrels came into use for storage and transportation in the late 18th century. It's likely that wood's effect on whisky's colour was first noticed by mistake, when a warehouse owner came across a long-forgotten cask, opened it and saw that the whisky within had miraculously darkened.

Today, of course, we have a better understanding of how oak can affect the spirit's colour (and taste), and how that transfer takes place. Many people are surprised to learn that, in most modern distilleries, when "new-make" spirit emerges from the still it is crystal clear. It gets most of its colour from being stored in oak.

ADDING COLOUR

Whisky can also get its colour from another source. Spirit caramel, otherwise known as E150a, is used to shade some, by no means all, Scottish and other whiskies for commercial consistency. It supposedly has no taste, but does impart a caramel colour. It is barred from use in US Bourbon and rye whiskeys, and many people would prefer it were not used for any whiskies, regardless of how little is used, or how arguably negligible its effect on flavour.

"TEARS" AND "LEGS"

You may have heard about a wine's "legs". These are the trails of liquid that cling to the glass when you swirl it around. In wine, this can tell you a lot about the alcohol content and viscosity of the product. With whisky – and spirits in general – things aren't so clear, as whisky is always high in alcohol. However, "tears", as they are called in the whisky industry, that run down the glass more slowly than other whiskies probably have a higher alcohol content. Be aware though, as this tells you nothing about the quality of the product.

◄ **Whisky "tears"** are predominantly water, as it has a higher surface tension, and is therefore "stickier" than alcohol.

Gin Clear

White Wine

Pale Straw

Light Gold

Pale Gold

Golden Straw

Yellow Gold

Pale Amber

Golden Amber

Rich Amber

Rich Gold

Burnt Amber

Burnished Copper

Chestnut/Oloroso Sherry

Russet/ Muscat

Tawny

Auburn

Mahogany

Burnt Umber

Old Oak

Brown Sherry

Treacle

▲ **WHISKY'S COLOURS**
This book uses the descriptions detailed here to describe the variety of whisky shades. They are terms widely used in the whisky-tasting world.

TASTING 01 / 20

TASTE WITH YOUR EYES

Can your eyes deceive you when tasting whisky? The answer is yes and no. Sight is your frontline sense and helps you form an opinion before you even begin to taste.

IF YOU CAN'T FIND THIS use Kilbeggan 8YO

WEIGHT 1	Scottish grain distillery, built 1963, owned by William Grant & Sons.

HOW IT WORKS

For this tasting, the lighter examples suggest storage in ex-Bourbon casks. Darker examples indicate ex-sherry barrels, while rose or antique copper colours usually mean port. If the whiskies are hazy or cloudy, it could mean they have not been chill-filtered to remove proteins or fatty acids. Putting your hand over the glass to see how long any bubbles remain indicates the dram's strength. Taste from left to right.

THE LESSON...

The big lesson here is realizing that whisky tasting is a process. As tempting as it may be to dive straight in and drink, it is more productive to take your time. That begins with looking at your drink. You will learn a huge amount, setting the tone for the tasting to follow. The more you look at whisky, the more you will "know" it.

THE BIG LESSON HERE IS REALIZING THAT WHISKY TASTING IS A PROCESS

 WHITE WINE

 VERY SUBTLE, soft caramel; milk chocolate

SWEET AND DELICATE vanilla; herbal notes; lemon

 **LONG,** delicate and subtle

FLAVOUR MAP

WOODY
PEATY
FRUITY
SPICY
FLORAL
CEREAL

 LIKE THIS? Try Bain's Cape Whisky

ARDBEG

10YO SINGLE ISLAY MALT

46% ABV

IF YOU CAN'T FIND THIS use
Talisker 57° North Single Malt

WEIGHT	
5	One of the world's most heavily peated single malts.

PALE STRAW

A RAGING FIRE on a peat bog!
Some sweeter notes

INTENSE, SMOKY; eucalyptus,
sweet mint, citrus

LONG, smoky sweet finish

LIKE THIS? Try Laphroaig 10YO

MAKER'S MARK

BOURBON

45% ABV

IF YOU CAN'T FIND THIS use
Eagle Rare 10YO Bourbon

WEIGHT	
4	Maker's Mark has been producing Bourbon since 1954.

GOLDEN AMBER

RICH AND SWEET; caramel, toffee;
cola sweets

LUSCIOUS; spiced poached fruit;
chilli chocolate

A LINGERING, sticky, spicy sweetness

LIKE THIS? Try Four Roses Single Barrel

GLENDRONACH

12YO "ORIGINAL" SINGLE HIGHLAND MALT

43% ABV

IF YOU CAN'T FIND THIS use
Mortlach Rare Old Single Malt

WEIGHT	
4	A cult classic for sherry-cask-loving whisky fans.

GOLDEN AMBER

DRIED APRICOTS, apple strudel,
cinnamon, cloves

SWEET FIGS; pear crumble; creamy
rice pudding

LONG AND LUXURIOUS, slightly dry,
spicy oiliness

LIKE THIS? Try Glen Moray Sherry Finish

▲ **Master at work.** Seiichi Koshimizu, Chief Blender at Suntory's Yamazaki distillery, puts his nose to use.

DETECTING WHISKY AROMAS

Your nose will be your best friend when it comes to selecting your favourite drams. It is important, then, to understand some of its physiology and how to use it when tasting. It is your "gateway" to whisky.

It may seem counter-intuitive to smell whisky before tasting it. But it is not just good sense, it is a vital first stage in perfecting the tasting experience.

Before we look at aromas or flavours, we need to understand how our sense of smell processes the information that allows us to identify individual elements.

MAKING SENSE OF SENSE

What is most important to realize is where the point of detection is, so that we can apply this information when we taste. The most sensitive data-gathering part of your palate is your olfactory system. Olfactory receptor nerve cells, each containing a single olfactory neuron and embedded high up in your nasal cavity, are agitated and stimulated by aroma molecules that exist around us.

Whether it is a summer meadow or your favourite coffee shop, everywhere we go is infused with its own set of aromas. Once a flavour has been detected, the neuron identifies the smell as best

YOUR MOUTH AND TONGUE ARE ACTUALLY QUITE INEFFICIENT AT DETECTING ALL BUT THE MOST BASIC FLAVOURS

it can and notifies your brain to process and sort the information. As there are many more flavours than receptors, the receptors usually work together to identify specific aromas.

The first pathway for these receptors is through your nostrils when you smell something. What you may not know is that a second pathway exists behind your tongue. When you taste something, the flavour molecules travel up the back of your throat to the olfactory receptors, going in the opposite direction to the food or drink you consume. If these receptors are blocked, as when you have a cold,

your sense of taste is hampered. In whisky-tasting terms, using your olfactory system to detect aromas is called "nosing".

TASTE WITH YOUR NOSE

Your mouth and tongue are actually quite inefficient at detecting all but the most basic flavours, such as salt, sweet, and bitter. But as these are precisely the things your olfactory system cannot detect, you can begin to see how your nose, tongue, and mouth are ultimately linked in the tasting process. Put simply, aroma plus taste equals flavour.

NOSING TIPS

Just like with cleansing your palate between each whisky tasting, so you should "correct" your olfactory system before nosing individual whiskies.

NOT IN BAD TASTE

Avoid strongly flavoured foods or smoking an hour before tasting. Both can deaden your palate, making it harder for your nose to detect more subtle aromas.

SAVE YOUR SKIN

If you find your palate overwhelmed, perhaps having tasted a number of whiskies, smell your non-watch-wearing wrist. This can help you "reset" your olfactory system.

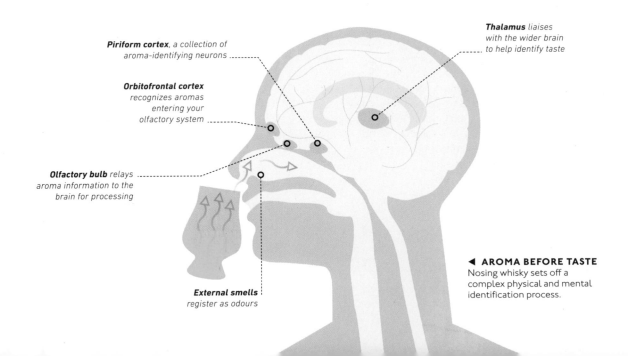

Piriform cortex, a collection of aroma-identifying neurons

Orbitofrontal cortex recognizes aromas entering your olfactory system

Olfactory bulb relays aroma information to the brain for processing

Thalamus liaises with the wider brain to help identify taste

External smells register as odours

◀ **AROMA BEFORE TASTE**
Nosing whisky sets off a complex physical and mental identification process.

TASTING 02 / 20

TASTE WITH YOUR NOSE

Now you know your olfactory system is responsible for most of your aroma-spotting skills, it's time to put it to the test. Here, we will ask you to focus on using your nose to detect aroma and flavour.

HOW IT WORKS

Here, the focus is on nosing: smelling the whisky to identify its aromas. Nose each whisky, undiluted, then add a few drops of water to each. Nose again, taking notes. Add more water (the whisky will eventually be diluted to at least 50/50, if not more) and make notes at each stage. You may not normally drink your whisky with this much water, but here you are analysing them for as many individual aromas as possible.

THE LESSON...

What you should take away from this tasting is how important your sense of smell is, and how to use it. To see how it is the driving force behind your ability to pick out key whisky flavours. You will have also learned the importance of using water to help draw out aromas. You don't have to always be so analytical, but now you know how to extract the maximum flavour!

NOSE EACH WHISKY, UNDILUTED, THEN ADD A FEW DROPS OF WATER

CHIVAS REGAL MIZUNARA FINISH

BLENDED SCOTCH
40% ABV

IF YOU CAN'T FIND THIS use Hibiki Harmony

| WEIGHT **3** | This Chivas Regal variant is finished in Japanese, or mizunara, oak casks. |

 GOLDEN STRAW

 FRAGRANT HERBS; cherry-blossom; pepper and toffee

 A LIGHT, slightly oily texture

 **LIGHT** and deft finish

FLAVOUR MAP

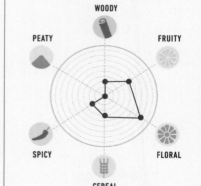

 LIKE THIS? Try Ballantine's 17YO

BALVENIE SB 12YO

SINGLE SPEYSIDE MALT

47.8%

IF YOU CAN'T FIND THIS use
Knappogue Castle 12YO

WEIGHT 2	Established 1892, the Grant family's second single malt distillery, after Glenfiddich.

PALE GOLD

DAISIES AND BUTTERCUPS; fresh honey on crusty bread

HONEY SWEETNESS; warming, velvety mouth feel

SWEET AND LONG finish

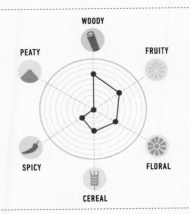

LIKE THIS? Try Glenkinchie 12YO

SAZERAC RYE

KENTUCKY RYE

45% ABV

IF YOU CAN'T FIND THIS use
Jim Beam Rye

WEIGHT 5	Produced at Kentucky's multi-award-winning Buffalo Trace distillery.

BURNISHED COPPER

SAVOURY BEEF JERKY, Parma ham, barbeque smoke, fragrant nuttiness

SWEET, SPICY, peppery and creamy

QUITE DRY and spicy

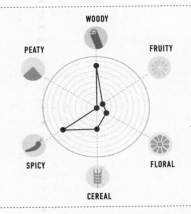

LIKE THIS? Try FEW Rye

LAGAVULIN 16YO

SINGLE ISLAY MALT

43% ABV

IF YOU CAN'T FIND THIS use
Ardbeg Uigeadail

WEIGHT 5	A highly regarded Islay single malt, with a robust "after-dinner" style.

GOLDEN AMBER

OLD LEATHER ARMCHAIRS, tobacco, chocolate, cinnamon; peat smoke

A GOLDEN syrup-like texture

LONG and smoky

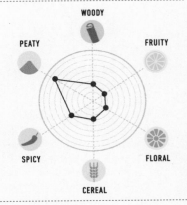

LIKE THIS? Try Wemyss Peat Chimney

WHISKY'S MAIN FLAVOURS

In any given whisky there is a complex set of tastes to discern. Using a flavour wheel is a great "at a glance" way to both identify whisky's main flavours and then go deeper, to explore the subtleties of what you taste.

No two whiskies taste the same. Each one, even if it's from the same distillery as the whisky alongside it, will have minute or big differences – or something in between.

GETTING YOU STARTED

The more fluent we can become in the language of tasting, along with an ever-expanding vocabulary of terms and descriptors, the more we can build truly individual notes for each individual spirit we try.

A useful tool that assists in this pursuit is what is known as a "flavour wheel". The example on the right is a good example of one you can use as a springboard for your own notes. It is not in any way

a definitive "chart" you should think of as set in stone. The most interesting notes, after all, are those extracted from your imagination.

In time, you will be able to produce tasting notes without resorting to aids such as these. Until then, and as a way of training your brain to think in terms of how

AS THE FLAVOURS RADIATE OUT FROM EACH OF THE SIX MAIN TASTE CATEGORIES THEY BECOME MORE AND MORE SPECIFIC

whisky's flavours are categorized, referring to a flavour wheel will prove highly useful.

THE BIG SIX FLAVOURS

One of the great benefits of using this tool is that it conveniently breaks down whisky's main flavours into manageable – and accurate – categories.

In whisky's case, it is agreed among experts that its flavours fall into six main groups:
- Woody
- Fruity
- Floral
- Cereal
- Spicy
- Peaty

Once you fix that breakdown in your mind you will be well on the way to understanding, and then exploring, the more profound mysteries of this fascinating spirit's ever-changing moods.

WHEN WHISKY GOES WRONG

Generally speaking, whisky is a pretty robust spirit, yet it is not unknown for it to, occasionally, take a turn for the worse.

While it is rarer to find "off" flavours in whisky than in, say, wine, it does happen. This is especially the case for whisky with cork stoppers. As with wine, this can lead to cork taint. Chlorophenol compounds (from pesticides and preservatives) are absorbed by the cork tree, converted into TCA (trichloroanisole), which then reacts with the whisky in the bottle to create a musty, nasty, damp aroma. It will not seriously damage your health, but it will certainly taste pretty foul. If your whisky smells bad, don't drink it.

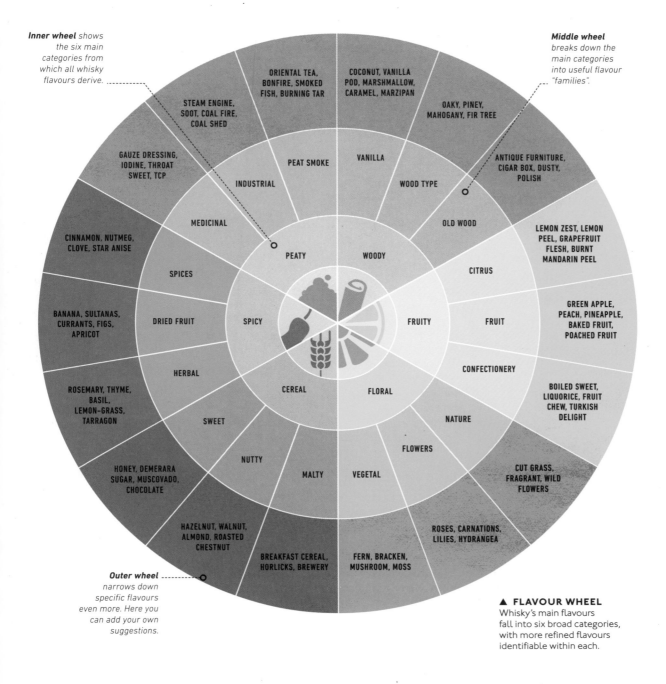

ORIENTAL TEA, BONFIRE, SMOKED FISH, BURNING TAR

COCONUT, VANILLA POD, MARSHMALLOW, CARAMEL, MARZIPAN

STEAM ENGINE, SOOT, COAL FIRE, COAL SHED

OAKY, PINEY, MAHOGANY, FIR TREE

PEAT SMOKE

VANILLA

GAUZE DRESSING, IODINE, THROAT SWEET, TCP

ANTIQUE FURNITURE, CIGAR BOX, DUSTY, POLISH

INDUSTRIAL

WOOD TYPE

MEDICINAL

OLD WOOD

CINNAMON, NUTMEG, CLOVE, STAR ANISE

LEMON ZEST, LEMON PEEL, GRAPEFRUIT FLESH, BURNT MANDARIN PEEL

PEATY

WOODY

SPICES

CITRUS

BANANA, SULTANAS, CURRANTS, FIGS, APRICOT

GREEN APPLE, PEACH, PINEAPPLE, BAKED FRUIT, POACHED FRUIT

DRIED FRUIT

SPICY

FRUITY

FRUIT

HERBAL

ROSEMARY, THYME, BASIL, LEMON-GRASS, TARRAGON

CONFECTIONERY

CEREAL

FRUITY

BOILED SWEET, LIQUORICE, FRUIT CHEW, TURKISH DELIGHT

SWEET

FLORAL

HONEY, DEMERARA SUGAR, MUSCOVADO, CHOCOLATE

NATURE

NUTTY

FLOWERS

CUT GRASS, FRAGRANT, WILD FLOWERS

MALTY

VEGETAL

HAZELNUT, WALNUT, ALMOND, ROASTED CHESTNUT

ROSES, CARNATIONS, LILIES, HYDRANGEA

BREAKFAST CEREAL, HORLICKS, BREWERY

FERN, BRACKEN, MUSHROOM, MOSS

▲ FLAVOUR WHEEL
Whisky's main flavours fall into six broad categories, with more refined flavours identifiable within each.

HOW THE WHEEL WORKS

Like spokes on a wheel, as the flavours radiate out from each of the six main taste categories they become more and more specific.

You can see, for example, that a "peaty" whisky does not have just one category of sub-flavours.

"Peaty", then, can mean a medicinal flavour, or something smoky, or even something "industrial" or metallic. And within those three sub-categories there are yet more tastes to explore. So, step-by-step, using a flavour wheel will assist you greatly in uncovering whisky's wonderful complexities.

TASTING
03 / 20

TASTE WITH YOUR TONGUE

Using the same whiskies as in the last tasting for continuity, we focus here on how your taste buds and olfactory system work together, with flavours and aromas combining in a complex sensory blend.

HOW IT WORKS

Taste the whiskies from left to right. Tasting at bottled strength (depending on how high or low this is, of course) can really numb your palate, making it difficult to taste subsequent whiskies. Add a few drops of water to each whisky to begin with. Taste and then add more water until you feel it has reached its "peak", balancing flavour and alcohol.

THE LESSON...

Having "tasted" these same whiskies with your nose, now that you have sampled them with your mouth you will see how the flavours in different whiskies display themselves on the tongue versus aromas in the olfactory system. The flavours should be enhanced and magnified. Little by little, you are training your powers of detection to identify and differentiate flavour.

YOU ARE TRAINING YOUR POWERS OF DETECTION TO IDENTIFY AND DIFFERENTIATE FLAVOUR

CHIVAS REGAL MIZUNARA FINISH

BLENDED SCOTCH
40% ABV

IF YOU CAN'T FIND THIS use Hibiki Harmony

| WEIGHT **3** | Aberdeen grocers the Chivas brothers began blending whisky in the 1850s. |

GOLDEN STRAW

SWEET FRAGRANT HERBS, cherry-blossom, pepper, toffee

GRAPE-LIKE sweetness; orange blossom honey; spice; mandarin, peach skins

LIGHT, slightly oily texture

FLAVOUR MAP

WOODY

PEATY

FRUITY

SPICY

FLORAL

CEREAL

LIKE THIS? Try Ballantine's 17YO

BALVENIE
SB 12YO

SINGLE SPEYSIDE MALT

47.8%

IF YOU CAN'T FIND THIS use
Knappogue Castle 12YO

WEIGHT

2

One of the last
Scottish distilleries to
malt at least some
of its own barley.

PALE GOLD

DAISIES AND BUTTERCUPS, fresh honey,
with the comb

VANILLA; lemon curd. Custard
doughnut. Add water for soft citrus

SWEET, long finish

LIKE THIS? Try Glenkinchie 12YO

SAZERAC RYE
KENTUCKY RYE

45% ABV

IF YOU CAN'T FIND THIS use
Jim Beam Rye

WEIGHT

5

This whiskey forms
the basis of the New
Orleans-invented
Sazerac cocktail.

BURNISHED COPPER

BIG, RICH, SPICY; beef jerky, Parma ham,
barbeque smoke; fragrant nuttiness

SPICY, HERBY, then fresh apples. Sweet
caramel, butterscotch, zesty fruit

QUITE DRY, spicy long finish

LIKE THIS? Try FEW Rye

LAGAVULIN 16YO
SINGLE ISLAY MALT

43% ABV

IF YOU CAN'T FIND THIS use
Ardbeg Uigeadail

WEIGHT

5

Quite simply one of
the great Islay peaty
whiskies.

GOLDEN AMBER

LEATHER, TOBACCO, chocolate,
cinnamon; peat-smoke

APRICOT JAM on toast. Herbs, aniseed,
cinnamon; peat smoke-infused fudge

COMFORTINGLY smoky long finish

LIKE THIS? Try Wemyss Peat Chimney

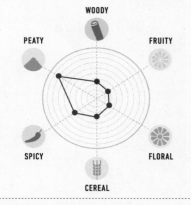

BODY AND FINISH

What do we mean when we talk about a whisky's body and finish? Let's look at what the final element of whisky tasting brings to the show and, in every sense, rounds off the experience.

UNDERSTANDING "BODY"

Of all the terms used to describe whisky, "body" is possibly the hardest to accurately put your finger on. It is also the easiest to understand. It is a sensory process, something you learn by doing.

Body, essentially, is how the whisky feels in your mouth, almost regardless of flavour. You can also use the words "weight" or "mouthfeel" in this context, as it is literally how heavy or light the whisky feels in your mouth. Don't worry, once you have got a few tastings under your belt and know more about what to look for, your whisky's body will be much easier to assess.

▼ **To appreciate whisky**, first enjoy how it looks and its aroma, then its taste and how it feels in your mouth, then savour its finish.

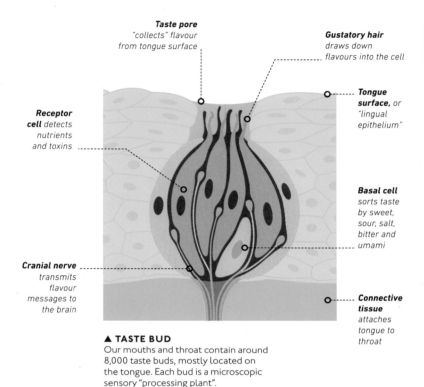

Taste pore
"collects" flavour from tongue surface

Gustatory hair
draws down flavours into the cell

Receptor cell *detects nutrients and toxins*

Tongue surface, *or "lingual epithelium"*

Basal cell *sorts taste by sweet, sour, salt, bitter and umami*

Cranial nerve *transmits flavour messages to the brain*

Connective tissue *attaches tongue to throat*

▲ TASTE BUD
Our mouths and throat contain around 8,000 taste buds, mostly located on the tongue. Each bud is a microscopic sensory "processing plant".

OUTSIDE INFLUENCES

Things that can affect a whisky's weight, or mouthfeel, include:

• **The whisky's cask type** and its "freshness". For example, a brand-new Bourbon American oak cask will contain more extractives, including lignin, which is quite naturally oily, than a well-used cask

• **Shorter stills.** Copper-pot stills of a more squat, stouter type will offer less opportunity for contact between the copper and the spirit, generally resulting in a "meatier" and possibly an oilier whisky

• **Alcohol content.** Sometimes, but not always, a higher ABV will give the impression that the whisky has a fuller body

• **Peat smoke** can also give the impression that a whisky is full of body, but not always

As with every other element of tasting, what body you detect is purely personal. Don't worry if you do not detect exactly what everyone else does. Sharing taste experiences is part of the fun.

Note that body is not an indication of quality, and there are as many lovely light-bodied whiskies as heavy-bodied ones.

DETECTING "FINISH"

The finish is the final piece of the tasting puzzle. It is not uncommon to nose and taste some seemingly incredible whiskies only for them to be let down by the finish.

As with the body or mouthfeel, the finish is not easy to describe or quantify without the experience of having tried a few whiskies.

Like many whisky matters, it is about relaxing and not being self-conscious. If you feel something, say it. "Oily"? "Meaty"? These, and more, are valid ways to talk about body and finish. You will eventually find your voice. What we are looking for in a finish is something almost intangible that ties any loose ends together and brings all of the flavours to a close.

As long as the finish does this well, it doesn't matter how long the finish lasts, as long as it is not over in a flash – always one of the biggest potential disappointments when tasting any whisky.

BODY, ESSENTIALLY, IS HOW THE WHISKY FEELS IN YOUR MOUTH, ALMOST REGARDLESS OF FLAVOUR

TASTING 04 / 20 | TASTE FOR BODY AND FINISH

CHIVAS REGAL
MIZUNARA FINISH

BLENDED SCOTCH
40% ABV

In the last of our three related tastings, using the same four whiskies, here we savour every aspect of the spirit in your mouth and in your throat, including its mouthfeel and finish.

IF YOU CAN'T FIND THIS use Hibiki Harmony

WEIGHT 3	Most of Chivas Regal's make comes from Speyside's Strathisla distillery.

HOW IT WORKS

Here you should analyse how the whisky feels, texture-wise, as it slips over your palate and down your throat. This is assessing body and finish. How do the flavours differ (if at all); how long do they last? This is the finish. You can use water, but be aware it can, and does, dilute the texture. Try sampling without first.

THE LESSON...

This is where you assemble the full tasting experience, making those final connections between how a whisky smells, how it tastes, and, now, what its body and finish are like. By now, you should be completely aware of what "taste" is – and how to put together a fully-rounded whisky taste profile.

GOLDEN STRAW

LUSH FRAGRANT HERBS; cherry-blossom, pepper, toffee

GRAPE-LIKE SWEETNESS; orange blossom honey; spice; mandarin, peach

LINGERING HONEY and citrus with a sweet, lightly oily texture

FLAVOUR MAP

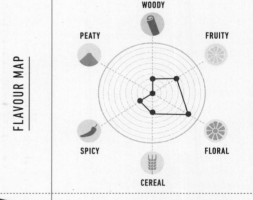

BY NOW YOU SHOULD BE COMPLETELY AWARE OF WHAT "TASTE" IS

LIKE THIS? Try Ballantine's 17YO

BALVENIE SB 12YO

SINGLE SPEYSIDE MALT

47.8%

IF YOU CAN'T FIND THIS use
Knappogue Castle 12YO

WEIGHT 2	Used, with Glenfiddich and Kininvie, in Grant's Monkey Shoulder.

PALE GOLD

DAISIES AND BUTTERCUPS, fresh honey, with the comb

SPICY VANILLA, lemon curd, caramel, custard; icing sugar, citrus

VANILLA, WARMING SPICES. Sweet, luscious finish. Velvety, creamy texture

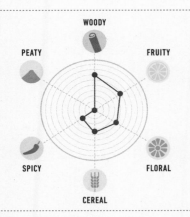

LIKE THIS? Try Glenkinchie 12YO

SAZERAC RYE

KENTUCKY RYE

45% ABV

IF YOU CAN'T FIND THIS use
Jim Beam Rye

WEIGHT 5	From the same family of Kentucky whiskeys as Eagle Rare, Van Winkle and Blanton's.

BURNISHED COPPER

BIG, RICH, spicy; beef jerky, barbeque smoke; fragrant nuttiness

SPICY AND HERBY; fresh apple. Butterscotch, caramel, zesty fruit

LIQUORICE, CINNAMON then sweet clove and vanilla. Thick, oily texture

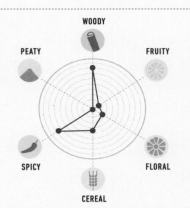

LIKE THIS? Try FEW Rye

LAGAVULIN 16YO

SINGLE ISLAY MALT

43% ABV

IF YOU CAN'T FIND THIS use
Ardbeg Uigeadail

WEIGHT 5	Gaelic for "hollow of the mill", Lagavulin sits on a lovely stretch of Islay coastline.

GOLDEN AMBER

LEATHER, TOBACCO, chocolate, cinnamon; peat smoke

APRICOT JAM on buttery, brown toast. Aniseed, cinnamon, dried herbs

PEAT SMOKE; Indian spices; menthol or eucalyptus; linseed oil-like texture

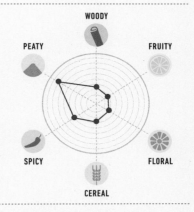

LIKE THIS? Try Wemyss Peat Chimney

CHAPTER | 3

TASTE
----- BY -----
STYLE

WHISKY IS A WONDERFULLY DIVERSE SPIRIT. "Scotch" is a single word that embraces single malts, single grains, and blended whiskies. American whiskeys are equally diverse, as are Irish whiskeys. And that's without mentioning Canadian, Japanese, and the rest of the world's whiskies. That's why we look here not so much at *where* a whisky is made but *how* it is made, and the style of spirit it represents. You'll discover what differentiates (and what links) malt whiskies, blends, Bourbons, rye, corn, and wheat whiskies, and more.

SCOTCH-STYLE WHISKIES

THINK OF SINGLE MALT WHISKY and Scotland is surely the first place that comes to mind. The range and quality of Scottish single malt whiskies is huge, from smooth to full-bodied examples, as well as the famed peated whiskies of producers such as Islay's Lagavulin (left). Then there's grain whisky. Scotland's adoption of this style led to its domination of the world whisky market. It also paved the way for blended whiskies, and the rise of Bourbon and other US whiskeys. As for Scotland's blended whiskies, they make up almost 90 per cent of Scotch whisky sales worldwide and, in large part, give Scotch-style whiskies a profile no other whisky-making nation can match.

MADE
AT 1
DISTILLERY
+
USES
MALTED
BARLEY
+
MADE IN
COPPER POT
STILLS
+
MATURED
MIN. 3
YEARS
+
BOTTLED
AT MIN.
40% ABV
=
SINGLE
MALT
WHISKY

WHAT IS SINGLE MALT WHISKY?

For many, it is the zenith of whisky types. Single malt is now produced around the world as well as in Scotland. But what exactly is it, and why is it so revered?

WHAT IS IT?

It can be difficult to process all of the rules of whisky making. The image above hopefully simplifies things. The key point for single malt whisky is the use of 100 per cent *malted* barley. It should also be noted that all of the whisky that goes into a bottle of single malt can come from different batches of production, but must come from just one distillery. That is what the "single" in single malt

EACH OF SCOTLAND'S MORE THAN 100 SINGLE MALT DISTILLERIES PRODUCES A DIFFERENT SPIRIT

▲ WHISKY AT A GLANCE
This greatly simplified image quickly and easily shows how single malt whisky is made.

means. In its traditional Scottish home, single malt is made across the country's five main whisky-producing regions of the Highlands and Islands, the Lowlands, Islay, Speyside, and Campbeltown.

WHY IS IT SPECIAL?

Single malt holds its iconic status for several reasons.

• **Provenance** It is the "original" form of whisky, the source from which all other whisky flows. Its appearance and taste have definitely changed since whisky first emerged hundreds of years ago, but there is a clear historical lineage, and a method of production, that leads directly to present-day single malts.

• **Place** Single malt distilleries are often situated in incredibly beautiful, almost mystical locations. The romance of where whisky is made certainly enhances its popularity – as any marketing person will enthusiastically agree. Whether the location contributes anything to a whisky's taste is a cause of much debate, though.

- **Diversity of flavour** Each of Scotland's more than 100 single malt distilleries produces a different spirit. While they all use the same basic techniques, they may use different barley, or vary their fermentation times; mashing, fermentation, and distillation equipment can be different in scale and shape – and that's not to mention the different cask types available. Just one distillery can produce quite diverse variants of its house style by manipulating one or more of its processes. The end result is an almost infinite combination of styles and flavours – the very thing that makes whisky so fascinating.

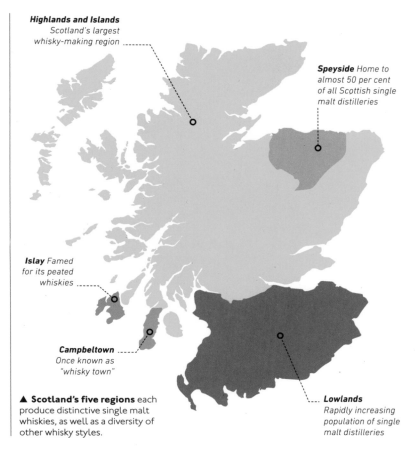

Highlands and Islands Scotland's largest whisky-making region

Speyside Home to almost 50 per cent of all Scottish single malt distilleries

Islay Famed for its peated whiskies

Campbeltown Once known as "whisky town"

Lowlands Rapidly increasing population of single malt distilleries

▲ **Scotland's five regions** each produce distinctive single malt whiskies, as well as a diversity of other whisky styles.

FOLLOW THE LEADER

While Scotland is by far the most historically and commercially important single malt whisky-making region, single malts are now made worldwide.

Japanese single malts, for example, are soaring in popularity and prestige, winning "World's Best" awards. Distilleries elsewhere in Asia include India and Taiwan, while Europe, North America, South Africa and Australasia are making highly notable single malt whiskies, too.

WORLD OF MALT ▶ Map highlighting the world's main single malt whisky-making nations.

TASTING 05 / 20

SCOTTISH SINGLE MALT WHISKIES

Scottish single malts are seen as the zenith of Scotch-style whiskies. However, they can vary widely in taste. Here we look at four single malts to show you exactly how much they can vary.

HOW IT WORKS

Taste the whiskies from left to right. They are arranged in this way for intensity of flavour – left is lighter, right is heavier. Nose and taste each without water, then add water and repeat. How different do they smell and taste, with and without water? These notes are a guide – what you taste is much more important.

THE LESSON...

This session shows just how different single malts can be. They are not all sweet and floral, or strong and peaty. Each distillery has its own "house style", but even this varies hugely from bottling to bottling. Once you've identified your favourite dram from this Tasting, or "flight", its flavour map will help lead you to others like it – and eventually to your perfect malt.

NOSE AND TASTE EACH WITHOUT WATER, THEN ADD WATER AND REPEAT

AUCHENTOSHAN 12YO

SINGLE LOWLAND MALT

40% ABV

IF YOU CAN'T FIND THIS use Glenmorangie 10YO

WEIGHT 2 A triple-distilling single malt whisky-maker on the outskirts of Glasgow.

 GOLDEN STRAW

 SWEET AND FRAGRANT honeysuckle, vanilla, and subtle citrus notes

 DELICATE, SWEET, easy-going. Crisp apples, peaches and cream

 LIGHT, FRUITY and lingering finish

FLAVOUR MAP

WOODY
PEATY
FRUITY
SPICY
FLORAL
CEREAL

 LIKE THIS? Try Dalwhinnie 15YO

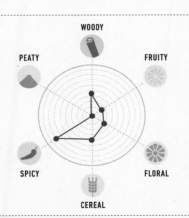
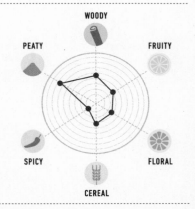

GLENFARCLAS 15YO

SINGLE SPEYSIDE MALT
43% ABV

IF YOU CAN'T FIND THIS use
Glendronach 12YO

WEIGHT
4

Family-owned Glenfarclas is known for using ex-sherry casks.

GOLDEN AMBER

DRIED RAISINS AND CURRANTS, with a light dusting of cinnamon

SUMPTUOUS, OILY MOUTHFEEL; Christmas pudding and brandy butter

THE FINISH IS LONG, dry, and spicy

WOODY
PEATY
FRUITY
SPICY
FLORAL
CEREAL

LIKE THIS? Try Aberlour 12YO

GLEN SCOTIA 15YO

SINGLE CAMPBELTOWN MALT
46% ABV

IF YOU CAN'T FIND THIS use
Springbank 10YO

WEIGHT
4

Recently revamped and rejuvenated distillery in the Mull of Kintyre.

GOLDEN STRAW

A BAG OF OLD-FASHIONED BOILED SWEETS. A slight sea-spray tang

TANGY AND COMPLEX, apricot jam, nougat, marzipan; subtle peat smoke

LONG AND SLIGHTLY bitter-sweet finish

WOODY
PEATY
FRUITY
SPICY
FLORAL
CEREAL

LIKE THIS? Try Oban 14YO

BOWMORE 12YO

SINGLE ISLAY MALT
40% ABV

IF YOU CAN'T FIND THIS
use Caol Ila 12YO

WEIGHT
4

Medium-peated spirit produced at Islay's oldest distillery.

GOLDEN STRAW

A BRACING WALK on a windswept beach. Peat smoke and pineapple chunks

PEAT-SMOKED POACHED PEARS; light herbal and citrus notes

MEDIUM-LONG FINISH with a smoky citrus end

WOODY
PEATY
FRUITY
SPICY
FLORAL
CEREAL

LIKE THIS? Try Talisker 10YO

WHAT IS SINGLE GRAIN WHISKY?

It was possibly the most important development in the whisky industry's evolution nearly 200 years ago. But what is it, and how did it allow for new styles, such as Bourbon, to be created?

WHAT IS IT?

The illustration below shows a simplified version of a complex process. The thing to remember is that single grain whisky, despite its name, is a mix of malted barley with other grains such as wheat, rye, or corn in a continuous method of distillation. The "single" refers to the fact that this all takes place at one single distillery.

BACKGROUND

Before the development of grain whisky there was only single malt whisky and blended malt whisky in

Scotland, and single pot still whiskey in Ireland.

In Scotland, the single malts were then more peaty or smoky than today, as peat was then the dominant fuel used for drying barley during the malting process.

The production of grain whisky was facilitated, and perfected, by three men. In 1822, Irishman Sir Anthony Perrier patented a "continuous" method of whisky making that allowed for cereals other than barley to be used in distillation. It inspired the Scot Robert Stein to develop his own "patent" still in 1828. Aeneas Coffey, an Irish ex-customs and

excise man, then built on Perrier and Stein's work, winning a patent for his twin-column continuous still in 1830. The Coffey, or column, still remains the mainstay of grain whisky and Bourbon-style whiskey making today.

HOW IT'S MADE

Coffey's design meant that a huge number of distillations could occur within the process (see illustration opposite), with ever-increasing alcohol content. However, grain whisky makers are limited to distilling to no more than 94.8% ABV, and US makers to 89% ABV.

 + + + =

USES MALTED BARLEY   AND OTHER CEREALS   CONTINUOUS DISTILLATION   MADE BY 1 DISTILLERY   SINGLE GRAIN

▲ **A SIMPLIFIED PICTURE**
The manufacture of single grain whisky relies on the use of a mix of grains, distilled continuously at just one distillery.

BLENDED GRAIN WHISKY

This little-known category exists as a "technicality".

It was designated in order to prevent distillers combining two completely different grain whiskies together and calling the result "Single Grain". That said, distillers such as Compass Box Whisky make some interesting blended grain whiskies in their "Hedonism" range that are well worth a look.

◄ **Column still**. It looks complex, but works by liquid condensing and distilling as it flows through the device.

Because it is a continuous (that is, "open") process, rather than a pot still-style batch (or "closed") method, the only production limit is how much raw material you can feed into the still. Coffey's still revolutionized how – and how quickly – whisky was made.

WHICH GRAINS?

Most Scottish distillers use wheat; in the US, mainly corn. Almost all use around 10 per cent malted barley, as its enzymes help with fermentation. Grain whisky is less complex than single malt, as its distillation process means most of its flavour is replaced with alcohol. This makes it reliant on the mainly ex-Bourbon oak casks it's stored in for flavour. When young, it is fresh, creamy, and often zesty; when aged it can become layered with rich toffee, spice, and more.

BEFORE THE DEVELOPMENT OF GRAIN WHISKY THERE WAS ONLY SINGLE MALT WHISKY AND BLENDED MALT WHISKY

WHAT IS BLENDED SCOTCH WHISKY?

Blended Scotch is the world's favourite style of Scottish whisky. How it is blended, and who decides what to blend, is a fascinating story – as is the tale of how it got to be so phenomenally popular.

WHAT IS IT?

Blended Scotch is a mix of one or more single malt whiskies with one or more single grain whiskies. Like all Scotch whiskies, a blended whisky must be matured in Scotland for a minimum of three years and then bottled at a minimum of 40% ABV, once again in Scotland.

A HISTORY OF BLENDS

It is the mid-1800s, and most Scottish single malts are being made using peated malted barley, a very distinctive style not to everyone's taste.

Enter grain whisky, created using newly-invented continuous stills, and everything changed. Whisky makers began blending this new,

THE AIM OF BLENDING IS TO CREATE A WHISKY BETTER THAN ITS CONSTITUENT PARTS

quite neutral, whisky with the more complex, flavoursome, and usually smoky single malts of the day to make a mild and "approachable" whisky that quickly found favour.

Many of these blending pioneers were grocers, purveyors of then-luxury items such as coffee, tea, and spices, men such as Kilmarnock's John ("Johnnie") Walker, John and James Chivas of Aberdeen, and George Ballantine from Glasgow. Their creations are still around and became the global brands we all now know.

WHY IS IT POPULAR?

There are many reasons that led to the world domination of Scotch blends. The major ones are:
- The Scotch industry's adoption of continuous distillation in the mid-1800s, making production faster and increasing volumes.
- The Irish industry's refusal to do the same until the 1900s.
- Phylloxera, a vine-killing pest, ravaged Western European vine stocks in the late 1800s, causing a gap in Cognac production.
- US Prohibition – not a problem, as Berry Brothers and others exported blended whiskies such as Cutty Sark into Canada and the Bahamas for easy access for US "importers".

HOW IT'S BLENDED

The aim of blending is to create a whisky better than its constituent parts. Distillers rarely reveal the proportions of malt versus grain in

SINGLE MALT + SINGLE GRAIN = BLENDED SCOTCH

◀ **EASY OPTION?**
Making blended Scotch is deceptively simple. The art lies in getting the right blend.

▲ **Johnnie Walker's** Blenders' Batch Red Rye Finish was launched in 2016. As the name suggests, it was finished in ex-rye whiskey casks.

their blends, but most commercial blends contain around 20–25 per cent malt whisky. Generally speaking, the more you pay for a blend, the higher its proportion of malt whisky and its age.

The person that decides which whiskies to blend, and in which proportion, is the Master Blender. They will nose thousands of samples annually, in order to concoct each batch. Once a blend has been developed in "miniature" it will then be scaled up in order to make the final blend.

PROFITING FROM MISFORTUNE

Whisky was the unwitting beneficiary of a devastating grape-destroying parasite.

In the late 1800s, the vineyards of France were infested with the *Phylloxera vastatrix* aphid, a tiny insect that practically wiped out wine and brandy production for several years. As stocks of grape-based alcohol ran low, European sales of whisky soared.

▲ **Wine, champagne and brandy** sales fell by 70 per cent following the outbreak, creating the 1880s' "whisky boom".

MONKEY
SHOULDER®

BATCH 27 SMOOTH AND RICH

BLENDED MALT SCOTCH WHISKY

ROOTED IN MALT WHISKY HISTORY, AND INSPIRED BY THE
MALT MEN WHO STILL TURN THE MALTING BARLEY BY HAND,
'MONKEY SHOULDER' IS BLENDED IN SMALL BATCHES OF
THREE FINE SPEYSIDE SINGLE MALTS THEN MARRIED TO
ACHIEVE A SMOOTHER, RICHER TASTE.

SELECTED BY OUR MALT MASTER

▲ **Monkey Shoulder** is a "simple" blend of three single malts. Other producers use many more – up to 16 in some cases.

WHAT IS BLENDED MALT WHISKY?

It seems counter-intuitive. Why blend one malt whisky with another malt whisky? But in an era in which finding new whisky tastes is ever-more important, it's a category growing in popularity.

WHAT IS IT?

This whisky style existed long before the now-dominant blended Scotch category. After all, once there were just single malts, so the only way to create new whiskies was to blend two or more single malts. Put simply, that's what blended malt whisky is: a blend of two or more single malt whiskies from two or more distilleries.

If you want to make your own blended malt, just pour the remains of one bottle of single malt into the remains of another from a different distillery. There. You now have a home-made blended malt!

WHY BLEND THEM?

Single malts were once characterized by peaty and smoky flavours. Blending them with

BLENDING SINGLE MALTS WITH EACH OTHER IS A GREAT WAY TO CREATE COMPELLING NEW WHISKY COMBINATIONS

whiskies made from other grains such as wheat, corn, and rye was seen as the ideal way to make them "softer" and more accessible.

Today, single malts have a much wider flavour range, so blending single malts with each other is a great way to create compelling new whisky combinations while retaining the character for which single malts are renowned.

For people who like the sweetness of single malt but want to try something a bit different, blended malts are a good option.

WHO DOES IT?

With a couple of notable exceptions, larger distillers rarely invest heavily in blended malt whiskies. This category is instead championed mainly by

independent bottlers - companies who do not (or originally did not) own distilleries but who instead buy casks of whisky to bottle under their own brand names.

This way of working allows independent bottling companies to experiment with blending, taking the risks that larger, established concerns will not.

As a result, the category has been steadily growing in popularity, with producers such as Compass Box and Douglas Laing issuing well-received product.

▼ **Glengoyne Distillery,** close to Glasgow, allows visitors to mix their own whiskies as part of the facility's unique "Malt Master Tour".

MADE IN TAIWAN

You may struggle to find blended malt whiskies displayed prominently at your local spirit supplier – unless you live in Taiwan, that is.

Taiwan is the largest market for blended malt whisky, with examples including Yushan, from the Nantou distillery. The country's taste for blended malt started in 1984, when Nantou began importing Scotch whisky to blend locally. In 2008 Nantou began releasing locally-made whiskies, too. Taiwan, now a growing whisky-making power, also produces excellent single malts, evidenced in 2015 when its Kavalan Solist Vinho Barrique was awarded the coveted "world's best" garland at the World Whisky Awards.

▲ **Taiwan's Yushan** blended malt, released in 2016, combines whiskies matured in ex-Bourbon and ex-sherry casks.

MAKING YOUR OWN BLENDS

Blending whiskies together perhaps seems like sacrilege, but master blenders do it all the time. It is a craft that takes years of practice. But that's no reason you can't try it for yourself.

BLENDING'S ORIGINS

Blending began in the mid-1800s as a way of balancing the flavours of single malts, which were much more of the peaty persuasion back then, by mixing them with the lighter, more neutral flavours of grain whisky.

In time, blending developed into a science, with master blenders mixing whiskies together in laboratory conditions, using highly specialized equipment, as well as their own senses. But what blending comes down to is creating a whisky that tastes better to you than the individual whiskies you put into it. Whether you're a master blender or enthusiastic amateur, the result is the same: are you satisfied with the final flavour?

YOUR BLENDING KIT

To try blending you'll need these tools:
• One small measuring jug, approx. 50ml
• One large measuring jug, approx. 500ml
• A few empty bottles with corks/screw-caps
• One or two graduated pipettes
• Half a dozen tasting glasses
• Pad and pen to keep notes
• Self-adhesive labels
• Up to six single malts of varying style and weight
• A young (8–12 year old) single grain whisky

Grain whisky isn't absolutely essential for all blending experiments. It does form an excellent "base" for blending whiskies, though, and it is what we have used here.

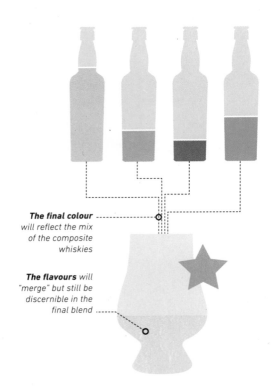

The final colour will reflect the mix of the composite whiskies

The flavours will "merge" but still be discernible in the final blend

▲ **YOUR CHOICE**
Each blend you make is 100 per cent personalized, as you control the number and the proportions of the whiskies in it.

GET BLENDING

The first thing you need to decide is: what style of blend do I want? The examples below have been created to get you started, showing you the whisky proportions needed for the three different styles highlighted.

There are no rules, except those you invent, so why not start by using the pipette to add an amount of the lightest style of whisky to the empty small jug. Add smaller amounts of each of the other whiskies, taking note of proportions and nosing – using the tasting glasses – at each change point.

When you reach a flavour combination you are happy with, scale it up into the larger measuring jug, ensuring your notes are up to date. Then, pour your blend into an empty bottle, label it, and enjoy.

Remember, the whisky will change in the bottle as the flavours marry together, hopefully for the better. Continue taking note of how it evolves, in case you need to make adjustments the next time you attempt a similar blend.

WHAT BLENDING
COMES DOWN TO
IS CREATING A
WHISKY THAT
TASTES BETTER
TO YOU

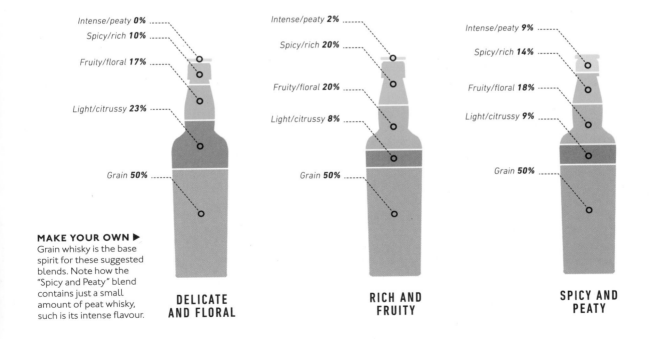

MAKE YOUR OWN ▶
Grain whisky is the base spirit for these suggested blends. Note how the "Spicy and Peaty" blend contains just a small amount of peat whisky, such is its intense flavour.

Intense/peaty **0%**
Spicy/rich **10%**
Fruity/floral **17%**
Light/citrussy **23%**
Grain **50%**

DELICATE AND FLORAL

Intense/peaty **2%**
Spicy/rich **20%**
Fruity/floral **20%**
Light/citrussy **8%**
Grain **50%**

RICH AND FRUITY

Intense/peaty **9%**
Spicy/rich **14%**
Fruity/floral **18%**
Light/citrussy **9%**
Grain **50%**

SPICY AND PEATY

TASTING 06 / 20

SCOTCH WHISKY

There is no one thing that can be called "Scotch whisky". It is in reality a range of styles, flavours, and tastes. The whiskies selected here represent, in part, that range.

HOW IT WORKS

This tasting is about contrasts. So many people go through their lives not realizing these different styles of Scotch whisky exist, let alone tasting them side by side. Remember to record the mouthfeel and finish, as these are often quite different between malt and grain whisky.

THE LESSON...

Hopefully you will see how varied Scotch whiskies can be. If you cannot perceive the big differences between the grain whisky and the malt whiskies then there may be no hope for us all! This is the perfect tasting to do with your whisky-hating friends. They'll see that not all Scotch, in fact not all whisky, tastes the same.

THIS IS THE PERFECT TASTING TO DO WITH YOUR WHISKY-HATING FRIENDS

LOCH LOMOND SINGLE GRAIN

SINGLE GRAIN WHISKY
46% ABV

IF YOU CAN'T FIND THIS
use Girvan "Patent Still"

WEIGHT 1	This single grain is made entirely from malted barley, but using Coffey stills.

PALE GOLD

SWEET, FRESH CITRUS gives way to a luscious tinned peach aroma

INITIALLY LIGHT AND DELICATE, then displays ripe, juicy tropical-fruit tones

CITRUS AND CREAM SODA. Mid-length finish and soft mouthfeel

FLAVOUR MAP

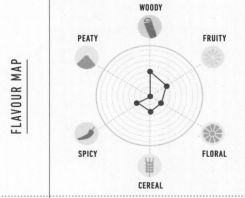

WOODY

PEATY

FRUITY

SPICY

FLORAL

CEREAL

LIKE THIS? Try The Norfolk "Parched"

ARRAN 10YO

SINGLE ISLAND MALT

46%

IF YOU CAN'T FIND THIS
use Scapa Skiren

WEIGHT	
2	One of the first "new wave" Scottish single malt distilleries, established in 1995.

PALE GOLD

WARM VANILLA gives way to citrus and freshly-picked green apples

VERY ZESTY AND FRESH, then a touch of vanilla and soft, warming spice

LIGHT SPICES finish off the citrus notes that run through this whisky

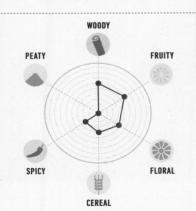

LIKE THIS? Try Tomatin 12YO

COMPASS BOX "GREAT KING ST" ARTIST'S BLEND

BLENDED SCOTCH

43% ABV

IF YOU CAN'T FIND THIS
use Johnnie Walker Black Label

WEIGHT	
3	Compass Box is a blending and bottling company, having no distillery of its own.

PALE STRAW

FRESH RED BERRY FRUITS, pear drops, very slight hint of smoke

SPICY, SMOKY custard on a Bakewell tart. Light, subtle, refreshing lemon

EVEN, BALANCED and quite a delicate, dry finish

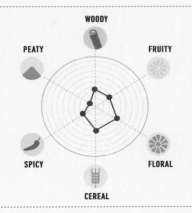

LIKE THIS? Try Cutty Sark "Prohibition"

WEMYSS "SPICE KING" 12YO

BLENDED MALT WHISKY

46% ABV

IF YOU CAN'T FIND THIS
use Douglas Laing "Scallywag" 10YO

WEIGHT	
4	In 2014, independent bottler Wemyss invested in a new distillery, Kingsbarns.

PALE GOLD

SWEET AND SALTY CARAMEL, white chocolate, aromatic pineapple

MOUTH-FILLING, spiced cooked apples. Hot, cinnamon-sprinkled pain au raisin

QUITE A LONG, DRY and peppery finish

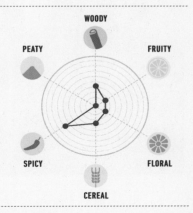

LIKE THIS? Try Compass Box "Spice Tree"

OLD BUSHMILLS DISTILLERY CO LIMITED
SINGLE MALT
1608
SINGLE MALT
1608

IRISH WHISKEYS

IRISH WHISKEY IS MADE in much the same way as Scotch whiskies, but with key differences. The most salient of these was the Irish industry's use of unmalted barley along with malted barley in the same mash bill. This created Ireland's unique single pot still style. Triple-distillation also played its part, with both Jameson and Bushmills implementing this process (along with one or two Scottish distilleries).

Now, the new distilleries popping up across the Emerald Isle are choosing their own paths. Whether it be carefully reproducing single pot still or even following a more Scotch-style blueprint. These are interesting times for Ireland's industry indeed.

MADE IN COPPER POT STILLS + MATURED FOR MIN. 3 YEARS + BOTTLED AT MIN. 40% ABV + MIN. 30% MALTED AND 30% UNMALTED BARLEY + MADE BY 1 DISTILLERY = IRISH "SPS" WHISKEY

WHAT IS IRISH WHISKEY?

Essentially, Irish whiskey was until recently synonymous with single pot still (SPS) whiskey. While today there is a greater variety of Irish styles, it is single pot still whiskey that made Ireland's name, and it is the focus here.

▲ **IRISH WHISKEY**
Also traditionally called single pot still whiskey, it's similar to Scotch, with key differences.

WHAT IS IT?

The illustration above is a neat summary of how single pot still Irish whiskey is made. As with other whisky styles with "Single" in their title, the word refers to the fact that the spirit must have been made at one single distillery, in a traditional copper pot still, in the same way as single malt whisky.

Along with the malted and unmalted mash bill shown above, it can also contain up to 5 per cent of cereals, such as corn, wheat, and rye. A 50–50 split between the two barley types is common.

WHY UNMALTED BARLEY?

In 1785, a tax on malted barley was introduced in Ireland, making whiskey production expensive and unviable for many. To maintain profit margins, distillers turned to cheaper unmalted barley to make up the mashbill, keeping a portion of malted barley to assist with fermentation and flavour.

The result of this cereal recipe is a whiskey that is often spicier and oilier than single malts.

UPS AND DOWNS

By the early 1800s, single pot still Irish whiskey was the world's favourite. By 1835, there were 93

AT ITS BEST, SINGLE POT STILL WHISKEY IS LUXURIOUSLY SWEET AND OILY, WITH A RICH, ALMOST HERBAL QUALITY

mostly single pot still Irish distilleries, with Dublin Whiskey particularly popular.

However, the big Irish whiskey makers refused to embrace the column-still revolution of the mid-1800s, the product of which they did not recognize as "real" whiskey. This, the Great Famine, the Irish War of Independence and US Prohibition, all contributed to the decline of demand for Irish whiskeys. By the 1970s, just two distilleries were left.

BACK ON TRACK

Since the millennium, single pot still whiskey has seen a resurgence. New distilleries have looked back into Ireland's glorious whiskey past and are distilling this style once again, often alongside single malt.

At its best, single pot still whiskey is luxuriously sweet and oily, with a rich, almost herbal, quality that is difficult to describe. The best way to discover it, as always, is to taste it.

TRIPLE DISTILLING

For much of its history, many thought it was the act of a third distillation that differentiated Irish whiskey from Scotch, which is usually double distilled.

It is more accurate to say the mix of single pot still's mash recipe with triple distillation creates its unique character. After all, some Scottish distilleries triple distil, too. Ireland and Scotland both also use pot stills, with Cork-based Jameson the owner of the world's largest example (below).

◄ **Cooper's Croze,** released in 2016, was created and named to celebrate the craft of Jameson's head cooper, Ger Buckley.

TASTING 07 / 20

"TRADITIONAL" IRISH WHISKEY

BUSHMILLS 10YO

SINGLE MALT WHISKEY
40% ABV

Bushmills and Jameson have stood firm through Irish whiskey's ups and downs. While the country is now enjoying a "new" whiskey boom, it's time to look at what these two stalwarts have to offer, too.

IF YOU CAN'T FIND THIS
use Quiet Man 10YO

WEIGHT 2

In 2008, the Bank of Ireland put the Old Bushmills Distillery on its new banknotes.

HOW IT WORKS

Bushmills, in Northern Ireland, triple-distils from malted barley; Jameson, in the Republic, triple-distils from malted and un-malted barley. These examples are arranged left to right to take you on a taste-based journey through traditionally produced Irish whiskey.

THE LESSON...

Not all of today's Irish whiskey makers use triple distillation. It is a process that both increases the alcohol content and, it's said, lightens the flavour profile. Did you detect that, against other, double-distilled whiskies from other Tastings? The other main contrast is between the single malt and the two single pot still whiskies. Did you notice any difference?

PALE GOLD

SOFT, SWEET RUNNY HONEY; light, fragrant lemon and herbs

FRESH, CRUNCHY APPLE; a hint of spice; a little vanilla and lemon curd

TANGY, BITTER-SWEET, slight acidity and medium-length finish

TRIPLE DISTILLING BOTH INCREASES THE ALCOHOL CONTENT AND, IT'S SAID, LIGHTENS THE TASTE

FLAVOUR MAP

WOODY

PEATY

FRUITY

SPICY

FLORAL

CEREAL

LIKE THIS? Try Bushmills 16YO

BUSHMILLS BLACK BUSH

BLENDED WHISKEY

40% ABV

IF YOU CAN'T FIND THIS
use Bushmills Original

WEIGHT **3**	Bushmills actually uses grain whiskey from Jameson for its blends.

PALE AMBER

TANGY, SWEET AND SPICY poached pear; peaches and pineapples

RIPE RED FRUIT; blackberry crumble and custard; slight acidity and pepper

QUITE LONG FINISH, with juicy acidity and a satisfying tang

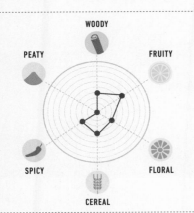

LIKE THIS? Try Teeling The Blend

MITCHELL'S GREEN SPOT

SINGLE POT STILL WHISKEY

40% ABV

IF YOU CAN'T FIND THIS
use Writers Tears

WEIGHT **2**	A single pot still whiskey from Jameson's Midleton distillery in Cork.

GOLDEN STRAW

AROMATIC APPLES AND PEARS give way to buttery, spicy vanilla and pineapple

EASY-GOING, with tropical fruit, oaky spices and a touch of fresh mint

LIGHT AND DEFT FINISH, with fruit and spices fading slowly

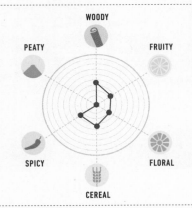

LIKE THIS? Try Teeling Pot Still

REDBREAST 12YO

SINGLE POT STILL WHISKEY

40% ABV

IF YOU CAN'T FIND THIS
use Powers John's Lane 12YO

WEIGHT **3**	Irish Whiskey Awards 2013 "Overall Irish Whiskey of the Year."

RICH GOLD

FRAGRANT HERB GARDEN; sweet, aromatic rosehip-infused honey

MOCHA COFFEE and marshmallow. Ripe peaches, apricots and crème fraîche

LIGHT, SWEET FINISH with a touch of bitterness; velvety mouthfeel

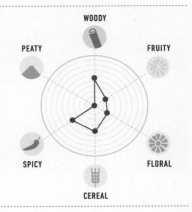

LIKE THIS? Try Redbreast 15YO

NORTH AMERICAN WHISKEYS

THERE'S A LOT HAPPENING in American whiskey. It has always been a country that is keen to innovate, and with around 300 years of whiskey-making experience, this vast nation has plenty of know-how to draw from and build upon.

And there's more to American whiskey than Bourbon, as hugely popular and important as that iconic spirit is. Corn, rye, wheat, and even malt whiskeys are becoming increasingly popular, especially alongside the rise of the micro-distillery and craft-whiskey movements. While the traditional areas of Tennessee and Kentucky remain vitally important, distilling hot spots are springing up all across the land of the free.

The main recognized types of American whiskey, as stipulated by the US Government, are:

BOURBON RYE WHEAT MALTED RYE CORN

Distillation. Scotch producers use the same continuous stills for grain whisky, but distil up to 94.8% ABV (190° US Proof), rather than the 80% ABV (160° US Proof) allowed in the US. This may seem like a small difference, but the more you purify and distil for increased alcohol, the more flavour you subtract.

WHAT IS "AMERICAN" WHISKEY?

There is no one American whiskey style. Instead, there are several categories – corn, rye, and wheat, among others, plus their variants and sub-categories. How are they made, and what makes them distinctive?

A BRIEF HISTORY

As soon as Scottish, Irish, and German settlers arrived in America from the late 1600s, whiskey making began. These immigrants took their European knowledge of spirit distillation and applied it to the familiar and not-so-familiar cereals and grains they found in the New World.

At first, they used home-made, rudimentary pot stills, and produced liquor almost exclusively for their own use. These stills were often portable, travelling across the great continent as their owners looked for places to put down roots.

It was not until the mid-1800s, when Irishman Aeneas Coffey's "continuous" distillation process was introduced, that the large-scale and commercial production of US whiskey could begin.

US WHISKEY CATEGORIES

The five major styles of US whiskey, as recognized in American law, are:
• Bourbon whiskey
• Rye whiskey
• Wheat whiskey
• Malted Rye whiskey
• Corn whiskey
   Each of these also has a "Straight" sub-category, for example, "Straight Bourbon". Along with a further guarantee that the bottled spirit is a minimum of two years old (although most don't display an age statement), it is also accepted as a "badge" of quality, and this was certainly the objective of the extra categorization when it was introduced.

There are also a number of categories aimed more at the cheaper "liquor store" end of the market, such as "Light Whiskey" and "Blended Whisky" (note the missing "e").

One little-known type of US whiskey is the "Bottled-in-bond" category. This was introduced in

Cereals. Corn, wheat, and rye are the most used grains for American whiskeys. Barley use is growing, as US tastes for malt whisky grows.

Casks. Except for corn whiskey, all US whiskey types use only brand-new charred oak casks. This has a dramatic impact on the final flavour.

Climate. The range of climates across the US results in differing rates of maturation.

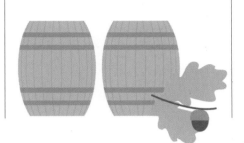

1897 by the American government to authenticate a whiskey that had not been adulterated in any way: in the late 1800s, some US distillers were known to add ingredients such as cheap grain spirit, iodine, or even tobacco to their whiskeys.

Bottled-in-bond whiskeys had to be made in a single distillery and matured in government-controlled (or "bonded") warehouses for at least four years. Whiskey makers who created spirit in this way were thus able to prove to buyers that their product was pure.

Bottled-in-bond whiskey, with its emphasis on provenance, has made something of a comeback on the back of the craft whiskey movement. Alongside this, with non–"traditional" whiskey styles such as single malts becoming more commonly produced by US domestic distillers, the question of what an "American" whiskey is has become an increasingly open one.

CORN 51%	RYE GRAIN 51%	WHEAT 51%	MALTED RYE 51%	CORN 80%
BOURBON	**RYE**	**WHEAT**	**MALTED RYE**	**CORN**

WHY "WHISKEY"?

Nobody knows exactly why the Irish and the US industries prefer, in general, to spell whiskey with an "e". A convenient and often quoted urban myth is that the Irish, in attempting to distance themselves from the "inferior" Scottish grain whisky products of the time, changed the spelling – which the

▲ THE RULES

Each US whiskey type must comprise a set minimum amount of its "named" grain. The main difference between Bourbon and corn whiskey is in how they are matured.

United States then inherited or followed. This, though, is pure conjecture. Or is it...?

HOW MUCH IS MADE?

Each year, the US produces around 37 million cases, or 444,000,000 bottles, of whiskey. It's short of Scotland's 1.2 billion bottles a year, but sales are growing as US whiskey becomes ever-more popular.

EXCEPT CORN WHISKEY, ALL US WHISKEY TYPES USE BRAND-NEW CHARRED OAK CASKS

WHAT IS CORN WHISKEY?

Overwhelmingly an American style, corn whiskey has been on the up since the millennium. This is partly due to the burgeoning US craft whiskey scene, with its taste for lighter whiskeys.

WHAT IS IT?

Corn whiskey must be distilled from a mash containing at least 80 per cent corn. The rest can comprise any other grains, such as wheat or rye. Traditionally, it contains around 10 per cent malted barley in order to use the enzymes for fermentation. Corn whiskey does not need to be aged, but where it is it must be in new, uncharred oak barrels, or used charred oak barrels. Put corn whiskey into a brand-new charred oak cask and it becomes Bourbon.

WHISKEY PIONEER

Corn whiskey is the forefather of Bourbon. Scots-Irish settlers – who began making whiskey using rye, due to the northerly latitude of where they arrived – found that as they travelled south and west, corn took over as the predominant and thriving grain.

These first whiskies were the ancestors of modern, unaged corn whiskey, albeit with fruits and spices sometimes added to make them more drinkable.

IS CORN WHISKEY THE SAME AS BOURBON?

Corn whiskey and Bourbon are closely related. They are both corn-dominated and distilled in the same way. Storage is where the real difference becomes clear. By US law, Bourbon, to be so-called, must have been stored and aged in new oak casks. Corn whiskey does not have this time restriction. Smaller, craft whiskey makers like this rule, as it means their corn whiskey will be ready as soon as it is distilled, meaning they can get it to market quickly.

WHAT DOES IT TASTE LIKE?

Due to the flexibility of maturation in corn whiskey, and the mix of non-corn grains, it is difficult to pin down one set of flavours. When unaged in oak it can be fresh, sweet

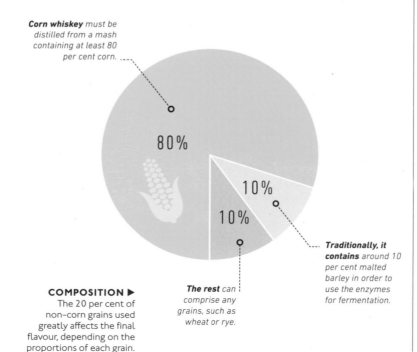

Corn whiskey must be distilled from a mash containing at least 80 per cent corn.

80%

10%

10%

COMPOSITION ▶
The 20 per cent of non-corn grains used greatly affects the final flavour, depending on the proportions of each grain.

The rest can comprise any grains, such as wheat or rye.

Traditionally, it contains around 10 per cent malted barley in order to use the enzymes for fermentation.

and buttery. With a couple of years in oak it becomes more complex and spicy, but still sweet.

CORN TYPES

Corn whiskey isn't made from the yellow sweetcorn that we commonly see in grocery stores. It is too moist and not starchy enough to be fermented. Most corn whiskey is made from white corn, though some craft distillers

▲ **Bourbon casks** must be new and charred; corn whiskey casks must be used or uncharred.

have experimented with other varieties, such as blue and red corn. These do not affect the colour of the whiskey, but do offer subtly differing flavours.

This is not entirely dissimilar to different grape varieties being used to make different styles of wine.

THE COLOUR OF CORN

When it was first made, often as illicit "Moonshine", corn whiskey was commonly known as "white whiskey" due to its lack of colour.

Any spirit, including whisky, when it leaves the still is completely clear and uncoloured – and, in theory, corn whiskey can be bottled straight from the still. Any colour a corn whiskey does have comes from its time spent in the cask. In general terms, the darker the corn whiskey, the more time it has spent maturing in a barrel.

CORN WHISKEY AND BOURBON ARE CLOSELY RELATED. THEY ARE BOTH CORN-DOMINATED AND DISTILLED IN THE SAME WAY

Bourbon is made in the US utilizing a mash recipe, or bill, of corn and any other cereal (usually rye; sometimes wheat).

51%

The mash bill must contain at least 51 per cent corn.

It can be distilled in pot stills, continuous stills, or a combination of both. Bourbon is generally continuously distilled. However, many distilleries employ a simple pot still (or a doubler) to finish off the spirit.

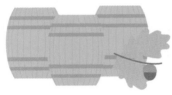

It must be matured in brand-new, charred oak casks.

WHAT IS BOURBON?

For many people American whiskey means Bourbon. But what is Bourbon, how and where is it made, and how does it differ from other US styles? It's a story that has helped this spirit become one of the world's favourites.

A HISTORY OF BOURBON

A branch of the French royal family – the Bourbons – left its mark in the southern US, where it once held colonies. Think of Bourbon Street in New Orleans, or Bourbon County in Kentucky – where the modern form of this whiskey was first produced in the late 19th century and where it may have acquired its name (no one knows for sure) to differentiate it from the rye whiskey produced in other US regions.

Equally mysterious is who thought of storing it in brand-new, charred oak casks. It's most likely the region's French-descended

◄ **Bourbons come in a range** of flavours. Maker's Mark, one of America's best-selling whiskeys, is at the sweeter end of the spectrum.

80%

It must be distilled to no more than 80% ABV (160° Proof).

40%

It must be bottled at a minimum of 40% ABV (80° Proof).

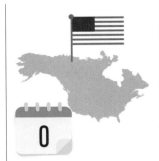

0

Except for "straight" whiskeys, there is no ageing requirement.

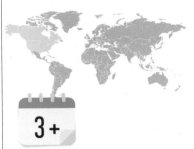

3+

In the EU, it must be aged for at least three years. Elsewhere, rules vary.

---

population knew about ageing Cognac in toasted casks and used that know-how for Bourbon.

There are flavour variations, but the use of brand-new, heavily charred casks tends to impart all Bourbon with very sweet, rich, spicy, and vanilla-heavy flavours.

TENNESSEE WHISKEY

Kentucky's neighbouring state of Tennessee produces whiskey that many people incorrectly think of as Bourbon. Tennessee whiskey, including Jack Daniel's, the world's best-selling US whiskey, is filtered, unaged, through charcoal pellets, giving, it's claimed, a softer, "purer" flavour than Bourbon. This is the "Lincoln County Process". Since 2013 it has been codified in US law to differentiate it from Bourbon production. Tennessee distillers who don't use this process can still call their whiskey Bourbon.

OLD AND NEW PLAYERS

Kentucky is Bourbon's "home", with Jim Beam and Heaven Hill alone distilling half of America's output. But, with the rise of craft distilling, makers across the US are now also producing Bourbons. Many "best of" Bourbon lists now regularly feature examples made as far from the US south as New York, Chicago, Utah, Michigan, and Ohio.

Bourbon is no longer purely a Kentucky, or even "Southern", spirit. It is now truly American.

BOURBON FACTS

In 1964, the United States Congress declared Bourbon to be America's only self-generated "native" spirit.

It is a status Bourbon's distillers, and the US economy, have greatly benefited from.

The number of Kentucky distilleries grew from 8 to 68 between 2009 and 2018.

Nearly 20,000 people are employed by the industry in Kentucky. That represents one-third of all distilling jobs in America.

95 per cent of the world's Bourbon comes from Kentucky.

1.7 million barrels of Bourbon were produced in 2018 – the highest figure for almost 50 years.

In 2017, sales of US whiskey grew by 8.1 per cent to $3.4bn.

KENTUCKY IS BOURBON'S "HOME", WITH JIM BEAM AND HEAVEN HILL ALONE DISTILLING HALF OF AMERICA'S OUTPUT

CASKS

Casks are vital to whisky production. Without their taste-affecting qualities the whisky world would be very different. So what are they made from, and what is done to them to make casks whisky-friendly?

▲ **American white oak.** A mature oak being felled in the Ozark mountain region of the USA, spread across Missouri, Arkansas and Oklahoma.

NEW/VIRGIN AMERICAN OAK

The main market for new, or virgin, oak casks is America, primarily for Bourbon, rye, and wheat whiskeys. All three styles can only, by law, be stored in new, charred casks made from white American oak (*Quercus alba*). The oak's freshly charred vanillins and lignin, coupled with Kentucky's hot, dry summers, give Bourbon-style whiskey its sweet, spicy and intense flavour set. Conversely, Scotch-style whisky makers rarely use new oak as it imparts too strong a flavour set.

SECOND-HAND BOURBON CASKS

There is a thriving market for ex-Bourbon casks for Scotch, Scotch-style, and Irish whiskey distillers. Whilst the US whiskey maker has already extracted the stronger flavours from these casks, plenty of subtle extractives remain. When an ex-Bourbon cask arrives in Scotland it receives its "first fill". Once that whisky has matured and been bottled the cask has its "second fill", and so on until the cask's flavour-imparting extractives have been exhausted. The re-used casks may also be periodically rejuvenated by re-charring.

EUROPEAN OAK AND WINE CASKS

Spicy, rich, sherry-cask-matured Scotch is quite different to spirit matured in ex-Bourbon casks. Sherry casks are mainly made from European *Quercus robur* or, increasingly, American oak. They are toasted rather than charred, a milder process that allows sherry to permeate the wood during maturation. This residue influences the flavour of whisky matured in ex-sherry casks. The same principle applies to ex-port, ex-Madeira, and ex-wine casks.

As ex-sherry casks are expensive, some whiskies are matured in ex-Bourbon casks first, for up to 10 years, then finished in sherry casks, typically for 6–24 months. This helps the ex-sherry casks last longer, while still imbuing whiskies with flavour. This is called "wood finishing" or, occasionally, "double maturation".

JAPANESE OAK

Also known as *Quercus mongolica*, or mizunara, Japanese oak is highly sought after for its tendency to imbue sweetly fragranced and aromatic characteristics. As it is not sustainable, Japan's distillers mainly use it to finish some of their whiskies, mostly, like Scotland, using ex-Bourbon and ex-sherry casks.

CASKS SHAPES AND SIZES

We may have heard of hogsheads, butts, and pipes, but maybe didn't know they are spirit cask sizes.

There are in fact eight "standard" cask sizes, but, in general, four are most commonly used.

200 LITRES (44 GALLONS)
ASB – American Standard Barrel
USA, rest of the world

250 LITRES (55 GALLONS)
Ex-Bourbon Hogshead
Scotland, Ireland, rest of the world

500 LITRES (110 GALLONS)
Ex-Sherry Butt
Scotland, Ireland, rest of the world

600 LITRES (132 GALLONS)
Ex-Port Pipe
Scotland, Ireland, rest of the world

◀ **Bourbon casks** being inspected. Once they have fulfilled their Bourbon-making duties, their next destination is probably Scotland, where they will be used to mature malt and grain whiskies.

TASTING 08 / 20

BOURBON

Here, quite simply, is an exploration of four very different Bourbons to help us understand how this important and big-selling style of US whiskey works – and how it tastes.

HOW IT WORKS

Bourbon, because of how it is made and matured, is subject to less in the way of "regional" variation than, say, Scottish single malts. But, there are differences. The examples here, from left to right, are: a "wheated" Bourbon, two corn-dominated whiskeys, and a rye-heavy Bourbon. Maybe add ice, perhaps after tasting. It's how these whiskeys were made to be drunk.

THE LESSON...

These whiskeys are all very intense, so dissecting them and their flavours is no mean feat. Don't be concerned if you felt there was very little – if any – difference between them. Bourbons, by their nature, are alike but never the same as each other. What you are looking for is how to find those nuances, so don't be quick to dismiss your palate or the whiskeys.

BOURBONS, BY THEIR NATURE, ARE ALIKE BUT NEVER THE SAME AS EACH OTHER

LARCENY STRAIGHT BOURBON

BARDSTOWN, KENTUCKY

46% ABV

IF YOU CAN'T FIND THIS
use Maker's Mark

WEIGHT 3 | 68% Corn, 20% Wheat, 12% Malted Barley.

 PALE AMBER

 SOFT ANISEED; sweet, restrained vanilla and spice. Slight, fresh leafy aroma

 BITTERSWEET, chewy liquorice; dry herbs; subtle, well-integrated spices

QUITE DRY, but tangy, fresh and medium-length finish

FLAVOUR MAP

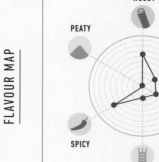

WOODY
FRUITY
PEATY
SPICY
FLORAL
CEREAL

 LIKE THIS? Try Old Fitzgerald 1849

GEORGE DICKEL NO.12 TENNESSEE WHISKEY

TULLAHOMA, TENNESSEE

45% ABV

IF YOU CAN'T FIND THIS
use Jack Daniel's Gentleman Jack

WEIGHT
3

75% Corn, 13% Rye, 12% Malted Barley.

BURNISHED COPPER

TOASTED MARSHMALLOWS; sour cherry; a hint of shoe polish!

TANGY, ACIDIC CHERRY, with a seam of bitter, dark chocolate and white pepper

SHORT, SWEET and peppery finish

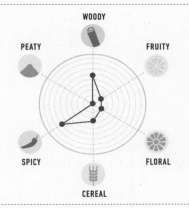

LIKE THIS? Try Jack Daniel's Single Barrel

MICHTER'S US*1 BOURBON

LOUISVILLE, KENTUCKY

50% ABV

IF YOU CAN'T FIND THIS
use Evan Williams Single Barrel

WEIGHT
4

79% Corn, 11% Rye, 10% Malted Barley.

RICH AMBER

SLIGHT NAIL-POLISH NOTES; sweet chocolate and caramel; gentle spice

CIGAR SMOKE; alcohol-soaked cherries and damsons; espresso with cream

LONG, SPICY FINISH; oily, aromatic mouthfeel

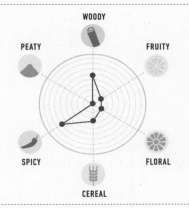

LIKE THIS? Try Elijah Craig Small Batch

FOUR ROSES SB BOURBON

LAWRENCEBURG, KENTUCKY

50% ABV

IF YOU CAN'T FIND THIS
use Bulleit Bourbon

WEIGHT
4

60% Corn, 35% Rye, 5% Malted Barley.

GOLDEN AMBER

DARK TREACLE, after-dinner mints; peppery spice; flora; creamy cocoa

SPICY, MACERATED DARK FRUIT, then mint chocolate, and dry black pepper

LONG AND DRY FINISH; plenty of lingering spice

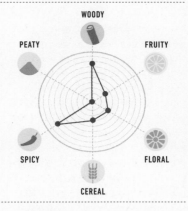

LIKE THIS? Try Woodford Reserve

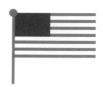

Also made in Canada, Denmark, Holland, and Germany, rye whiskey is most associated with the US. That's the version focused on here.

51%

Rye whiskey is made using a mash bill of rye and any other cereal (usually corn and malted barley). The mash bill must contain at least 51% rye.

It can be distilled in either pot stills, continuous stills, or a combination of both.

 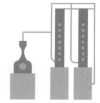

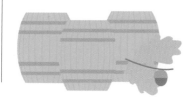

It must be matured in brand-new, charred oak barrels.

WHAT IS RYE WHISKEY?

It was until recently seen as the poor relation to Bourbon and other US whiskeys. Not anymore, and modern rye whiskey makers are showing just how good it can be.

A BRIEF HISTORY OF RYE

Rye was the first whiskey-type to be made by European settlers in the USA, who found this cooler-climate-loving grain was dominant in the north-eastern states of Pennsylvania and Maryland. This possibly suited the settlers, many of whom would have had experience of rye in Europe. Monongahela rye, named after the river of the same name, hailed from Pennsylvania and generally followed a rye-heavy mash bill; Maryland ryes tended

to contain more corn, giving a lighter, sweeter style.

While Bourbon is today seen as the archetypal US whiskey, rye was the nation's original and favourite style. Indeed, President George Washington himself made his own rye whiskey, at his home in Mount Vernon, Virginia, in 1797. It is still made on the same site today.

RYE'S FALL FROM GRACE

A local excise tax on liquor in 1791 ultimately forced many north-eastern US rye makers to switch

▲ **George Washington** took up the commercial distilling of rye whiskey in the same year that he retired from the Presidency of the United States.

production to Kentucky. In the 1800s, America's corn farmers benefited from crop subsidies, whereas rye growers did not. Rye production suffered further with the introduction of Prohibition in 1920. The illicit alcohol American drinkers could get their hands on tended to be lighter Scotch, Canadian and blended American

80%

It must be distilled to no more than 80% ABV (160° proof).

40%

It must be bottled at a minimum of 40% ABV (80° proof).

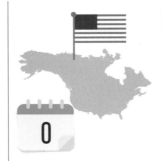

0

There is no minimum ageing requirement for the US and Canada.

3+

In the EU, it must be aged for at least three years. Elsewhere, rules vary.

WHILE BOURBON IS TODAY SEEN AS THE ARCHETYPAL US WHISKEY, RYE WAS THE NATION'S ORIGINAL AND FAVOURITE STYLE

whiskies. When Prohibition was repealed in 1933, rye whiskey had been largely left behind.

RYE ON THE RISE

Today, consumers are interested in rye again, and not just in the US. Craft whiskey makers led the way, and the big Kentucky distilleries followed suit.

It's doubtful that rye will ever threaten Bourbon or Tennessee whiskey sales, as it once did, but it is great to see this historic US whiskey style resurrected and in a healthy state, its trademark peppery flavour and earthy, aromatic character stimulating palates once more.

▼ **The Sazerac cocktail** was invented in late-1800s New Orleans. It's a heady blend of rye whiskey, bitters, lemon peel, sugar, and absinthe.

TASTING 09 / 20 — RYE WHISKEY

They are well known in the US, but rye whiskeys are increasing in popularity beyond the shores of America. This tasting investigates what this spicy, interesting style has to offer.

HOW IT WORKS

With rye on the rise, if you have not tasted any yet then now is the time – especially as they are easier to get hold of outside the US than ever before. If you want to add ice after nosing and tasting neat, feel free. They were made to be drunk this way.

THE LESSON...

The differences between the whiskeys here may be hard to spot or put your finger on. Don't worry, as this would be a challenge for even the most experienced taster. What you should have recognized is that rye whiskeys are a distinct "family", with a unifying spicy, peppery flavour set. Detecting the differences behind those dominant flavours will take time.

RYE WHISKEYS ARE A DISTINCT "FAMILY", WITH A UNIFYING SPICY, PEPPERY FLAVOUR SET

WILD TURKEY RYE WHISKEY

LAWRENCEBURG, KENTUCKY

40.5% ABV

IF YOU CAN'T FIND THIS
use Pikesville Rye

WEIGHT 3	51% Rye, 37% Corn, 12% Malted Barley.

 PALE AMBER

 CREAMY VANILLA AND CITRUS, with rye's spicy, peppery notes in the background

SUBTLE, DRIER, peppery notes. Sweet orchard fruits and soft vanilla

 MEDIUM-LENGTH finish, with the sweet vanilla lasting well

 FLAVOUR MAP

WOODY

PEATY

FRUITY

SPICY

FLORAL

CEREAL

 LIKE THIS? Try Peerless Rye

RITTENHOUSE BOTTLED IN BOND STRAIGHT RYE

BARDSTOWN, KENTUCKY
50% ABV

IF YOU CAN'T FIND THIS
use Catoctin Creek Roundstone Rye 92

WEIGHT 4	51% Rye, 35% Corn, 14% Malted Barley.

PALE AMBER

SWEET, alcohol-infused damsons. Mint and citrus mingle with subtle vanilla

SOFT NUTTINESS, then tiramisu; dark chilli chocolate, coconut, white pepper

LONG AND FRESH FINISH. Velvety mouthfeel

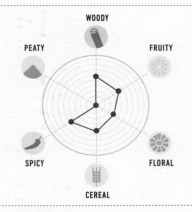

LIKE THIS? Try Jack Daniel's Rye

FEW SPIRITS RYE WHISKEY

EVANSTON, ILLINOIS
46.5% ABV

IF YOU CAN'T FIND THIS
use Russell's Reserve 6YO

WEIGHT 4	70% Rye, 20% Corn, 10% Malted Barley.

RICH AMBER

AROMATIC, COMPLEX, NUTTY. Marzipan. Soft citrus balances the sweetness

LEMON CURD; fresh mint or eucalyptus. Cardamom, smoked almonds, pepper

LONG, COMPLEX FINISH. Nice balance of sweet and dry

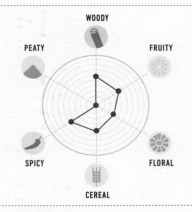

LIKE THIS? Try New York Ragtime Rye

RESERVOIR RYE WHISKEY

RICHMOND, VIRGINIA
50% ABV

IF YOU CAN'T FIND THIS
use Sonoma Distilling Co. Rye ·

WEIGHT 5	100% Rye.

TAWNY

RICH, FRAGRANT spices. Cinnamon, aniseed. Strong strawberry compote

MOUTH-FILLING. Luscious warm jam doughnut, with a peppery balance

LONG FINISH with fruit acidity and light peppery oiliness

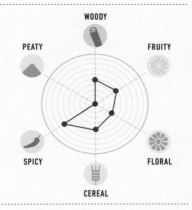

LIKE THIS? Try Koval Rye

◄ **Dillon's of Ontario** ages its "Three Oaks" rye whisky in three different types of oak cask for a minimum of three years.

RYE WHISKY IN CANADA AND EUROPE

Rye is an American whiskey, right? Correct, but the US doesn't have a monopoly on rye. It's also important to Canadian and European whisky makers, and is a style gaining in popularity.

CANADIAN RYE

Spirit production in Canada began in the late 1700s, with European settlers distilling rum. The emphasis only shifted to whisky as settlers moved westwards, making the importation of Caribbean molasses for rum less viable.

Wheat was originally the grain of choice, due to its light and sweet nature, but spicier rye was gradually introduced into the recipe at the behest of drinkers looking for more character. "Rye Whisky", as it began to be called, was, and is – in regards to Canadian whiskies – the same product, technically, as Canadian rye whisky and Canadian whisky.

Canadian rye whisky, officially, is a distilled product made from a mash of cereal grains that must be aged in "small wood" for a minimum of three years. Interestingly, it does not have to be made from a rye-dominant mash

CANADIAN WHISKY BECAME THE DARLING OF US WHISKY DRINKERS, OUTSELLING US WHISKIES ON DOMESTIC SOIL

(unlike American rye, for example), so Canadian whiskies typically vary widely in their rye content.

COMING TO AMERICA

Regardless, Canadian whisky became the darling of US whisky drinkers, outselling US whiskeys on domestic soil, before, during, and well after Prohibition. This was mainly due to its lighter, less intense nature. This made it particularly well-suited to the cocktail scene that developed after Prohibition, for example.

EUROPEAN RYE

It is likely that the first-ever rye whiskies were distilled in Europe. Rye is indigenous to Europe and distilling took place there long before it did in the US or Canada. Rye is a hardy grain, too, able to withstand bad weather and disease better than most other crops. However, it either never caught on, or, more likely, got lost among the malt-based Scotch and Irish whiskies that took over the world.

HANDLE WITH CARE

Rye is also notoriously difficult to deal with, becoming a sticky mess if not treated correctly, rendering it un-distillable. In wine terms, it is the Pinot Noir of the whisky world in that it's very difficult to get right.

But, despite these challenges, there has been a revival of rye whisky styles outside North America. European distillers – even a handful in Scotland – have decided it is worth the risk. Some, such as Austria's J.H. Distillery, have been producing it for over 20 years, others, like Germany's Spreewood, are just getting started. English distilleries, such as The Oxford Artisan Distillery (TOAD) and Norfolk's English Whisky Co. are also experimenting with rye. As whisky tastes continue to diversify and develop, the rye style has been one of the main beneficiaries of this change.

HOME GROWN?

Rye whiskies don't get more American than Wild Turkey.

Uncork a bottle and nose – it is unmistakably a Kentucky Rye. It may come as a surprise, then, to learn that Wild Turkey, among other US distillers, buys its rye grain from Germany. Perhaps this played a part in why some German whisky makers, especially following the craft whisky boom, began producing their own home-grown rye whiskies.

◀ **St George's Distillery,** in Roudham, Norfolk, released the rye-based limited edition single grain Malt 'n' Rye in 2017.

51%

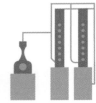

It can be distilled in either pot stills, continuous stills, or a combination of both.

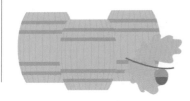

It must be matured in brand-new, charred oak barrels.

Wheat is the predominant grain used for Scottish grain whiskies, but it is the US version of this style that we focus on here.

Wheat whiskey is made using a mash bill of wheat and any other cereal (usually corn and malted barley). The mash bill must contain at least 51% wheat.

WHAT IS WHEAT WHISKEY?

Unlike Bourbon or rye, wheat whiskey is a relatively new concept, generally associated with the ever-growing craft distillation movement in America. Its popularity is growing as whiskey makers get to grips with it.

A BRIEF HISTORY OF WHEAT

The idea of commercial whiskeys produced via a wheat-dominant mash bill is recent, but wheat has been used to make whiskey in the US, especially Bourbon, for years.

The main reason that wheat was not used as much as corn or rye is that it was expensive. It was also in greater demand for flour and bread production, and still is. It should be remembered that whiskey was originally an agricultural by-product, made from left-over grain. It made little sense for farmers to "waste" valuable crops such as wheat to make whiskey.

THE GROWTH OF WHEAT

Wheat has been an important addition to the mash bills of a number of established brands,

◀ **Wheat yields** around one metric tonne per acre, and results in up to 400 litres of spirit per tonne. That's 533 75cl bottles of whiskey.

80%

It must be distilled to no more than 80% ABV (160° proof).

40%

It must be bottled at a minimum of 40% ABV (80° proof).

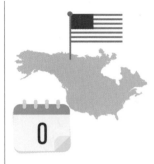

0

There is no minimum ageing requirement for the US and Canada.

3+

It must be aged for at least 3 years to be sold outside North America.

such as Maker's Mark, Heaven Hill's Old Fitzgerald and Buffalo Trace products like Pappy Van Winkle for many years.

Many of these are in high demand due to the wheated recipe, which many people prefer over a rye-orientated mix, due to the lighter, less "challenging" nature of wheat over rye.

WHO'S MAKING IT?

Actual wheat whiskeys are rare in comparison to Bourbon and rye. Only one of the established Kentucky distillers produces a wheat whiskey: Heaven Hill's Bernheim "Original". The main producers of wheat whiskeys are the smaller craft distilleries that are more willing to experiment with grain types – including wheat - such as Dry Fly in Washington State and Sonoma County Distilling in California.

One or two are also experimenting with other more unusual grains, such as triticale (a cross between wheat and rye). Wheat whiskey is not yet in the mainstream, but it may ultimately get there.

WHAT DOES IT TASTE LIKE?

Wheat whiskey has a much lighter and sweeter profile than rye, for example. This approachability could be a reason why it is becoming popular as a style of its own, as people look for something more "sociable" to drink.

Taste-wise, it tends towards mellow flavours, soft fruits, and buttery sweetness.

▼ **Dry Fly** distillery in Washington State makes a range of whiskeys. Its Cask Strength Straight Wheat Whiskey is its best-seller.

THE MAIN PRODUCERS OF WHEAT WHISKEYS ARE THE SMALLER CRAFT DISTILLERIES THAT ARE MORE WILLING TO EXPERIMENT

THE CRAFT WHISKY MOVEMENT

You may have heard of the worldwide craft whisky movement.
But what exactly is it? How are craft whiskies different from
their commercial counterparts?

▲ **A crafty business.** Though completely legal, the craft whisky movement draws inspiration from Prohibition-era American bootleggers.

It is a lively, vibrant market, with a hint of "moonshine" about it, but craft whiskies are just as legitimate as all other whiskies and are subject to the same distilling and maturation regulations.

WHAT IS CRAFT WHISKY?

There is no official definition, but craft whisky generally means small-scale production by enthusiast-led distillers pushing technical boundaries or lovingly re-creating whiskies from the past. Beware, though: "craft whisky" can also mean fast-buck businesses buying whisky from established distilleries, bottling it with a funky label and selling it on to unsuspecting customers.

Unless they have financial backing, craft whisky-makers often put aside some of their spirit to produce gin or vodka. These can be made and sold quickly, providing income and helping to build a brand while their whisky matures.

THE US LEADS THE WAY

It began as a grass-roots movement, a few makers experimenting with production. The spirits they created were not necessarily indigenous to their own states, or even to the USA. Many focused on making single malts, for example, though Bourbon was also popular. In 2010 there were around 200 US craft distillers; by 2017 there were more than 1500. Most US craft spirit-makers sell their product from their visitor centres, reinforcing their "authenticity" but making expansion tricky. Craft whiskeys are often little-known outside their localities. Some, though, have achieved national or international renown, such as Balcones from Texas, Chicago's KOVAL, High West from Utah, and Illinois' FEW.

CRAFTING AROUND THE WORLD

While popular in Europe, many Continental distillers do not call themselves "craft" whisky-makers, an indication perhaps of their desire to one day join the mainstream. Germany is a small-scale whisky-making hotspot. Its 200-plus makers include Berlin's Spreewood and the Hammerschmiede distillery in the northern Harz region. In the UK, Daftmill, in Fife, and the Cotswolds Distillery, from the area of the same name, are just two members of the ever-growing "craft" whisky network.

▲ **Pioneering spirit.** Spreewood is the oldest whisky distillery in the Berlin region, and the first rye-whisky distillery in Germany.

◀ **Art and labour.** Craft distilling involves whisky makers skilfully, and often artistically, preparing their grains for use.

TASTING 10 / 20

NORTH AMERICA'S MAIN STYLES

This should be interesting. Sample the four main traditional styles of US whiskey side by side and see the differences for yourself. There is a wide variety of taste experiences on offer.

HOW IT WORKS

Corn, Bourbon, wheat, and rye whiskeys all have their own histories and production methods – and tastes. What's interesting here is to see if and how each individual whiskey is distinct from the others. Start from the left, nose the whiskeys first, then taste, possibly adding water or ice as you go.

THE LESSON...

The whiskey that should stand out is the corn, as it has its own set of maturation rules; or the rye, due to its particular flavour. What's key is that you detect the differences *between* the four styles. Taste another four whiskeys from each category and you may find another four differences, giving you an insight into the flavour range within each style.

SEE IF AND HOW EACH INDIVIDUAL WHISKEY IS DISTINCT FROM THE OTHERS

BERNHEIM WHEAT WHEAT WHISKEY

BARDSTOWN, KENTUCKY
46.5% ABV

IF YOU CAN'T FIND THIS use Dry Fly Washington Wheat

WEIGHT 2	51% Wheat, 37% Corn, 12% Malted Barley

 RICH GOLD

 FRESH, SWEET DOUGHNUTS, Lightly spiced ginger cake

 HARD TOFFEE, red-berries; slightly salty savoury note, like unsmoked bacon

 **SHORT, DRY** and spicy finish

FLAVOUR MAP

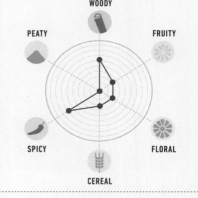

 LIKE THIS? Try Reservoir Wheat

MELLOW CORN
CORN WHISKEY

BARDSTOWN, KENTUCKY
50% ABV

IF YOU CAN'T FIND THIS use Balcones Baby Blue

| WEIGHT **3** | 80% Corn, 8% Rye, 12% Malted Barley |

GOLDEN STRAW

LIGHT AND FRESH, subtle vanilla essence, sweet popcorn

SOFT AND MELLOW SWEETNESS, luscious and lightly spiced

A LIGHT, REFRESHING short finish

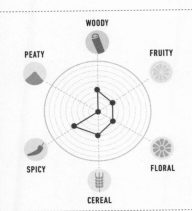

LIKE THIS? Try Platte Valley 3YO

WOODFORD
RESERVE DS
BOURBON

VERSAILLES, KENTUCKY
43.2% ABV

IF YOU CAN'T FIND THIS use Angel's Envy Bourbon

| WEIGHT **4** | 72% Corn, 18% Rye, 10% Malted Barley |

RICH AMBER

ICING SUGAR, caramelized lime, slight peppery, herbal

CUSTARD CREAMS, soft, velvety vanilla slice with a sprinkle of white pepper

DELICATE, SWEET and with no end in sight

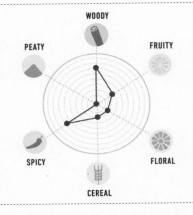

LIKE THIS? Try Bulleit 10YO Bourbon

KOVAL RYE SB
RYE WHISKEY

CHICAGO, ILLINOIS
40% ABV

IF YOU CAN'T FIND THIS use Bulleit Rye

| WEIGHT **5** | 100% Rye |

BURNT AMBER

CHOCOLATE MARSHMALLOW; burning fern and bracken; fruit-infused toffee

SUCCULENT, lightly smoked, spiced pear and peach. Hints of Turkish Delight

LONG, SWEET, elegant and gently peppery

WOODY

PEATY   FRUITY

SPICY   FLORAL

CEREAL

LIKE THIS? Try Jack Daniel's Rye

CHAPTER 4

TASTE

----- BY -----

PLACE

FROM ITS HEARTLAND in Scotland and Ireland, whisky making has spread across the globe – to the USA, of course, then on to the rest of the New World and beyond. In this chapter we will look at the whisky-making world today, taking in countries, states, and regions to survey the world's favourite spirit, from new start-ups and "craft" distillers to the established and best-known whisky makers. On the way we will find out how location and history both play their part, and where whisky may be going in the future.

SCOTLAND

THE DEBATE CONTINUES whether whisky's origins are Celtic or Caledonian. But for many, if not most, whisky's spiritual home is Scotland. The variety and quality of its whiskies is what the rest of the whisky-making world aspires to. Its distilling heritage has a depth, breadth, and longevity other nations can only dream of.

Old pretenders have come and gone. New nations are on the rise. But Scotland endures. And evolves. Scottish distillers could, given their strength and lineage, simply continue on as they have done for centuries. But they are investing in the future instead. Illustrious stalwarts and new distillers are constantly innovating, looking at how to further enhance and improve the world-famous single malts, delicious grains, and amazing blends that make Scotland *the* global whisky powerhouse.

Scotland's five whisky-making regions encompass a land like no other, embracing the rugged beauty of the Highlands and Islands (left, Glencoe), the rolling Lowlands, historic Campbeltown, the "whisky isle" of Islay, and ever-popular Speyside.

THE LOWLANDS

Often, and unfairly, thought of as more "lowly" than, say, the Highlands, this underrated region of Scotland produces excellent single malts.

FIRST WHISKY PRODUCTION Late 15th century

MAIN WHISKY STYLE Single malt

KEY DISTILLERIES
- Auchentoshan
- Bladnoch
- Glenkinchie
- Daftmill
- Clydeside

NUMBER OF DISTILLERIES 20

KEY

POT STILL

LOCATOR

12YO SINGLE MALT

AUCHENTOSHAN
Triple-distilled whisky made in Glasgow

DAFTMILL
One of Scotland's newest and smallest distilleries

GLASGOW DISTILLERY
Founded in 2014 in the city's north-west

LINDORES ABBEY
Re-opened 2017, after 523 years

EDEN MILL
Award-winning St Andrews distillery

KINGSBARNS
Sited on a formerly derelict farm building

River Clyde

Grangemouth

Linlithgow

Gifford

Edinburgh

CLYDESIDE
Docklands-based distillery using water from nearby Loch Katrine

Glasgow

THE LOWLANDS

River Tweed

BLADNOCH
Scotland's most southerly distillery

Merrick, *the highest peak in the Southern Uplands at 843m (2,765ft)*

Girvan

Dumfries

GLENKINCHIE
Diageo-owned distillery close to Edinburgh

15YO "ADELA" SINGLE MALT

River Nith

The Southern Uplands *includes the Cheviot, Moffat and Moorfoot Hills*

LOCATION

In whisky terms, the Scottish Lowlands are divided from the Highlands by a border running from Greenock to Dundee.

This imaginary line was demarcated and confirmed by the Scottish Whisky Association (SWA) in 2009. It should not be confused with the nearby "Highland Fault Line", a geological specification which describes a series of tectonic breaks between the two regions that helps to explain their differing landscapes. Much of the Lowlands is very flat and is great farming country, with much of Scotland's barley for malting grown here, including on at least one distillery's land, the farm-based Daftmill, in Cupar.

THE DISTILLERIES

Until recently, you could count the number of single malt Lowland distilleries on the fingers of one hand.

Whilst there were some great, historic names associated with the area, such as St Magdalene, Littlemill and Rosebank, the development of new Scottish distilleries happened in more "fashionable" areas. That has now changed, with the likes of the Clydeside Distillery, the Glasgow Distillery, Eden Mill, Lindores Abbey and Kingsbarns joining the one that quietly started the current Lowland "revolution" in 2005: Daftmill. The established distilleries of Auchentoshan, Glenkinchie and Bladnoch finally have new neighbours.

▲ **Clydeside Distillery,** opened in 2017, was Glasgow's first new dedicated single malt distillery for more than 100 years.

▲ **Barley fields** make up a large part of the Lowland landscape, in stark contrast to the mountainous Highlands "next door".

BACKGROUND

The Lowlands was formerly considered a hotbed for the mainly Irish method of triple-distillation.

The practice, though, had largely died out when brewing historian Alfred Barnard carried out his famous survey of Scotland and Ireland's distilleries in 1886. Today, only Auchentoshan triple distils. By the time of Barnard's survey, consumers had fallen out of love with Lowland whiskies, which were deemed lighter and less sophisticated than Highland single malts. Only Auchentoshan and Glenkinchie survived, later joined by the re-opened Bladnoch in the 1990s, and later still by today's new wave of distillers.

▲ **Auchentoshan's product** is sometimes called "the breakfast whisky" due to its sweet and delicate flavour.

THE HIGHLANDS & ISLANDS

This region has always been at the forefront of whisky making, with established distilleries making more whisky than ever and new distilleries carving a niche for themselves. But what makes this diverse region special?

FIRST WHISKY PRODUCTION
15th century

MAIN WHISKY STYLE Single malt

KEY DISTILLERIES
- Highland Park
- Talisker
- Glenmorangie
- Glendronach
- Old Pulteney

NUMBER OF DISTILLERIES
Approx. 40

TALISKER
Oldest working distillery on the Isle of Skye

DISTILLER'S EDITION

DORNOCH
Crowdfunded distillery founded in 2016

HIGHLAND PARK
Orkney-based, it is Scotland's most northerly distillery

"VIKING HONOUR"

North-west Highlands, a series of glacier-carved peaks

OLD PULTENEY
Self-described "Maritime Malt" distillery

GLENMORANGIE
World-famous single malt

18YO SINGLE MALT

GLENDRONACH
One of Scotland's oldest distilleries, established in 1826

Ullapool

Lairg

The Grampians include the Cairngorms and Lochaber

Invergordon

Inverness

DALWHINNIE
Scotland's highest distillery, based in the Cairngorms

KEY

POT STILL

Aviemore

Loch Ness

LOCATOR

Fort William

Ben Nevis 1,345m (4,412ft), Britain's highest mountain

THE HIGHLANDS & ISLANDS

GLENGOYNE
Most southerly distillery of the Highlands

LOCATION

The Highlands has probably the most richly varied and diverse landscape in Scotland.

Dramatic mountains and hills, studded with long, glacially eroded valleys and lochs, dominate the north and west, rolling down toward flatter coastal areas. This whisky region also includes Orkney, Shetland and the Western Isles (apart from Islay), encapsulated in the rugged beauty of the volcanic Isle of Skye. The climate is temperate, but changeable, with "four seasons in one day" not uncommon.

▶ **Eilean Donan Castle** on the Kyle of Lochalsh in the Western Highlands looks out and across to the Isle of Skye.

▲ **Dalwhinnie** sits on the border of the Highland and Speyside regions, but is classed as a Highland distillery.

THE DISTILLERIES

There are more than 40 malt distilleries spread across this large region.

Like the landscape, the Highlands' whiskies are very diverse. From soft and fruity Glengoynes and Dalwhinnies, through to the more robust Pulteney (or Old Pulteney, to give it its proper brand name), and from the rich and spicy Glendronach, to the peaty, and often explosive, Ardmore and Talisker, there is something for everyone. There are new distilleries, too, with spirit already being produced at Dornoch, as well as several others. It's a thriving, and growing, region.

BACKGROUND

Until the early 1800s, the Highlands was the poor relation of the Scotch whisky industry.

In contrast to the more sedate Lowlands, this region was wild and untamed, teeming with illicit stills. The topography of the land helped, making it easier for outlaw distillers to hide and disguise their activities – and harder for the authorities to find and punish them.

However, as the whiskies grew in reputation and popularity, the Highland distillers had to evolve. The Excise Act of 1823 had a huge effect, legitimizing whisky-making in Scotland, and assisting in making Highland single-malt whisky the regional and global phenomenon it is today.

PEAT AND WHISKY

Peat and Scotch whisky go back a long way, but what is this organic substance that appears to sit somewhere on the spectrum between earth and coal? And how it is used to make whisky smoky?

▲ **Cut peat** is usually piled for initial drying in situ. This, like much else in traditional peat cultivation, is a practice that has not changed in centuries.

WHAT IS PEAT?

Peat is decomposed bio-matter that has compressed and matured over hundreds, if not thousands, of years. Give it another few million years and it eventually becomes coal. It grows in wetlands worldwide, covering 3 per cent of the world's surface. In Scotland and Ireland, it was – and still is for some – a domestic, and occasionally industrial, heat source. It was dug up, cut into long briquettes, left to dry then burned over an open fire. For early Scottish whisky distillers, barley was dried on peat fires. When burnt, peat produces a thick, rich smoke, full of phenolic compounds that are absorbed into the skin of the still-damp barley. It's this process, scaled-up but still carried out today, that gives the barley, then the mash, then the wash, and eventually the spirit, the smoky, medicinal characteristic some Scotch single malts are known for. The best known Scottish peated whiskies include Laphroaig, Bowmore, Talisker, Ardbeg, Lagavulin, and Caol Ila. From further afield, peated "world whiskies" include Amrut, from India, Kavalan from Taiwan, Yoichi from Japan, and Sweden's Mackmyra.

WHICH DISTILLERIES USE IT?

A lot of people think that all Scottish whiskies are smoky and peaty. In fact, very few single-malt distilleries use peated barley in their mash recipes anymore. This tradition – born from necessity and not originally as a desire to deliberately create "smoky" whiskies – is now mostly limited to the majority of the distilleries of Islay, as well as a handful of other island and mainland distilleries. Where "peaty" whiskies are made elsewhere, especially in Asia and the Far East, peated barley is often imported from Europe, due to either the lack of native peat or the facilities to process peat locally.

PRESERVING PEAT

Peat doesn't grow quickly – around 1mm a year – and its rate of renewability is a question occupying whisky makers' minds. One estimate, for example, predicts that the island of Islay will run out of peat by the early 2020s and distillers are actively looking at alternative ways of peating their whisky, including importing peat to Scotland from some of the less disturbed peatlands of Canada, Siberia, and the Congo region of Africa.

VERY FEW SINGLE-MALT DISTILLERIES USE PEATED BARLEY IN THEIR MASH RECIPES ANYMORE

▲ **Peat is burned** in a kiln and the fragrant smoke produced is used to dry barley. This was once how all barley for Scotch whisky was prepared for use.

◀ **With Scottish peat** supplies allegedly running low, Canada's unspoiled peatlands (left) are being eyed by some Scottish distillers.

TASTING 11 / 20

PEATY WHISKIES

Peat is one of the building blocks of Scotch whisky making. Some whiskies are bound to it, reliant upon its smoke-giving goodness for their undoubtedly "unique" flavours; others use it as a "seasoning".

HOW IT WORKS

Tasting peated whisky is the simplest and the hardest aspect of whisky tasting. Simple because peat is the easiest flavour to spot; hard because, once you've sampled peated whisky, it's difficult to taste anything else. Peat's strong, smoky flavour is present even in blended whiskies. Start with the unpeated whisky on the left as a control sample.

THE LESSON...

Hopefully, this Tasting will show you the massive impact of peated barley. Around 150 years ago, most single malt whiskies were peated. Today, you have a choice, from heavily peated to unpeated and everything in-between. Peaty whiskies are now made all over Scotland – and worldwide – such is the turf's popularity.

TASTING PEATED WHISKY IS THE SIMPLEST AND THE HARDEST ASPECT OF WHISKY TASTING

THE GLENLIVET 12YO

SPEYSIDE SINGLE MALT

40% ABV

IF YOU CAN'T FIND THIS
use Strathisla 12YO

WEIGHT 2	The oldest licensed Speyside distillery and the biggest-selling single malt in the US.

👁 PALE STRAW

👃 **SUMMER MEADOW;** freshly mown lawn; vanilla

👄 **TANGY LEMON-GRASS.** No peat. Use as this flight's baseline

LONG, SILKY; dry

FLAVOUR MAP

WOODY
PEATY
FRUITY
SPICY
FLORAL
CEREAL

LIKE THIS? Try Nikka Miyagikyo

SPRINGBANK 10YO

CAMPBELTOWN SINGLE MALT

46% ABV

IF YOU CAN'T FIND THIS
use Craigellachie 13YO

| WEIGHT **3** | Campbeltown's oldest operating distillery. |

PALE GOLD

BOILED SWEETS, tinned pineapple, peaches. Soft but distinct peat smoke

SEARED ORANGE MARMALADE; dried spice; peat smoke-imbued fruit cake

SLIGHTLY SMOKY; citrus. Oily texture

LIKE THIS? Try Westland Peated

BENROMACH PEAT SMOKE

SPEYSIDE SINGLE MALT

46% ABV

IF YOU CAN'T FIND THIS
use BenRiach Curiositas

| WEIGHT **4** | Benromach distillery was revived by Gordon & MacPhail in 1993. |

LIGHT GOLD

SWEET AND LUSCIOUS; fresh vanilla; citrus; cured ham

SPICED APPLES, pears; sweet lemon. Smokiness from a distant peat fire

FRUITY SWEETNESS and peaty smokiness. Slightly oily

LIKE THIS? Try Ardmore Legacy

KILCHOMAN "MACHIR BAY"

ISLAY SINGLE MALT

46% ABV

IF YOU CAN'T FIND THIS
use Laphroaig 10YO

| WEIGHT **5** | Established 2005, Islay's first new distillery since 1881. |

PALE GOLD

SWEET, RICH biscuit aroma gives way to a whiff of peat smoke

WATER enhances the peat. Cereal and citrus notes wrapped in pungent smoke

LONG, smoky, oily

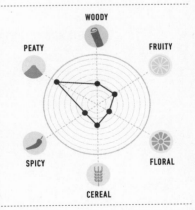

LIKE THIS? Try Ledaig 10YO Single Malt

ISLAY

Scotland's "Whisky Isle", Islay houses nine working distilleries. Its whiskies are often associated with fiery and peaty flavours, but is that all that Islay has to offer?

FIRST WHISKY PRODUCTION
Late 15th century

MAIN WHISKY STYLE Single malt

KEY DISTILLERIES
- Ardbeg
- Bowmore
- Bruichladdich
- Lagavulin
- Laphroaig

NUMBER OF DISTILLERIES 9

ARDNAHOE
Islay's newest distillery, opened in 2019

BUNNAHABHAIN
Distillery's name means "mouth of the river"

KILCHOMAN
Established 2005, one of Islay's newest and smallest distilleries

CAOL ILA
Islay's largest distillery, established in 1846

Port Askaig

River Laggan

ISLAY

River Abhainn Ghlas

BOWMORE
Home to the world's oldest maturation warehouse: the No.1 Vaults

15YO "DARKEST"

Bowmore

Beinn Bheigeir 491m (1,610ft), Islay's highest peak

Port Charlotte

BRUICHLADDICH
Produces mainly unpeated single malts, as well as gin

Portnahaven

ARDBEG
Distils, they claim, "the ultimate Islay single malt"

River Glenedgedale

Port Ellen

KEY

POT STILL

LOCATOR

LAPHROAIG
Established in 1815 by farmers Donald and Alexander Johnston

10YO SINGLE MALT

LAGAVULIN
Diageo's crown jewel distillery on Islay

LOCATION

Islay's terrain is more like that of the Lowlands or Campbeltown than its neighbouring islands.

The southernmost of the Inner Hebrides, its landscape is generally soft, green, and undulating. All but two of Islay's distilleries are by the sea. This was originally so that whisky could be more easily exported from the island by boat. These days, Islay's whisky leaves the island via the main ferry ports at Port Ellen and Port Askaig. As an island known for the production of peaty, smoky whiskies, Islay is covered in peat bogs with much of the main road from Bowmore to Port Ellen built on top of a seemingly endless stretch.

▶ **Port Ellen** in the south is one of Islay's main whisky shipping points along with Port Askaig.

THE DISTILLERIES

Islay's nine distilleries produce quite different whiskies that go beyond just peat.

Ardbeg, Kilchoman, Lagavulin, Laphroaig and the new distillery Ardnahoe focus on a very heavily peated, smoky spirit. Then you have the medium-peated whiskies from Caol Ila and Bowmore. Finally, there are the sweeter, fruitier unpeated whiskies made by Bunnahabhain and Bruichladdich, though both distilleries also make limited amounts of peated whiskies, with Octomore from Bruichladdich the best-known.

▲ **Lagavulin's name** derives from the Gaelic for "hollow of the mill", describing the distillery's location in a sheltered cove.

BACKGROUND

Some believe that the distilling of whisky came to Scotland from Ireland, via Islay.

With Islay only 14.5km (9 miles) off the coast of Northern Ireland, with many of the distilleries on the island among the oldest in Scotland, there may be some truth in this. What is certain is that Islay gives us a glimpse of life and distilling how it used to be. All Scottish whiskies were once made using peated, malted barley. When smokeless fuel and other whisky styles emerged, many whisky makers diversified. But Islay remained true to peat and, generally, still does.

CAMPBELTOWN

There are just three distilleries in the Campbeltown region, but it is an extremely important whisky-making area of Scotland.

FIRST WHISKY PRODUCTION Late 1600s

MAIN WHISKY STYLE Single malt

KEY DISTILLERIES
- Glengyle (Kilkerran)
- Glen Scotia
- Springbank

NUMBER OF DISTILLERIES 3

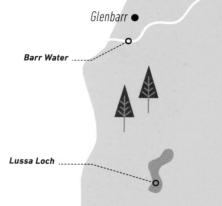

Glenbarr

Barr Water

Carradale

Saddell

Lussa Loch

CAMPBELTOWN

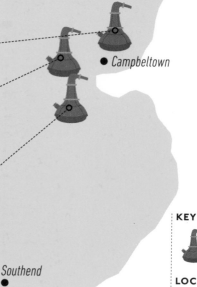

● *Campbeltown*

GLEN SCOTIA
Distillery founded in 1832

DOUBLE CASE SINGLE MALT

GLENGYLE
Its whisky uses the brand name Kilkerran

South Kintyre Marilyns

SPRINGBANK
Established in 1828 on an old illegal-still site

10YO SINGLE MALT

Southend

KEY

POT STILL

LOCATOR

LOCATION

Campbeltown is, in many ways, the end of the world. The Scotch whisky-making world that is.

If you have driven there, perhaps from Glasgow, past the great Lochs, Lomond and Fyne, through Inveraray and along the beautiful winding road that leads you all the way to Campbeltown, you can go no further. It is situated at the tip of the Mull of Kintyre amongst beautiful and fertile farmland, bordered by the sea. Campbeltown was once Scotland's "Whisky Town" – a small seaside settlement with over 30 distilleries. Most are now gone, but the three remaining distilleries retain their importance to this day.

▶ **Campbeltown** lies at the bottom of the Kintyre peninsula, a finger of land around 48km (30 miles) long.

THE DISTILLERIES

Glen Scotia was in business from 1832, and, following a brief closure from 1984 to 1989, is once again distilling a quality spirit.

Glengyle, under the brand name Kilkerran, produces a soft and sweet style, plus some smoky stuff too. However, it is Springbank which is perhaps the most iconic. This institution still makes whisky the old-fashioned way, the last established distillery to undertake every process on-site, from malting the barley, to distilling the spirit and bottling the whisky. Springbank is as much a working museum as a distillery.

▲ **Springbank** is Scotland's oldest independent family-owned distillery, stretching back over five generations.

BACKGROUND

Campbeltown was a massively important whisky-making area until the mid-to-late 1800s.

The whiskies made at most of its 30+ distilleries were peaty and "industrial" and fell out of favour when grain whisky and more subtle single malts began to challenge them. The closure of a local coal mine and the effects of Prohibition in the US caused distillery after distillery to close. By 1934, just Springbank and Glen Scotia remained. Springbank's owners resurrected the Glengyle distillery in 2004, signalling something of a revival in the region's fortunes.

SPEYSIDE

Speyside, geographically, is part of the Highlands, but in whisky terms has its own "appellation" in recognition of its standing in the Scotch-whisky world.

FIRST WHISKY PRODUCTION
Late 1700s

MAIN WHISKY STYLE Single malt

KEY DISTILLERIES
- Aberlour
- Glenfarclas
- Glenfiddich
- The Glenlivet
- The Macallan

NUMBER OF DISTILLERIES
Approx. 45

**RARE CASK
SINGLE MALT**

THE MACALLAN
*Once a hidden gem,
now a global giant*

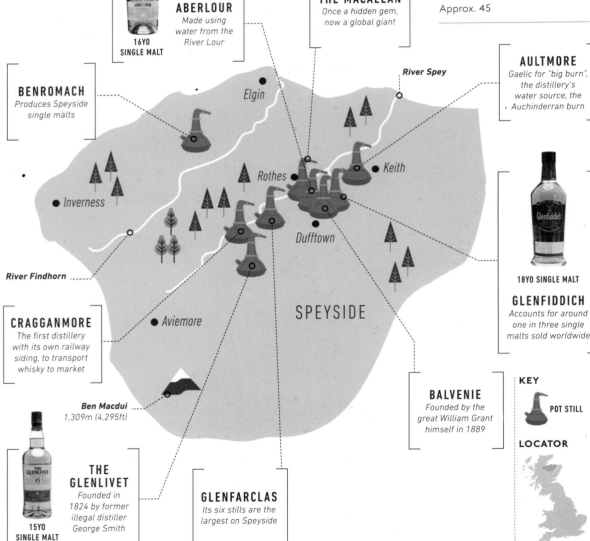

**16YO
SINGLE MALT**

ABERLOUR
*Made using
water from the
River Lour*

BENROMACH
*Produces Speyside
single malts*

River Spey

AULTMORE
*Gaelic for "big burn",
the distillery's
water source, the
Auchinderran burn*

Elgin

Rothes

Keith

Inverness

Dufftown

River Findhorn

SPEYSIDE

18YO SINGLE MALT

GLENFIDDICH
*Accounts for around
one in three single
malts sold worldwide*

CRAGGANMORE
*The first distillery
with its own railway
siding, to transport
whisky to market*

Aviemore

BALVENIE
*Founded by the
great William Grant
himself in 1889*

KEY

POT STILL

LOCATOR

Ben Macdui
1,309m (4,295ft)

**15YO
SINGLE MALT**

**THE
GLENLIVET**
*Founded in
1824 by former
illegal distiller
George Smith*

GLENFARCLAS
*Its six stills are the
largest on Speyside*

LOCATION

Speyside is sited roughly between the northern boundary of the Cairngorms and the Aberdeenshire coast.

It is a beautiful, soft and tranquil area of mainly agricultural land. The mighty Spey river and its many tributaries run through it like life-giving arteries, providing water for the region's many distilleries, famed for their smooth and complex product. This, along with the existence of great whisky making towns and sub-areas, such as Rothes, Dufftown, Aberlour and Keith, make Speyside one of the world's great whisky areas.

▶ **Speyside** takes its name from the Spey river, and many of its distilleries are located among the waterway's surrounding glens.

THE DISTILLERIES

There are nearly 50 very varied operating distilleries in this small area.

Glenlivet represents the lighter, floral, citrus side, while more "middleweight" distilleries, including Balvenie, Aultmore, and Cragganmore, produce more rounded, "plump" and fruitier styles. For lovers of rich, spicy, and robust whiskies, there's Glenfarclas and Macallan, among others. There are even some distillers, such as Benromach, still using peated malted barley, a tip of the hat to Speyside's old way of doing things.

▲ **Macallan's new distillery,** with its high-tech still room, shown here, opened in 2018, at a cost of £140 million.

BACKGROUND

Speyside is not a geographical or political location. It exists purely for whisky-making purposes.

It was created by the enthusiasm and passion of one man: whisky author Michael Jackson. Due in part to Jackson's advocacy, the SWA (Scotch Whisky Association) designated Speyside as a whisky region in the early 1990s. There was a movement then to classify single malts by region and style, as with wine. With many distilleries today diversifying from their original flavour specification, those hard and fast categories are becoming more fluid.

TASTING 12 / 20

HIGHLAND SINGLE MALTS

Many believe Scotch single malts can be classified, taste-wise, according to the distillery's region. So, are regional "types" relevant? This tasting examines Highland single malts as an example.

HOW IT WORKS

We are looking here for taste differences, big and small, as well as similarities. Use your palate to guide you and try to make up your own mind as to whether traditional regional classifications are still relevant when choosing your next whisky.

THE LESSON...

Where a whisky comes from is important, along with the region's landscape and history – it is all part of the distillery's provenance. Hopefully, after this tasting you will view regionality in a new light. Taste is much more about what flavour or style each individual distiller wishes to achieve. They may wish to adhere to a region's "traditional" style – or they may not.

HOPEFULLY, AFTER THIS TASTING YOU WILL VIEW REGIONALITY IN A NEW LIGHT

GLENGOYNE 12YO

(SOUTHWEST HIGHLANDS)

43% ABV

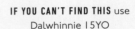

IF YOU CAN'T FIND THIS use Dalwhinnie 15YO

WEIGHT 2	Situated just north of the Highland/Lowland line, whisky making began in 1833.

PALE GOLD

RUNNY HONEY AND CITRUS; vanilla and coconut

LEMON TART, vanilla custard, toffee apples and shortbread

DRIED FRUITS and cinnamon; medium-length finish

FLAVOUR MAP

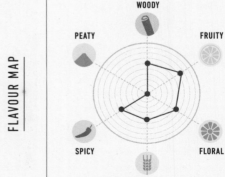

WOODY
PEATY
FRUITY
SPICY
FLORAL
CEREAL

LIKE THIS? Try Kavalan "Classic"

GLENMORANGIE 'QUINTA RUBAN'

(TAIN, ROSS-SHIRE)

46% ABV

IF YOU CAN'T FIND THIS use
Tomintoul 15YO Port Finish

WEIGHT	
3	This whisky is finished for several months in Port casks (or pipes).

BURNT UMBER

WINTER SPICES; cloves, cinnamon; vanilla pods

CHERRY-LIQUEUR filling; a touch of clove and aniseed spice

QUITE DRY, spicy, medium-length finish

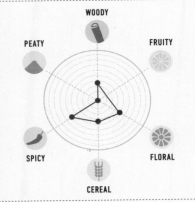

LIKE THIS? Try Balvenie 21YO Port Finish

CLYNELISH 14YO

(NORTHEAST HIGHLANDS)

46% ABV

IF YOU CAN'T FIND THIS use
Old Pulteney 12YO

WEIGHT	
3	Clynelish distillery was built in 1819, but was superseded by a new one in 1969.

PALE GOLD

CITRUS, FLORAL NOTES. Briny tang reflects Clynelish's coastal proximity

SEAWEED AND SMOKE; zesty citrus, spicy honey, vanilla

LONG, REFRESHING FINISH; slightly oily texture

WOODY
PEATY   FRUITY
SPICY   FLORAL
CEREAL

LIKE THIS? Try The Hakushu Single Malt

LEDAIG 10YO

HIGHLAND SINGLE MALT (ISLE OF MULL)

46.3% ABV

IF YOU CAN'T FIND THIS use
Ardbeg 10YO

WEIGHT	
5	This distillery was built in 1798, later closed, then revived in 1982.

RICH GOLD

PACKS A SMOKY WALLOP; alluring citrus tones

PUNGENT PEAT SMOKE; juicy citrus

ZINGY, clinging citrus and peat smoke

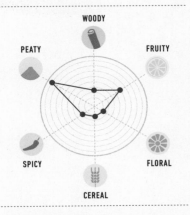

LIKE THIS? Try Amrut Peated

THE STORY BEHIND...

TYPES OF STILL

Whisky-making stills can generally be split into two types: pot stills and column stills. Both make distinctive whisky types but operate in similar but different ways. Here's how they work.

▲ ▶ COPPER POT STILLS
They have been the basis of whisky distillation for centuries, dominating the process until column stills were developed in the 1830s.

THE POT STILL

A pot still is the oldest, most traditional still for making whisky, especially single malts. Like a kettle, liquid "wash" or "beer" is heated to become steam which rises into a spout. The rising vapour is fed via a "swan-neck" pipe towards a cold condenser that turns the steam back into a more concentrated liquid

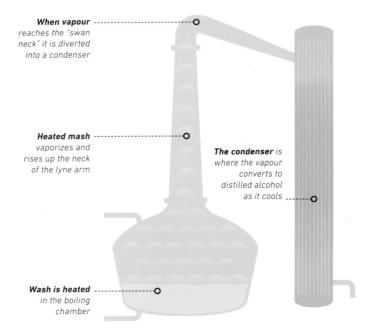

When vapour reaches the "swan neck" it is diverted into a condenser

Heated mash vaporizes and rises up the neck of the lyne arm

The condenser is where the vapour converts to distilled alcohol as it cools

Wash is heated in the boiling chamber

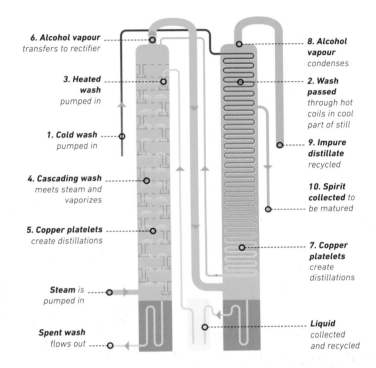

6. **Alcohol vapour**
transfers to rectifier

3. **Heated wash**
pumped in

1. **Cold wash**
pumped in

4. **Cascading wash**
meets steam and vaporizes

5. **Copper platelets**
create distillations

Steam *is
pumped in*

Spent wash
flows out

8. **Alcohol vapour**
condenses

2. **Wash passed**
through hot coils in cool part of still

9. **Impure distillate**
recycled

10. **Spirit collected** *to be matured*

7. **Copper platelets**
create distillations

Liquid
collected and recycled

◄ ▲ A COLUMN STIILL
This diagram (left) shows in numbered steps the main processes that occur, often simultaneously, inside a column still.

alcohol state. Pot stills are usually made of copper, as no other metal conducts heat as effectively while being able to remove unpleasant sulphur compounds from the liquid.

THE COLUMN STILL

Also known as patent, Coffey, or continuous stills, they create a purer spirit with higher alcohol levels. The wash, or beer, enters the top of the column and the liquid cascades down a series of platelets while hot steam is pumped upwards, causing mini-distillations. Column stills are used for distilling grain whisky for Scotch-style whiskies, and for US whiskeys such as Bourbon.

Other still types include the "Doubler", traditionally used for some Bourbon-style whiskeys in America. It is essentially a pot still that finishes off the spirit after column distillation. Hybrid stills combine the two technologies in one piece of equipment.

Column stills, though usually made of steel, feature copper in the condensing dome to help remove sulphur, as with a pot still.

COLUMN STILLS, THOUGH USUALLY MADE OF STEEL, FEATURE COPPER IN THE CONDENSING DOME TO HELP WITH SULPHUR REMOVAL

IRELAND

IRELAND'S RECORD OF PRODUCING globally popular whiskeys is enviable. But, like much else in Irish history, the tale of its distilling heritage is one of ups and downs – and then of rebirth, renewal, and, ultimately, of hope for a happier future.

Based on a tradition of single pot still whiskey-making, a tradition that made Irish whiskeys some of the best-known and best-selling in the UK and America, Ireland's distillers failed at first to embrace the nineteenth-century revolution that introduced the column still and continuous distillation to the whiskey-making process. While Ireland's devotion to the old way of doing things was culturally admirable, it was economically ruinous, sending the Irish whiskey industry into an almost terminal decline. Almost, but not quite. Irish whiskey making survived and, today, thrives. New producers are now joining the ranks of long-standing distillers Jameson in the Republic of Ireland and Bushmills in Northern Ireland, based just a stone's throw from the Giant's Causeway (left).

IRELAND

The love for Irish whiskey, particularly in the USA, is palpable. What drives this industry, older than Scotland's, and where does it stand today?

FIRST WHISKEY PRODUCTION
1700s

MAIN WHISKEY STYLES Single malt, single pot still, single grain, blended

KEY DISTILLERIES
- Jameson (Cork)
- Bushmills (Antrim)
- Cooley (Louth)
- Teeling (Dublin)
- Dingle (Kerry)

NUMBER OF DISTILLERIES 21

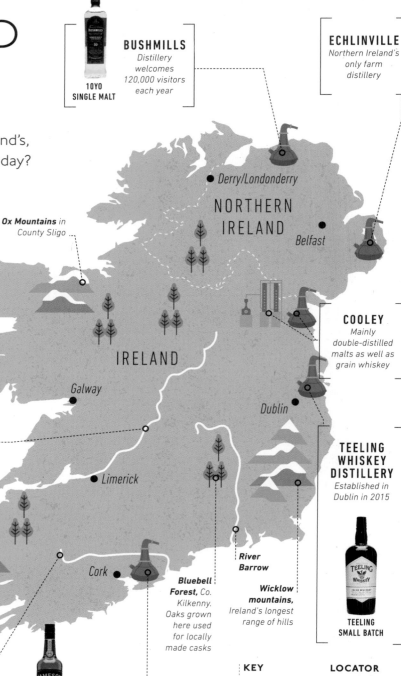

BUSHMILLS
Distillery welcomes 120,000 visitors each year

10YO
SINGLE MALT

ECHLINVILLE
Northern Ireland's only farm distillery

Ox Mountains in County Sligo

Derry/Londonderry

NORTHERN IRELAND

Belfast

COOLEY
Mainly double-distilled malts as well as grain whiskey

IRELAND

Galway

Dublin

TEELING WHISKEY DISTILLERY
Established in Dublin in 2015

River Shannon is Ireland's longest, at 360km (224 miles)

Limerick

TEELING
SMALL BATCH

DINGLE
"Artisan" distillery based in a converted sawmill

SINGLE MALT

Cork

Bluebell Forest, Co. Kilkenny. Oaks grown here used for locally made casks

River Barrow

Wicklow mountains, Ireland's longest range of hills

Carrauntoohil 1,039m (3,409ft), Ireland's highest peak

River Blackwater

STOUT EDITION

JAMESON
Originally based in Dublin, now distilled in Cork

KEY

COLUMN STILL

POT STILL

LOCATOR

LOCATION

The "emerald isle" is well-named. Outside of cities such as Dublin, Belfast, and Cork, Ireland consists of mainly green, arable farmland.

It is mostly low-lying, its rolling hills generally gentle and low rather than rugged and high. The climate is temperate-oceanic, meaning mild, wet winters and cool summers. The west of the island, facing the Atlantic and bearing the brunt of the transatlantic Gulf Stream, experiences double the rainfall of the east. The result is a lush landscape, in places rich in peat — although it is not widely used in Irish whiskey making.

▶ **Ireland's countryside** is a patchwork of subsistence-level smallholdings, rather than large-scale farms.

THE DISTILLERIES

Until the late 1980s, the Irish whiskey industry was all about Bushmills and Jameson.

They were joined in 1987 by Cooley, a former potato-alcohol processing plant. The family behind this venture, the Teelings, made well-received whiskey before selling their concern to Jim Beam in 2012. The Teelings then opened the Teeling Whiskey Distillery in Dublin, in 2015. Teeling, along with notable others, such as Dingle in Kerry and Echlinville in County Down, led the way in Ireland's post-millennium whiskey revival.

▲ **Bushmills' Black Bush** is aged in ex-Oloroso Sherry casks. It is 80 per cent malt and 20 per cent grain whiskey.

BACKGROUND

Ireland distilled whiskey before Scotland, but its industry has fared less well over the years.

This was partly due to historic harsh tax regimes and production regulations. However, the main reason for Ireland's decline against Scotland was that Irish whiskey makers refused to accept the Coffey-still "revolution" of the 1830s, remaining true to single pot still distilling, their products seen as outdated and expensive. By the 1980s, just two distilleries remained. Today, though, more than 20 are in operation and Ireland's whiskey revival continues.

IRELAND'S WHISKEY REVIVAL

Ireland, alongside Scotland, was once at the forefront of whisky making. Then it wasn't. What happened and, more importantly, how is it getting back on track?

▲ **Bushmills proudly** proclaims itself the world's oldest licensed whisky maker going back to 1608 – older even than any Scottish distillery.

UP TO THE 1970s

From a glorious past, by the 1970s Ireland's distillery industry was in a bad place. Where there had once been scores of makers, just two, admittedly large and high-quality, distilleries remained: Bushmills in Northern Ireland and Jameson in the Republic. They kept Ireland's whiskey flag flying while the rest of the country slowly reconfigured itself to adapt to changes in whiskey production and whiskey-drinking habits.

THE 80s REVIVAL

Things began to change in 1987, when Irish businessman John Teeling and his two sons converted a lowly potato-alcohol processing plant in County Louth into the whiskey-producing Cooley Distillery. Eschewing the "traditional" Irish whiskey-making path of triple-distilling malted and unmalted barley, Cooley took the Scottish route by double-distilling malted barley only. They also decided to create something no other Irish

FROM A GLORIOUS PAST, BY THE 1970s IRELAND'S DISTILLERY INDUSTRY WAS IN A BAD PLACE

distiller had done for a century: a peated Irish whiskey. From the start, Cooley was an inventive and interesting whiskey maker, one that other Irish distillers looked to for inspiration.

ENTER THE MILLENNIUM

2010 saw Cooley's owners reopen Kilbeggan, the oldest working distillery in Ireland. When the Teelings sold their business to Jim Beam for $95 million the following year, it was clear the big boys were waking up to Irish whiskey's potential.

From that point on it seemed as though a new Irish distillery opened each week. At the "macro" end, the historic Tullamore distillery, which had closed in 1954, was bought by Scotland's William Grant & Sons and reopened in 2014. In "micro" terms, places such as Echlinville in County Down, Northern Ireland, and The Shed Distillery in the Republic's County Leitrim, took up craft distilling. Both also produce gin, and market themselves as tourist destinations for general visitors and the whiskey-curious.

Returning to where Ireland's whiskey renaissance began, in 2015 the Teeling family rejoined the fray, opening the Teeling Whiskey Distilllery in Dublin.

HOW DO THEY DO IT?

Irish whiskey once meant single pot still distillation. But the picture is wider now.

Some, such as Teeling, Connacht, Shed, and Dingle are reviving the glories of single pot still distillation – alongside "normal" single malt production in some cases. Others are specializing in double- or triple-distilled single malts. Many newer distillers bottle and sell product made at larger and established distilleries, whilst their own spirit matures. From the monolithic industry that it once was, Irish whiskey making is now a model of diversity for others to learn from.

◀ **Dublin's Teeling** distillery is the latest venture by the Teeling family. It opened in 2015 and its aim is to produce around 500,000 litres of whiskey annually.

TASTING 13 / 20

"MODERN" IRISH WHISKEY

Single pot still whiskey held sway in Ireland for centuries. Now the picture is more diverse, with a range of styles making Irish whiskey worth investigating beyond the usual suspects.

HOW IT WORKS

This tasting takes in Cooley, Jameson, and Teeling, three distilleries representing what is happening with "modern" Irish whiskeys that are currently available (much "new" Irish whiskey is still being aged at the time of writing). These give an indication of the innovations and different styles that are being embraced.

THE LESSON...

Although a "traditional" single pot still whiskey, the Method and Madness is aged in alternating oak and chestnut wood barrels. Did that affect what you tasted? The three other whiskies also offer new takes on what "Irish" whiskey is, and all four whiskies tasted here reflect the changes occurring in Ireland.

ALL FOUR WHISKEYS TASTED HERE REFLECT THE CHANGES OCCURRING IN IRELAND

TEELING SINGLE GRAIN

SINGLE GRAIN WHISKEY

46% ABV

IF YOU CAN'T FIND THIS
use Kilbeggan 8YO

WEIGHT 2 | From one of only two distilleries currently with mature grain whiskey.

 GOLDEN STRAW

 LIGHT, ZESTY CITRUS. Candy floss, vanilla and a touch of cinnamon

 TANGY FRUIT the nosing didn't hint at. Fruity acidity and white chocolate

 THE CITRUSSY FINISH goes on, seemingly forever

 **FLAVOUR MAP**

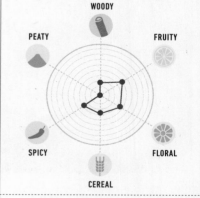

 LIKE THIS? Try Method and Madness SG

METHOD AND MADNESS SPS

SINGLE POT STILL

46% ABV

IF YOU CAN'T FIND THIS
use Green Spot Léoville Barton Finish

| WEIGHT **3** | Matured in ex-Bourbon and ex-sherry casks, then French chestnut casks. |

RICH GOLD

ROASTED PEARS and cloves. Boiled sweets. Burnt demerara and cinnamon

A REAL FRUIT BOMB of pineapple, peach and kiwi. Then vanilla and dried fruit

LONG, LASTING FINISH. A refreshing, acidic mouthfeel

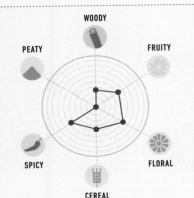

LIKE THIS? Try Powers John's Lane

KNAPPOGUE CASTLE 12YO

SINGLE MALT WHISKEY

40% ABV

IF YOU CAN'T FIND THIS
use Teeling Single Malt Whiskey

| WEIGHT **2** | This whiskey is aged in casks beneath 15th century Knappogue Castle. |

PALE STRAW

EASY-GOING VANILLA and citrus. Slightly nutty; a touch of marzipan

SOFT, SWEET FRUIT and delicate spices. A hint of muscovado sugar

LONG AND ALLURING; creamy mouthfeel

LIKE THIS? Try Knappogue Castle 16YO

CONNEMARA PEATED IRISH WHISKEY

SINGLE MALT

46% ABV

IF YOU CAN'T FIND THIS
use Bunnahabhain Toiteach

| WEIGHT **4** | The first peated Irish single malt produced in Ireland for over a century. |

LIGHT GOLD

SMOKED AND BURNT APPLE PIE. Soft peat smoke. Honeyed, malted barley

THE PEAT is more apparent; additional floral flavours and a whiff of mint

LONG AND STRONG in smoke. Quite dry

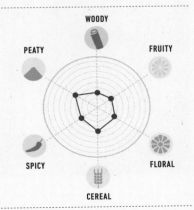

LIKE THIS? Try Connemara 12YO

NORTH AMERICA

ANY WHISKEY-BASED survey of North America has to begin with Kentucky, the home of Bourbon and one of the world's great whiskey-making powerhouses. It's also the perfect jumping-off point to discover what the rest of the New World has to offer.

The next stop is Tennessee, another American whiskey giant, then on to the emerging regions of western, central and the eastern United States (left, Brooklyn Bridge, New York City). Then we head north, to see what Canada can do.

It's a survey of the North American scene that embraces Bourbon, corn and rye whiskey, wheat whiskey, blends and more. The following pages also look at the growing micro-distillery movement, to see how that's both conserving traditional whiskey-making techniques and pushing back the boundaries of what whiskey is and how it should be distilled and aged.

KENTUCKY

Almost certainly the birthplace of Bourbon and definitely the state that produces most of it, Kentucky has cemented its importance in the whisky world.

FIRST WHISKEY PRODUCTION
Mid-1700s

MAIN WHISKEY STYLES Bourbon, corn, rye, wheat

KEY DISTILLERIES
- Buffalo Trace (Frankfort)
- Four Roses (Lawrenceburg)
- Heaven Hill (Bardstown)
- Jim Beam (Clermont)
- Wild Turkey (Lawrenceburg)

NUMBER OF DISTILLERIES
Approx. 70

KEY

Column still

COLUMN STILL

Pot still

POT STILL

LOCATOR

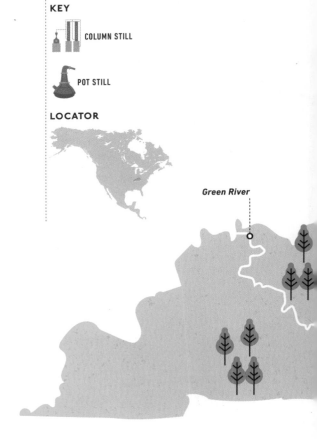

Green River

LOCATION

Kentucky borders seven states, including fellow whiskey powerhouse Tennessee.

The climate in the state varies slightly from north to south, but it is generally warm and sub-tropical. It is not as hot as more southerly states, like Mississippi or Alabama, but warmer in winter than more northerly states, such as Michigan and Pennsylvania. Water is quite abundant, and all of Kentucky's rivers flow into the Mississippi. Kentucky is a green, fertile state with a long history of farming, especially for corn.

▲ **Almost half** of Kentucky is forested, indicating a warm, wet climate ideal for making – and maturing – whiskey.

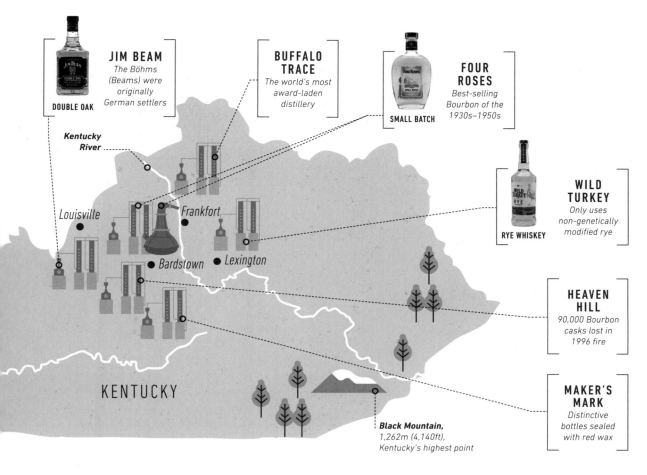

JIM BEAM
*The Böhms
(Beams) were
originally
German settlers*

DOUBLE OAK

**BUFFALO
TRACE**
*The world's most
award-laden
distillery*

**FOUR
ROSES**
*Best-selling
Bourbon of the
1930s–1950s*

SMALL BATCH

*Kentucky
River*

Louisville

Frankfort

Bardstown

Lexington

**WILD
TURKEY**
*Only uses
non-genetically
modified rye*

RYE WHISKEY

**HEAVEN
HILL**
*90,000 Bourbon
casks lost in
1996 fire*

**MAKER'S
MARK**
*Distinctive
bottles sealed
with red wax*

KENTUCKY

*Black Mountain,
1,262m (4,140ft),
Kentucky's highest point*

THE DISTILLERIES

**Until the early 2000s there was
only a handful of whiskey
distilleries in Kentucky.**

However, like Buffalo Trace and Heaven
Hill, for example, each produced a
plethora of different brands and
bottlings, possibly giving the impression
of more whiskey makers than there
really were. Today, the craft whisky
revolution sweeping the world has
left its mark on Kentucky, too, and there
are now more than 70 separate
distilleries in the state, either fully
operational or in process.

▲ **Jim Beam** began selling Old Jake
Beam whiskey in 1795, named after the
company's founder, Jacob Beam.

BACKGROUND

**Whiskey has been made in
Kentucky since European settlers
arrived in the late 1700s.**

With corn grown state-wide, there was
plenty left after harvest to make corn
whiskey. This was replaced by Bourbon
when oak casks began being used for
maturation, not just storage. Bourbon is
now, after Scotch, the world's most
heavily exported whisky. Most of
Kentucky's large commercial producers
have grown from humble beginnings.
Maker's Mark, for example, is still made
in a distillery dating from 1773.

LOCATION

The distilleries of Tennessee are mainly centred near Nashville in the west, Knoxville in the east, and Fayetteville in the south.

Tennessee has a similar humid, sub-tropical climate to Kentucky, but is a few degrees warmer in summer and winter. It is an agricultural and manufacturing area, exporting cattle, poultry and producing transportation and electrical equipment. The mighty Mississippi river borders the west of the region and the Appalachian Mountains skirt the east of the state.

▲ **Nashville** is known as America's country music capital, but is also at the heart of Tennessee's whiskey production.

TENNESSEE

Aside from a certain whiskey by a certain Mr Daniel, what do we know about Tennessee and its whiskeys? There is a lot more to it, that's for sure.

FIRST WHISKEY PRODUCTION
Late 18th century

MAIN WHISKEY STYLES Tennessee whiskey, Bourbon, corn, rye, wheat

KEY DISTILLERIES
• Jack Daniel's (Lynchburg)
• George Dickel (Tullahoma)
• Benjamin Prichard's (Kelso)
• Corsair (Nashville)
• Nelson's Green Brier (Nashville)

NUMBER OF DISTILLERIES Approx. 30

KEY

COLUMN STILL

POT STILL

LOCATOR

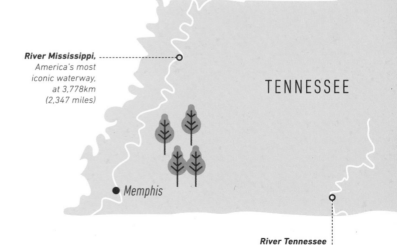

River Mississippi,
America's most iconic waterway, at 3,778km (2,347 miles)

TENNESSEE

● *Memphis*

River Tennessee

THE DISTILLERIES

From only two post-Prohibition distilleries – Jack Daniel's and George Dickel – Tennessee now has around 30.

Many are fairly new, craft whiskey makers. In 2013, the "Lincoln County Process" was enacted, stating that all Tennessee whiskeys, to be so labelled, must be charcoal-filtered. Ironically, the Benjamin Prichard Distillery, the only Tennessee whiskey maker not subject to this rule (for complex legal reasons), is the only distillery actually located in Lincoln County.

▲ **Jack Daniel's** charcoal burner. The distillery burns maple wood on site to make charcoal to filter its whiskey.

BACKGROUND

Tennessee was populated by the same European immigrants that settled neighbouring Kentucky.

But their whiskey-making fortunes varied. Tennessee was the first US state to outlaw whiskey production, in 1909, 10 years before Prohibition, and only legalized it in 1939, six years after Prohibition. The Jack Daniel's distillery re-opened a year later, as did George Dickel in 1958. The Benjamin Prichard distillery opened in 1997, followed by the new wave of craft distillers helping fuel the state's whiskey-making boom.

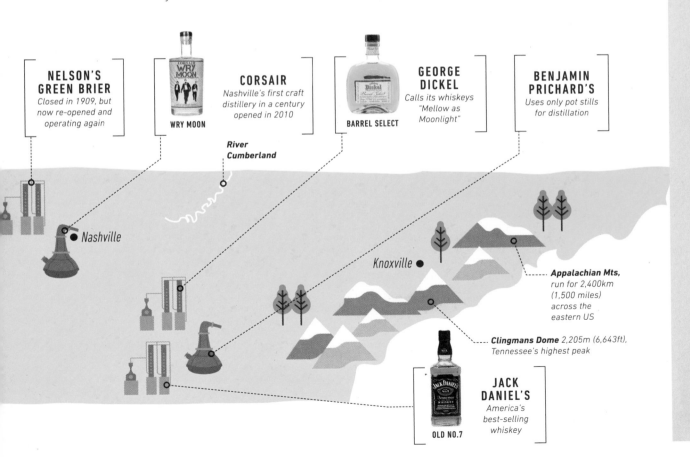

NELSON'S GREEN BRIER
Closed in 1909, but now re-opened and operating again

CORSAIR
Nashville's first craft distillery in a century opened in 2010

WRY MOON

River Cumberland

GEORGE DICKEL
Calls its whiskeys "Mellow as Moonlight"

BARREL SELECT

BENJAMIN PRICHARD'S
Uses only pot stills for distillation

● Nashville

Knoxville ●

Appalachian Mts, run for 2,400km (1,500 miles) across the eastern US

Clingmans Dome 2,205m (6,643ft), Tennessee's highest peak

JACK DANIEL'S
America's best-selling whiskey

OLD NO.7

WESTERN USA

The west of America may not spring to mind when thinking about whiskey. Here we look at the California, Washington, Utah, and Oregon distilleries putting this region on the whiskey map.

FIRST WHISKEY PRODUCTION 1790s

MAIN WHISKEY STYLES Single malt, Bourbon, corn, rye, wheat

KEY DISTILLERIES
- Hotaling and Co. (Calif.)
- St George Spirits (Calif.)
- Dry Fly (Wa.)
- High West (Utah)
- Clear Creek (Oregon)

NUMBER OF DISTILLERIES
Approx. 230

Cascade Mts. Volcanic range of peaks

Columbia River

CLEAR CREEK
Produces peated single malts, among others

THE EDGEFIELD DISTILLERY
Established in 1998

DRY FLY
Produces vodka, gin, and whiskey

BOURBON 101

ST GEORGE SPIRITS
Also makes Absinthe and other liquors

SINGLE MALT

HIGH WEST
Utah's first post-Prohibition distillery

WASHINGTON
Seattle
Spokane
Portland
OREGON
IDAHO
NEVADA
Salt Lake City
UTAH
San Francisco
Sacramento River
HOTALING AND CO.
Makes rarely produced rye pot still whiskey
CALIFORNIA
Los Angeles
San Diego
Sierra Nevada range contains three national parks

Mt. Whitney 4,418m (14,495ft), highest peak in the Sierra Nevada

KEY

COLUMN STILL

POT STILL

LOCATOR

LOCATION

The western USA is roughly bordered by the Pacific ocean to the west and the Rocky Mountains to the east.

It is a huge area covering more than 1.8 million sq km (700,000 sq miles), with a wide variety of landscapes and climates, from inland deserts, temperate northern forests, tropical southern coastlines and lush, verdant plains and valleys. Most of the ever-growing number of western US distilleries are centred around the major cities of Seattle and Portland in the north, down to San Francisco and Los Angeles further south, with many whiskey makers (with a few notable exceptions) based close to or on the Pacific coast.

▶ **San Francisco** and its surrounding Bay Area is home to almost 20 whiskey distilleries.

THE DISTILLERIES

Western America has no old working distilleries. Prohibition swept them all away.

But with typical American drive, whiskey makers simply started again. San Francisco led the way in 1982; its St George's Spirits claiming to be the "first small American distillery since Prohibition". Other early pioneers of micro-distilling include San Francisco's Anchor Distillery (now Hotaling and Co.), and The Edgefield Distillery in Troutdale, Oregon, both distilling well before the craft whiskey movement that exploded after the new millennium.

▲ **High West's Rendezvous Rye** is an award-winning "rye-heavy" spirit, making for a spicy but smooth drink.

BACKGROUND

America's western states were never prime whiskey-making areas. Grains needed to create the spirit were grown further east.

Prohibition reinforced this, closing down what whiskey distilleries there were. It's best, then, to look forward. Without the same whiskey-making weight of tradition, local distillers have a blank slate on which to write a new history. And they are, creating, for example, "unlikely" whiskeys such as American single malts. This region today is making some of the most innovative and exciting whiskeys in America.

CENTRAL USA

Some of the most exciting and interesting whiskeys are coming from the central US states. Here, we look at Texas, Arkansas, Illinois, Wisconsin, and Missouri to find out why.

FIRST WHISKEY PRODUCTION 1790s

MAIN WHISKEY STYLES Bourbon, rye, single malt

KEY DISTILLERIES
- Balcones (Waco, Texas)
- Rock Town (Little Rock, Arkansas)
- FEW (Evanston, Illinois)
- Great Lakes (Milwaukee, Wisconsin)
- Holladay (Weston, Missouri)

NUMBER OF DISTILLERIES Approx. 140

WISCONSIN

River Mississippi

GREAT LAKES
Award-winning, multi-spirit making distillery

Milwaukee

Madison

River Missouri

Chicago

Springfield

ILLINOIS

Kansas City

MISSOURI

HOLLADAY
Set up in 1856 by the founder of Wells Fargo

Missouri white oak *is a major source for US Bourbon casks*

Ozark Plateau

ARKANSAS

Little Rock

RYE WHISKEY

FEW
This small-batch distiller's slogan is "By the few, for the few"

BOURBON

ROCK TOWN
Arkansas' first legal distiller since Prohibition

Dallas

TEXAS

BRIMSTONE CORN WHISKEY

BALCONES
Began distilling in 2009

Houston

KEY

COLUMN STILL

POT STILL

LOCATOR

LOCATION

There's a wide variety of landscapes in this group of states covering more than 1.3 million sq km (515,000 sq miles).

It is temperate in the north and humid and sub-tropical in the south. The central states are subject to extreme weather events, such as tornadoes, while the southern coastal states experience periodic hurricanes. In general, the land is fertile, largely flat, and the economy is agriculture-based. Illinois, Wisconsin, Missouri, and Minnesota, for example, are among America's main corn-producing states and form part of the country's "corn belt" – resulting in a fair amount of locally produced corn-based whiskey.

▶ **Severe tornadoes** are common in this region. These can decimate wheat, rye, and other whiskey-making crops.

THE DISTILLERIES

Like much of the US, this region's whiskey history was deeply affected by Prohibition.

One exception is Missouri, possibly due to its proximity to the traditional whiskey-making states of Kentucky and Tennessee. The Holladay Distillery in Weston, Missouri, has been operating since 1856, under a variety of names and owners. Nowadays, Texas is the main distillery state, with more than 50 producers, and Missouri, Minnesota, and Illinois are hotbeds of craft whiskey. Many smaller regional producers only sell their product locally.

▲ **Carrie Nation (1846-1911)** was one of Texas' most formidable Temperance leaders. Her influence abides there today.

BACKGROUND

Before Prohibition, the anti-alcohol Temperance Movement held sway in many of these states.

Even today, there are several counties in Texas and Arkansas, for example, where it is illegal to sell alcohol. Generally speaking, America's "dry'" counties are clustered in the central states, covering 18 million citizens. That said, distillers here are now as innovative as any US whiskey makers. Helped by lower alcohol-licensing costs and national and state deregulations for small-batch producers in particular, American craft whiskey is currently thriving.

EASTERN USA

The Eastern US has a long whisky-distilling history. Here we look at New York, the Virginias, Pennsylvania, and Indiana, to see what's going on in North America's oldest settled region.

FIRST WHISKEY PRODUCTION
Early 1700s

MAIN WHISKEY STYLES Bourbon, rye, single malt

KEY DISTILLERIES
- Tuthilltown (Gardiner, NY)
- Smooth Ambler (Maxwelton, W. Virginia)
- A. Smith Bowman (Fredericksburg, Virginia)
- Dad's Hat (Bristol, Pennsylvania)
- MGP (Lawrenceburg, Indiana)

NUMBER OF DISTILLERIES
Approx. 200

KEY

COLUMN STILL

LOCATOR

OLD SCOUT

SMOOTH AMBLER
Appalachian-based distillery founded in 2009

PENNSYLVANIA RYE

DAD'S HAT
Award-winning rye whiskey specialists

HUDSON BABY BOURBON

TUTHILLTOWN
Distillery based on the site of a 200 year old grist mill

NEW YORK STATE

PENNSYLVANIA

● Pittsburgh

New York ●

Philadelphia

INDIANA

Indianapolis ●

OHIO

● Columbus

● Cincinnati

WEST VIRGINIA

Ohio River

Richmond ●

VIRGINIA

MGP
Supplies whiskeys to many "sourced" craft whiskey brands

Appalachian Mountains

A. SMITH BOWMAN
Family-owned distillery dating from 1935

LOCATION

The eastern US has a longer history, a larger population and, traditionally, more industry than the central and western regions.

Venerable cities such a New York, Boston, Washington, and Philadelphia dot the eastern seaboard. The climate, being similar to Scotland and Ireland's, makes the region suitable for whisky making. It is colder in the north, with woods, forests, and rugged coastlines, temperate in the middle, and tropical in the south, low-lying with swamplands in Florida, for example. The landscape is dominated by the Appalachian Mountains, which run through most of the eastern US and into Canada.

▶ **New York City** has at least ten whiskey distilleries, mostly around "hip" Brooklyn, but also in Manhattan.

THE DISTILLERIES

Rye whiskey production began in Pennsylvania and Maryland in the early 1700s.

Today, those two areas are re-igniting interest in this classic, spicy style through distilleries such as Dad's Hat in Bristol, Pennsylvania. Virginia and West Virginia, as neighbours of whiskey powerhouse Kentucky, are hives of distilling action, with start-ups emerging since the new millennium. Further north, New York's Hudson Whiskeys, from the Tuthilltown distillery, has been creating a buzz with its rye, corn, Bourbon, and malt whiskeys.

▲ **Hudson's** Baby Bourbon and New York Corn whiskeys both use grain grown locally to their upstate New York distillery.

BACKGROUND

New York's first distillery was opened by Dutch settlers in 1640 making genever, or gin.

When the British took over in 1664, rum became the favoured spirit, followed by whiskey post-US independence. Further south, President George Washington founded a whiskey distillery in Mount Vernon, Virginia, in 1797. American alcohol production was hampered for the next 150 years by restrictive taxes, the Civil War, and Prohibition. The legacy of this history is a new tradition of smaller-scale distilling, with an inventive approach to whiskey making.

TASTING 14 / 20

US REGIONAL CRAFT WHISKEYS

Here we taste product from newer US distillers in less traditional whiskey-making areas. They are testing the boundaries of what "American" whiskey is – so, what do they taste like?

HOW IT WORKS

It's not easy to pin down four spirits representing the buzz around the new wave of US distillers. This quartet gives a good idea of the range of whiskeys being produced by some of the smaller, more innovative makers. It's a range that is growing year by year.

THE LESSON...

Did you taste where these new-wave whisky makers are going? They should not have tasted better or worse than any "traditional" US whiskeys you have already tasted, but hopefully you discerned both differences and similarities. Californian Bourbon? American single malts? The smaller distillers have cast off the shackles and are embracing new ways of doing things.

DISTILLERS HAVE CAST OFF THE SHACKLES AND ARE EMBRACING NEW WAYS OF DOING THINGS

SONOMA DISTILLING BOURBON

BOURBON

CALIFORNIA
46% ABV

IF YOU CAN'T FIND THIS
use Dry Fly Bourbon

| WEIGHT **3** | Operating since 2010, its whisky is made using traditional copper pot stills. |

 RICH GOLD

 CREAM SODA, seared raspberry coulis, Morello cherry, fresh basil

FLAT CHERRY COLA, chopped mint, black pepper, clove hints

 **SPICY AROMATICS**, sweet vanilla essence; medium-length finish

FLAVOUR MAP

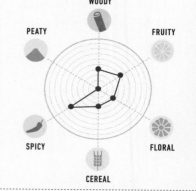

 LIKE THIS? Try Old Fitzgerald Bourbon

BALCONES
NO. 1 SINGLE MALT

SINGLE MALT WHISKY

WACO, TEXAS
53% ABV

IF YOU CAN'T FIND THIS
use Wasmund's Single Malt

WEIGHT 4	Texas' first post-Prohibition whiskey maker. Pot stills handmade on-site.

GOLDEN AMBER

QUITE MEATY AND SAVOURY; dark, spices; sweet, seared tarragon

CHEWY, SATISFYING. Rum and raisin ice-cream, drizzled with PX Sherry

SMOKY HONEY, burnt orange zest; long, dry finish

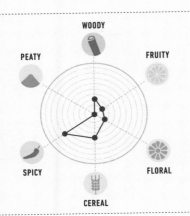

LIKE THIS? Try Aberlour A'bunadh

HUDSON
MANHATTAN RYE

RYE WHISKEY

GARDINER, NY STATE
46% ABV

IF YOU CAN'T FIND THIS
use Redemption Rye (Sourced)

WEIGHT 5	Hudson whiskeys hail from New York's Tuthilltown Distillery, established in 2005.

BURNT AMBER

AROMATIC AND SPICY PEARS, cigar smoke

HEAVILY SPICED, burnt apple pie with cinnamon custard. Seared orange peel

LONG, DRY, CHEWY. Very satisfying finish

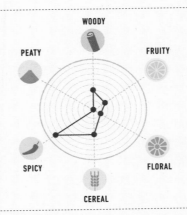

LIKE THIS? Try Jack Daniel's SB Rye

WESTLAND
PEATED

SINGLE MALT WHISKEY

SEATTLE, 46% ABV

IF YOU CAN'T FIND THIS
use McCarthy's Peated Oregon Malt

WEIGHT 4	One of the only US distilleries to focus purely on single malt production.

GOLDEN STRAW

PEAT SMOKE, wrapped in orange zest; a touch of clove and cinnamon

SPICY, SMOKED PEAR in a hot pie with mint sprigs and white chocolate flakes

LONG, DRY, finish; lightly smoky, very well-balanced

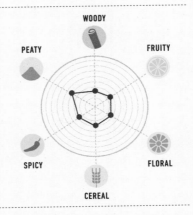

LIKE THIS? Try Caol Ila 12YO

KEY

COLUMN STILL

POT STILL

LOCATOR

GLENORA DISTILLERY
Its Glen Breton Rare is a single malt whisky

Rocky mountains, Canada's longest and highest range

CANADA

Vancouver

Winnipeg

Quebec

Montréal

Halifax

Albany River

Ottawa River

Appalachians run from Canada to the US Deep South

GIMLI DISTILLERY
Makes Crown Royal, Canada's best-selling whisky

FORTY CREEK DISTILLERY
Produces small batch whisky

"OLD TIME" RYE WHISKY

ALBERTA DISTILLERS
Makes 100 per cent rye whiskies

CANADIAN CLUB
Founded in 1848, its whisky is aged for six years in oak

BLENDED

CANADA

Canada is often overlooked in the North American context as a whisky maker. Yet this vast country has a long tradition of distilling, and continues to produce fine quality whiskies.

FIRST WHISKY PRODUCTION Late 1700s

MAIN WHISKY STYLES Canadian rye, blended, single malt

KEY DISTILLERIES
• Alberta Distillers (Calgary, Alberta)
• Canadian Club (Windsor, Ontario)
• Forty Creek Distillery (Grimsby, Ontario)
• Gimli Distillery (Gimli, Manitoba)
• Glenora Distillery (Glenville, Nova Scotia)

NUMBER OF DISTILLERIES Approx. 50

LOCATION

It is the second largest country in the world, yet 60 per cent of Canada is sub-arctic.

The country's colder regions are ideal for *drinking* whisky but not for cultivating the crops necessary to make it, apart from rye, which is grown mainly in western Canada. This hardy grain thrives in cold conditions, so it's no surprise that rye is Canada's main whisky style. The Appalachian Mountains, the Great Lakes, and the vast Hudson Bay dominate the east of the country, while the towering Rockies border western Canada. In between lie the great plains, the country's "bread bowl", producing wheat, corn, and rape seed.

▶ **Banff National Park** lies in the Rocky Mountains and is a vast area of peaks, glaciers, ice fields, and forests.

THE DISTILLERIES

Canada's whisky industry was traditionally dominated by a handful of large distilleries.

Hiram Walker, a Detroit-based US businessman, opened what eventually became the Canadian Club Distillery in Windsor, Ontario, in 1854, and other makers soon followed suit. Today, there are innovative distillers such as Glenora, which claims to have been making North America's first single malt since 1989, under the brand name Glen Breton. There's a fair number of craft distillers, too, especially in Nova Scotia in eastern Canada and elsewhere.

▲ **Once Canada's** largest distiller, Gooderham & Worts stopped producing in the 1990s but remains an iconic brand.

BACKGROUND

Who brought distilling to Canada is a matter of debate. Some say it was the Scots or the Irish.

Others say it was English, or possibly German, immigrants. Regardless, with its softer flavours, Canadian whisky was, and remains, popular in the US. To this day Canadian whiskies are the second biggest-selling category of whisky in America, after Bourbon. Production-wise, unlike their American neighbours, Canadian makers distil rye, corn, and wheat whiskies separately, then blend them together, rather than mixing the grains together in the mash bill.

MICRO-DISTILLERIES

Putting the word "craft" in front of a whisky calls to mind cleverly marketed brands and fancy-labelled bottles. But who actually makes craft whisky, and how – and what exactly is a micro-distillery?

▲ **The Stein Distillery** in Joseph, Oregon, opened in 2009. It grows its own grains and makes its Bourbons, rye whiskeys, and blends by hand.

A QUESTION OF INTERPRETATION

Although no legal definition exists for this category of whisky making, micro-distilling notionally means spirits produced on a small scale using a small-batch process often from local and, possibly, organic ingredients. Often micro-distilleries are passion projects undertaken by whisky enthusiasts who have decided to make spirits for themselves. It is even the case that some micro-distillers are self-taught, bringing new ideas with them to the spirit-making process.

Micro-distilleries vary in size and provenance. Some are one-person operations, doing it for love (and, hopefully, a living); others may be small commercial distilleries, supported by a bigger business possibly hoping to share in the popularity of the "craft" whisky movement.

SMALL IS BEAUTIFUL?

It is considerably easier to start a small distillery than it once was. In the US in particular, there has been a relaxation of local laws on producing strong alcohol and this has given micro-distillers a leg-up they have enthusiastically accepted.

Not subject to the pressures of larger commercial whisky makers, micro-distillers take a more relaxed approach to their craft, experimenting with new or unusual grain combinations and testing new flavour blends. As for sales, they are by necessity usually kept local, often only available from the micro-distillery's shop.

For truly small micro-distilleries the whisky-making equipment they use is often compact enough to fit into one

▲ **Dry Fly,** like many small distilleries, also make spirits such as gin and vodka. This is due to a love of those spirits, but also to earn funds while their slower-ageing whiskeys mature.

room of a house; at the larger end of the micro-distillery scale, a business could fill a warehouse. It is probably easier to say that what makes a distillery "micro" is the attitude of the people making the whisky.

INVENTING A NEW TRADITION

There is a frontier spirit in micro-distilling and the whisky rule book is being torn up by those involved in it. Want to make a single malt in Germany? Why not? Or Bourbon in California? Go for it. Everything is to play for. The main things to bear in mind are local laws and international trademarks. Bourbon, for example, can only be labelled as such if it is from the US. It is the same with Scotch-style whiskies made outside Scotland. For safety's sake, it is best to steer clear of using the word "Scotch" in the labelling and avoid including "Glen" in the brand name.

OFTEN, MICRO-DISTILLERIES ARE PASSION PROJECTS UNDERTAKEN BY WHISKY ENTHUSIASTS

PIONEERING MICRO-DISTILLERIES

These are some of the world's earliest or most exciting craft distillers, along with their "signature" whiskies:

- Balcones (US): Texas Single Malt Whiskey
- Chichibu (Japan): "Peated" Single Malt
- Corsair (US): 100% Rye
- Cotswolds (England): Single Malt
- Daftmill (Scotland): 2006 Winter Release
- Spreewood (Germany): Stork Club Rye
- High West (US): Rendezvous Rye

ASIA

ASIAN WHISKY HAS BEEN ON THE RISE since before the turn of the millennium. Japan has been at the centre of the surge of interest in Eastern drams, but newer producers in India and Taiwan in particular are following hot on their heels.

Although largely inspired by Scottish whisky-making methods, Asian distillers have quickly learned to make the most of their particular climates and local ingredients. Whether it is India's Himalayan-grown barley, or the barrels made from aromatic Japanese mizunara oak, some of which is grown on the slopes of Mt. Fuji (left), Asia's whisky offers something very different to its counterparts produced in more traditional environments. And that's before we even get to Taiwan's sub-tropical climate that encourages rapid spirit maturation.

The result is a range of flavourful whiskies that has captured the whiskey-drinking public's imagination. And the experts agree, too, with Asian whiskies now regularly winning awards around the world.

JAPAN

Japanese whisky is acknowledged as among the best in the whisky world. Much of its output is now up there with the finest of Scotland and Ireland.

FIRST WHISKY PRODUCTION 1923

MAIN WHISKY STYLE Single malt

KEY DISTILLERIES
- Yamazaki (Osaka)
- Yoichi (Sapporo)
- Hakushu (Hokuto)
- Miyagikyo (Sendai)
- Chichibu (Saitama)
- Karuizawa (Miyota)

NUMBER OF DISTILLERIES 64

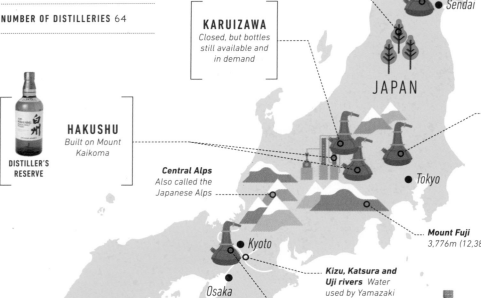

YOICHI
Japan's most northerly distillery

Sapporo

Mizunara oak forests *Source of aromatic cask wood*

Hokkaido mountains *High, volcanic plateaux*

Aomori

Ou mountains *Japan's longest range*

MIYAGIKYO
Makes Nikka's soft, floral malts

MIYAGIKYO
SINGLE MALT

Mizunara oak forests *Source of aromatic cask wood*

Sendai

CHICHIBU
Producer of award-winning whiskies

2016 PEATED

KARUIZAWA
Closed, but bottles still available and in demand

JAPAN

HAKUSHU
Built on Mount Kaikoma

DISTILLER'S
RESERVE

Central Alps
Also called the Japanese Alps

Tokyo

Mount Fuji
3,776m (12,388ft)

Kyoto

Kizu, Katsura and Uji rivers *Water used by Yamazaki*

Osaka

Hiroshima

YAMAZAKI
Japan's first distillery, est. 1923

THE YAMAZAKI
12YO SINGLE
MALT

KEY

 COLUMN STILL

 POT STILL

Fukuoka

Kyushu mountains
Stunning volcanic range

LOCATION

Japan has almost 7,000 islands. The four principal ones are: Honshu, Kyushu, Hokkaido, and Shikoku.

Japan is mountainous and is mainly covered in forest, apart from the cities and coastal zones. The climate is relatively warm, ranging from humid, subtropical-to-tropical rainforest in the south, to cooler conditions in Hokkaido. Japan is susceptible to earthquakes and tsunami as it sits on a series of tectonic fault lines. The country's distilleries are mostly on the main island of Honshu, some close to cities or coasts, others "hiding" in forests and nestling in high mountain areas.

▶ **Mount Fuji.** The country's highest mountain in the Central Alps is also a national symbol of Japan.

THE DISTILLERIES

Two big distilleries dominate Japan's whisky industry: Nikka and Suntory, who own two distilleries each.

They also have grain whisky-making facilities. They produce single malts, blended malts, and single grain whiskies. Unlike in Scotland, where distillers will swap casks of whisky for blending, Nikka and Suntory do not. The country also has a new wave of distillers, enjoying the huge popularity of Japanese whisky in recent years. Of the new distilleries, Chichibu is a good example of what's happening now in Japanese whisky.

▲ **Out with the old.** New pot stills installed at the Hakushu distillery in 2014 – the company's first upgrade for 33 years.

BACKGROUND

Japan's regulations allow producers to add whiskies from other countries into "Blended Japanese" whiskies.

Some do this to take advantage of the good will and publicity generated by the genuine product. Most well established and respected distillers no longer do this and, indeed, are trying to change these rather out-dated regulations from within. Be aware when you buy anything labelled as "Japanese Blended Whisky" from a producer that you do not know or has not been recommended by a trusted source.

TASTING 15 / 20

JAPANESE WHISKIES

For this tasting, we are focusing on the two established Japanese distillery giants, Nikka and Suntory, and their celebrated single and blended malt whiskies.

HOW IT WORKS

Nikka and Suntory are the Japanese whiskies most widely available. From Suntory, there's the distillery that started it all – Yamazaki – plus a whisky from the highly versatile Hakushu. There's a Nikka blended malt, named after the founder, and a single malt from Yoichi.

THE LESSON...

Did you spot the differences between the single malts? Yamazaki is the sweetest and most fragrant, with rich, honeyed, and floral characteristics. Hakushu is quite restrained in comparison, slightly smoky and with more citrus. Yoichi is the peatiest. The Taketsuru, a blend of Yoichi and Miyagikyo, is a nice example of how to combine whiskies from only two distilleries.

DID YOU SPOT THE DIFFERENCES BETWEEN THE SINGLE MALTS?

THE HAKUSHU DISTILLER'S RESERVE

SINGLE MALT
JAPAN
43% ABV

IF YOU CAN'T FIND THIS
use Allt-A-Bhainne

WEIGHT **3**	Built in 1973, Hakushu was the world's largest-capacity distillery.

GOLDEN STRAW

MANDARINS; sweet, subtle vanilla and coconut; hints of smoky peat

ORANGE CITRUS, then mouth-tingling spice; distant, lingering peat smoke

LONG; JUICY ACIDITY; a hint of smoke

FLAVOUR MAP

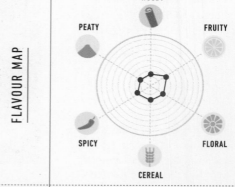

WOODY
FRUITY
PEATY
SPICY
FLORAL
CEREAL

LIKE THIS? Try Kilkerran 12YO

THE YAMAZAKI DISTILLER'S RESERVE

SINGLE MALT

JAPAN
43% ABV

IF YOU CAN'T FIND THIS
use Hibiki Harmony

WEIGHT **3**	The oldest whisky distillery in Japan, established in 1923.

YELLOW GOLD

SCENTED and fragrant. Tropical and orchard fruit. A hint of spiced vanilla

GRAINY HONEY; marmalade. Peaches and cream. A touch of ginger and spice

LONG, QUITE SPICY and complex

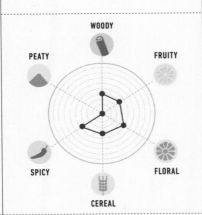

LIKE THIS? Try Craigellachie 13YO

NIKKI YOICHI

SINGLE MALT

JAPAN
45% ABV

IF YOU CAN'T FIND THIS
use Bunnahabhain 12YO

WEIGHT **3**	Distillery's Hokkaido base was selected for its "Scottish" weather and landscape.

PALE STRAW

SMOKED ORCHARD FRUIT; zesty, with fresh lime and sugared pink grapefruit

FLESHY, SEARED PEACHES, white pepper, a touch of vanilla. Background smoke

LONG, SWEET, complex and elegant

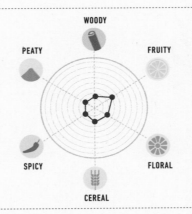

LIKE THIS? Try Glenglassaugh Revival

NIKKA TAKETSURU PURE MALT

BLENDED MALT

JAPAN
43% ABV

IF YOU CAN'T FIND THIS
use Nikka Pure Malt Black

WEIGHT **3**	Blended malt named after one of Japanese whisky's most influential figures.

PALE AMBER

SMOKED HAM; oranges, apricot jam; Jamaican ginger cake, clotted cream

FLORAL NOTES; malty cereal, smoked almonds, toasted marshmallow, spices

DELICATE, medium-length finish. A touch of smoke

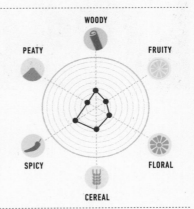

LIKE THIS? Try Great King St Blend

THE RISE OF JAPANESE WHISKY

In just 100 years Japan has gone from no whisky to some of the most highly respected and decorated whiskies in the world. And it's largely the result of the vision of two great men.

▲ **Masataka Taketsuru** is a revered figure in Japanese – and world – whisky circles. There is even a bronze statue of him in his adopted city of Yoichi.

FROM JAPAN TO SCOTLAND AND BACK AGAIN

Masataka Taketsuru (1894–1979) was born into a sake-making family in Hiroshima, Japan, in 1894. But whisky was his obsession, leading him to join Settsu Shuzo, an innovative sake firm that was experimenting with whisky making.

Knowing of Taketsuru's whisky enthusiasm, Settsu Shuzo's president sent him to Scotland in July 1918 to learn how to make it. In just three years, while studying at Glasgow University, Taketsuru gained valuable insight, knowledge, and experience while on placement with several distilleries, such as Longmorn in Speyside and Hazelburn in Campbeltown. He also found time in Glasgow to meet and marry Rita Cowan, the sister of a young man he was teaching judo to. The couple returned to Japan in 1921, so that Taketsuru could apply what he'd learned there.

After helping establish Japan's first malt whisky distillery (see below), Taketsuru and Rita moved to the Japanese north island of Hokkaido, whose landscape and climate is most similar to the Highlands of Scotland.

In 1934, Taketsuru opened the Yoichi distillery, a business that would eventually become the Nikka Whisky Company.

JAPAN ON THE WHISKY MAP

Today's size, scale, and global reach of Japanese whisky is largely because of one man: Shinjiro Torii (1879–1962). Originally a pharmaceutical wholesaler, Torii understood the chemistry of distillation. He set up a wine and liqueur business in 1899, but moved on to whisky making when he saw the commercial possibilities it offered. When Masataka Taketsuru returned to Japan after his Scottish sojourn in 1921, Torii lured him away from Settsu Shuzo. Under Torii's guidance, they created Yamazaki, Japan's first malt whisky distillery, which started production on 11 November 1924.

While Taketsuru eventually left Yamazaki to found Yoichi, Torii, an astute entrepreneur, continued on his path and built up what would ultimately become the Japanese global whisky superpower, Suntory.

The foundations laid by these two men, Taketsuru and Torii, helped to make Japanese whisky what it is today – which is, quite simply, among the best in the world. Their achievements should be even more loudly applauded when it's remembered that the country's whisky industry is less than 100 years old.

THESE TWO MEN, TAKETSURU AND TORII, HELPED TO MAKE JAPANESE WHISKY WHAT IT IS TODAY

▶ **Yoichi Single Malt.** The distillery describes its taste as bold and strong, and "pleasantly peaty", with a "briny hint" from its coastal location.

◀ **Yamazaki whiskies** have won two "World Best" awards in 2013 and 2015, and are among the most sought-after worldwide.

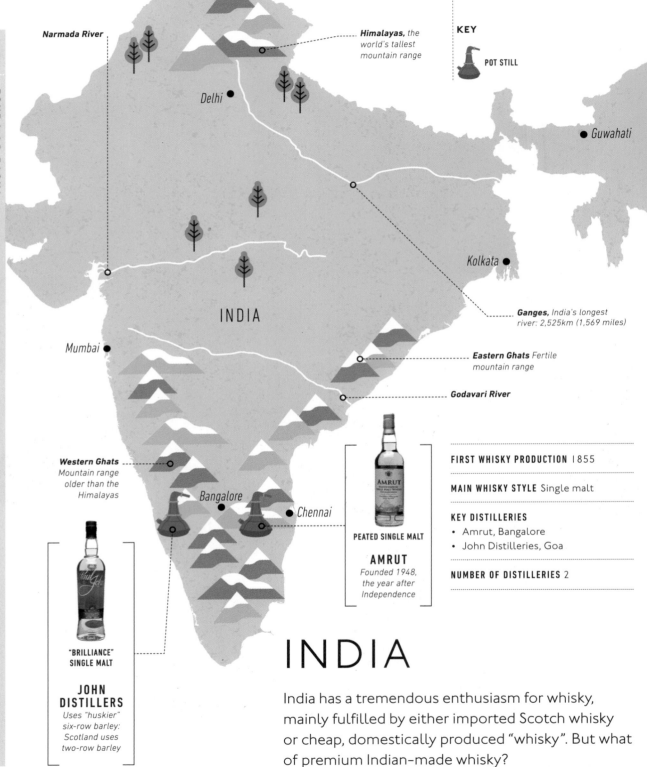

Narmada River

Himalayas, *the world's tallest mountain range*

KEY

POT STILL

Delhi

Guwahati

INDIA

Kolkata

Ganges, *India's longest river: 2,525km (1,569 miles)*

Mumbai

Eastern Ghats *Fertile mountain range*

Godavari River

Western Ghats
Mountain range older than the Himalayas

Bangalore

Chennai

PEATED SINGLE MALT

AMRUT
Founded 1948, the year after Independence

FIRST WHISKY PRODUCTION 1855

MAIN WHISKY STYLE Single malt

KEY DISTILLERIES
• Amrut, Bangalore
• John Distilleries, Goa

NUMBER OF DISTILLERIES 2

**"BRILLIANCE"
SINGLE MALT**

**JOHN
DISTILLERS**
Uses "huskier" six-row barley: Scotland uses two-row barley

INDIA

India has a tremendous enthusiasm for whisky, mainly fulfilled by either imported Scotch whisky or cheap, domestically produced "whisky". But what of premium Indian-made whisky?

LOCATION

India is a south Asian country mainly surrounded by sea to the south, east, and west.

India borders Pakistan, China, Nepal, and Bangladesh, among others, and is home to 1.2 billion inhabitants. The Himalayas lie to the north and India is quite mountainous generally. However, being a vast sub-continent of 3.29 million sq km (1.27 million sq miles), there are also vast deserts, fertile plains, especially along the watercourses of the Ganges and Narmada rivers, and low-lying marshlands prone to flooding in the monsoon season. The climate is warm: from temperate/cold in the north to tropical in the south, which speeds up whisky maturation times.

▶ **The holy city of Varanasi,** as seen from India's most sacred river, the Ganges.

THE DISTILLERIES

Indian premium whisky is on the rise, but there are also many bogus distillers making spirit from molasses and selling it as whisky.

Here we'll focus on India's two main distillers: Amrut, in Bangalore, and John Distilleries, from Goa. Amrut, initially a producer of cheaper Indian "whisky", began making their well-received single malts in the early 1990s, finding that Goa's humid climate helped with quick maturation. John Distilleries' Original Choice blend is its biggest seller, but their single malts, first released in 2012, are increasingly popular.

▲ **Founded in 1996,** Paul John Whisky grew rapidly. It now makes the world's seventh best-selling whisky.

BACKGROUND

Kasauli, India's first distillery, was built in the mid-1850s by British settler Edward Dyer, 1,829m (6,000ft) high in the Himalayas.

Dyer's aim was "to produce a malt whisky as fine as Scotch whisky". Today, though, most whisky produced in India is pretty basic stuff, with affluent whisky aficionados preferring imported "status" brands such as Johnnie Walker. New, quality craft distilleries are coming through, but Amrut and John Distillers prefer to direct their attention on sales to the UK, Europe, and the US rather than their home market.

TAIWAN

Unlike Japan and India, Taiwan has no history of whisky making. But today, it is creating that history from scratch. So why Taiwan? And why now?

FIRST WHISKY PRODUCTION 2006

MAIN WHISKY STYLES Single malt, single pot still, blended whisky

KEY DISTILLERIES
- Kavalan
- Nantou

NUMBER OF DISTILLERIES 2

KAVALAN
Its award-winning whiskies include "Concertmaster", shown here

SINGLE MALT

Tamsui River

Taipei

OMAR
SINGLE MALT

NANTOU
State-owned distillery founded in 2008

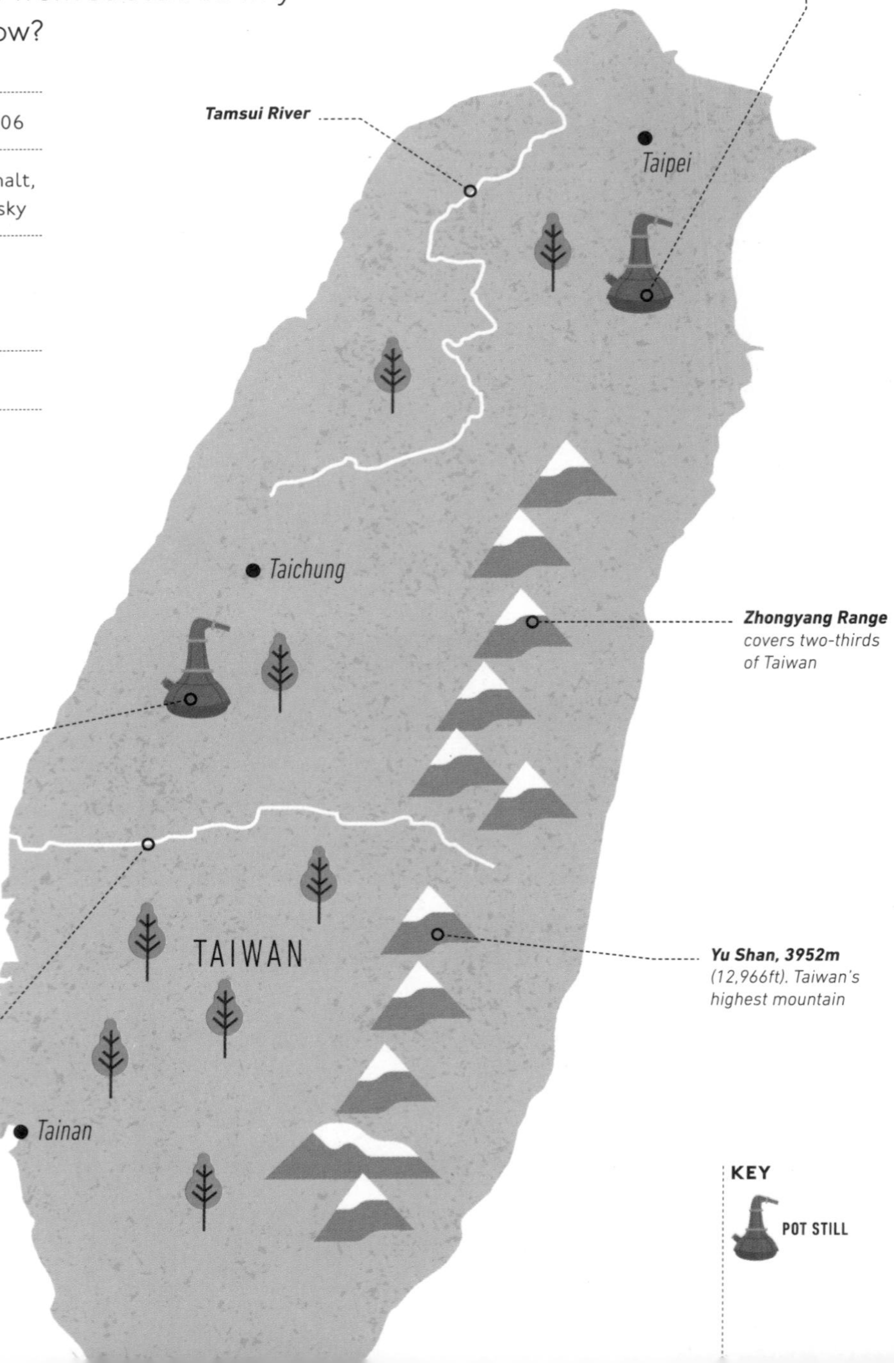

Taichung

Zhongyang Range
covers two-thirds of Taiwan

TAIWAN

Yu Shan, 3952m
(12,966ft). Taiwan's highest mountain

Zhuoshui River,
186km (116 miles). Taiwan's longest river

Tainan

KEY

POT STILL

LOCATION

Taiwan is an island 160km (100 miles) from the south-eastern coast of China.

Just 394km (245 miles) long, Taiwan, formerly known as Formosa, is covered in high, verdant mountains in the east. The remaining third of the country is generally flat plains in the west. The south of the island is warm, with a tropical monsoon climate, whereas the north experiences more rain with wider temperature variations. The Kavalan distillery is in the hot, humid north-east, which means the whisky matures relatively quickly. Omar is made at the Nantou distillery, in central Taiwan, where the cooler climate and hilly landscape is more "Scottish".

▶ **Taipei,** Taiwan's capital, and its surrounding areas, is home to around one third of the country's 23.5 million citizens.

THE DISTILLERIES

When Taiwan joined the World Trade Organization (WTO) in 2002 its business laws were relaxed.

This allowed for the opening of Kavalan, the country's first non-state-owned distillery. Its driving force was T.T. Lee, founder of the King Car Group, who dreamed of a distillery whose product would rival Scotland's. Kavalan produced its first whisky in March 2006. Taiwan's other distillery, Nantou, is state-owned. Originally a brewery and winery, the installation of four Forsyths-made copper pot stills in 2008 allowed Nantou to begin making Omar whisky.

▲ **Lee Yu-Ting** CEO of Kavalan samples the company's wares in the distillery's cask-lined tasting room.

BACKGROUND

When Kavalan's owners wanted to build a distillery they turned to whisky guru Dr Jim Swan.

Swan, who died in 2017, played an integral part in countless distillery start-ups, including Kilchoman, Penderyn, and The Cotswolds in the UK, and Amrut in India. His speciality was in creating rounded spirits that matured quickly. In Taiwan, Swan had the ideal country in which to do this. Taiwan's hot and humid climate means that whisky matures rapidly in the cask, and Kavalan, and now Omar, whiskies, though recent, are increasingly well regarded.

TASTING 16 / 20

ASIAN WHISKY

Here we taste four would-be world-beating single malts from Taiwan and India, two Asian regions with relatively short but interesting histories of whisky making.

HOW IT WORKS

While not "traditional" whisky-making nations, Taiwan's and many of India's distilleries have earned their spurs, trouncing more established whisky-producing areas in blind tastings. All the whiskies here are produced in the "Scottish" method of double-distillation of malted barley in pot stills.

THE LESSON...

None of these whiskies is more than four years old. Is that too young? Not necessarily, as whiskies in hot and humid regions mature more quickly than those in temperate areas, with flavour extracted from the cask at an accelerated rate. That's a key lesson: that age, while very important, is also closely tied to provenance.

AGE, WHILE VERY IMPORTANT, IS ALSO CLOSELY TIED TO PROVENANCE

KAVALAN CLASSIC

SINGLE MALT

YILAN, TAIWAN
40% ABV

IF YOU CAN'T FIND THIS use Glenmorangie 10YO

WEIGHT
2

This is Kavalan's flagship bottling, matured mainly in ex-Bourbon casks.

GOLDEN AMBER

SWEET AND FRAGRANT tropical fruit salad. Subtle menthol note

JUICY PEACHES, apricots, Seville orange marmalade, sweetened almonds

LONG AND MELLOW with a light spicy touch

FLAVOUR MAP

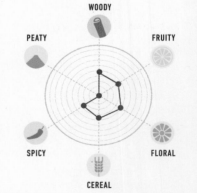

WOODY

PEATY

FRUITY

SPICY

FLORAL

CEREAL

LIKE THIS? Try Solist Bourbon Cask

OMAR BOURBON CASK

SINGLE MALT
NANTOU, TAIWAN
46% ABV

IF YOU CAN'T FIND THIS use
Nikka Miyagikyo

| WEIGHT 3 | The second brand of whisky made in Taiwan. Distillery is state-owned. |

GOLDEN STRAW

SEARED LEMON PEEL, strawberry liquorice; a touch of aniseed

APPLE PIE with sultanas and lemon peel. Slight savoury notes

SPICES AMASS like fine cigar smoke and linger

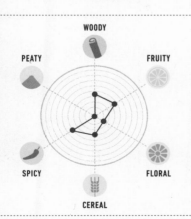

LIKE THIS? Try King Car Conductor

AMRUT FUSION

SINGLE MALT
BANGALORE, INDIA
50% ABV

IF YOU CAN'T FIND THIS use
Ardbeg Uigeadail

| WEIGHT 4 | A fusion of Indian malted barley with Scottish peated malted barley. |

PALE AMBER

BURNT ORANGE MARMALADE, cinnamon, cloves and ham hock

PEAT SMOKE-infused honey. Spiced, like an Indian street market

LONG, LUSCIOUS, SWEET. Quite oily on the finish

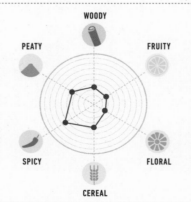

LIKE THIS? Try Paul John Peated

PAUL JOHN BOLD

SINGLE MALT
GOA, INDIA
46% ABV

IF YOU CAN'T FIND THIS use
Port Charlotte 10YO

| WEIGHT 4 | The company's Goa-based distillery uses Indian-made copper pot stills. |

PALE AMBER

SMOKED ALMONDS, smoky bacon crisps, eucalyptus hints

APRICOTS AND PASSION FRUIT wrapped in peat smoke; fresh mintiness

THE MINT PERSISTS, "protecting" the palate from the background spice

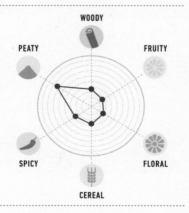

LIKE THIS? Try Amrut Peated

SOUTHERN HEMISPHERE

UNTIL RECENT TIMES whisky created south of the Equator did not appear on many "best of" lists. That's now changing.

Leading the way is Tasmania, one of the world's most vibrant and innovative whisky-making regions. That's why we've detached it from Australia and given "Tassie" its own entry. That's not to say the rest of the antipodes aren't worth exploring, too. Mainland Australia and New Zealand (left, Lake Tekapo) are also examined, especially how their temperance-influenced histories have both hampered and helped whisky making there.

Then there's South Africa, a country that is emerging from decades of unrest and uncertainty and is now forging its own whisky-distilling identity.

If you don't already know about southern hemisphere whiskies, it's now time to put that right.

TASMANIA

This island is to Australia what Islay is to Scotland. In fact, Tasmania is probably even more important to the Australian whisky industry, its products held in high esteem.

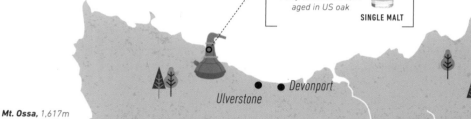

HELLYERS ROAD
Its Original Roaring Forty (shown here) is aged in US oak

SINGLE MALT

Devonport

Ulverstone

Mt. Ossa, 1,617m (5,305ft)

Launceston

TASMANIA

South Esk River *is Tasmania's longest, at 252km (156 miles)*

Derwent River *flows through the capital, Hobart*

SINGLE MALT

OVEREEM
Uses locally produced barley for its whiskies

WILLIAM McHENRY AND SONS
Australia's most southerly family-run distillery

Hobart

FIRST WHISKY PRODUCTION 1822

MAIN WHISKY STYLE Single malt

KEY DISTILLERIES
- Lark Distillery
- Sullivans Cove
- Hellyers Road
- William McHenry and Sons
- Overeem

NUMBER OF DISTILLERIES Approx. 20

LARK
Founded by the "Godfather" of Tasmanian whisky, Bill Lark

SINGLE MALT

SULLIVANS COVE
"World's Best" winner in 2014

LOCATION

Tasmania's temperate climate is closer to that of the UK or New Zealand than mainland Australia.

Little wonder, then, that Tasmania is known as the antipodes' "Whisky Isle". Conditions there are ideal for whisky making, and Tasmania has become something of a regional superpower for distilling. Lying 240km (150 miles) from the mainland, Tasmania is mountainous and heavily forested, though there are also large tracts of fertile arable land, especially in the island's central regions. Significantly, barley is grown locally and plentifully, and is one of the reasons why the island is making a name for itself as a producer of very high quality single malt whiskies.

▶ **Southwest National Park** is a World Heritage Area. A true wilderness, there is just one short road running through it.

THE DISTILLERIES

In 2014 Tasmania had nine whisky distilleries. Today, it has more than 20, producing other spirits as well.

The island's first modern whisky maker was Lark, which opened in 1992, closely followed by Sullivan's Cove in 1994. Most of Tasmania's whisky makers focus on small batch and single cask releases. Tasmania's highly respected whisky distilleries turn out around 200,000 litres (44,000 gallons) annually. Islay produces 100 times that amount. For Tasmanian whisky makers, the focus is on quality over quantity, as testified by their growing pile of "Best of" awards.

▲ **Sullivans Cove.** Its 2014 French Oak Cask whisky was the first outside Scotland or Japan to be voted the world's best.

BACKGROUND

Tasmania, like mainland Australia, had a budding whisky industry in the early 1800s.

However, in 1839, Australia's Distillation Prohibition Act banned all production. Tasmania's whisky stills would not fire up again for more than 150 years. The man that re-started it all was Tasmanian native Bill Lark, who, while out trout fishing one day, realized that the island was ideal whisky-making country. After getting the Prohibition Act overturned in 1992, Lark set up his own single malt distillery, and then lent a helping hand to others that wanted to do the same.

AUSTRALASIA

Mainland Australia and New Zealand have long whisky-making traditions. Here we'll see what they are doing today – excluding Tasmania, which we looked at earlier.

FIRST WHISKY PRODUCTION Early 1800s

MAIN WHISKY STYLES Single malt, corn-based, and rye whiskies

KEY DISTILLERIES
- Starward, Victoria (Aus)
- Great Southern Distilling Co., Western Australia (Aus)
- Archie Rose, NSW (Aus)
- Thomson Whisky Distillery, Riverhead (NZ)
- Cardrona Distillery, Otago (NZ)

NUMBER OF DISTILLERIES Approx. 90

Darwin

Cairns

Uluru, 863m (2,831ft), also called Ayers Rock

River Darling

Alice Springs

AUSTRALIA

Brisbane

ARCHIE ROSE
Allows customers to "design" their own whisky blends

Adelaide

Sydney

River Lachlan

Melbourne

River Murray

SINGLE MALT

STARWARD
Based in wine-making country

Perth

WHIPPER SNAPPER
Produces US-style whiskey

GREAT SOUTHERN DISTILLING CO.
Established in 2004

Limeburners

LIMEBURNERS SINGLE MALT

THOMSON WHISKY DISTILLERY
Founded in 2014

Auckland

Aoraki/Mount Cook, 3,764m (12,349ft), New Zealand's highest mountain

Wellington

KEY

COLUMN STILL

POT STILL

NEW ZEALAND

Christchurch

CARDRONA DISTILLERY
100 per cent family-owned and operated

Queenstown

LOCATION

Australia's 7.7 million sq km (3 million sq mile) landmass includes deserts, tropical forest, and snow-capped mountains.

The climate varies from "warm desert" in the interior, to "tropical savanna" in the far north and "warm oceanic/temperate" in the south-east. Most distilleries are along the coast, close to major cities, or slightly inland in the cooler south-east – all good whisky-making areas. New Zealand is 1,900km (1,200 miles) south-east of Australia. The south island is dominated by the Southern Alps, while the north island is mostly volcanic plateau and plains. Its climate is wet in the west of the south island, to hot and dry further north.

▶ **The Blue Mountains** spread out from close to Sydney, Australia, and include seven national parks and a nature reserve.

THE DISTILLERIES

The relaxation of Australia's distilling regulations in the 1990s boosted its whisky industry.

Whipper Snapper, in East Perth, and Archie Rose, in Sydney, make US-style and Scotch-style whiskies. Starward, in Melbourne, is bringing wine-casked matured single malts to an international audience. New Zealand's micro-distillery "boom" is small but significant. A long-time distilling ban meant the country couldn't exploit its favourable whisky-making climate. Today, a growing group of distillers is creating a new tradition of whisky making.

▲ **Archie Rose** is a craft distillery making a range of innovative spirits, including a white rye whisky and a smoked gin.

BACKGROUND

Australian whisky making began in 1822, in Tasmania, pre-dating some Scottish distilleries.

The first major mainland distillery, Corio opened in 1929 in Melbourne. Corio closed in 1989, but at its peak produced more than 2.2 million litres (484,000 gallons) of whisky – four times the total of all Australia's current whisky distilleries. After New Zealand lifted its whisky-making ban, Willowbank was the most significant new maker, opening in 1974. Although it closed in 1997, Willowbank's product is still popular and – here and there – still available.

SOUTH AFRICA

With, until recently, only one distillery of note, South African whisky making was quite a niche concern. But it is a growing niche, and one worth investigating as its industry grows.

DRAYMAN'S
Micro-brewery since 1997, now making single malt whisky

"SOLERA" BLENDED

FIRST WHISKY PRODUCTION Late 19th century

MAIN WHISKY STYLES: Blended whisky, single malt, single grain

KEY DISTILLERIES
- James Sedgwick Distillery
- Drayman's
- Boplaas

NUMBER OF DISTILLERIES: 3

Orange River, South Africa's longest waterway, at 2,200km (1,367 miles)

Vaal River

Pretoria ●

Johannesburg ●

Bloemfontein ●

Cape Fold Belt, Dramatic range including Table Mountain

SOUTH AFRICA

Durban ●

Cape Town ●

Drakensberg Mts, the eastern edge of South Africa's Great Escarpment

Mafadi, South Africa's highest peak, at 3,450m (11,320ft)

KEY

COLUMN STILL

POT STILL

LOCATION

BAIN'S SINGLE GRAIN

JAMES SEDGWICK DISTILLERY
Whisky released under the Three Ships and Bain's labels

BOPLAAS
Its blended whisky is aged in ex-brandy casks

LOCATION

South Africa is surrounded by the South Atlantic and Indian oceans.

It also borders Namibia, Botswana, Zimbabwe, Mozambique and Swaziland. Its landscape is dominated by a high central plateau. The coastal lowlands that surround it include celebrated wine producing areas, and are also home to two of the three main distilleries. The plateau is split into distinct regions, with micro-climates of desert in the north-west, to grasslands in the east, where the third main distillery is located, in an area designated as "tropical" (ideal for the fast maturation of whisky). The overall climate is "hot desert" in the north-west and "oceanic" in the south-east.

▶ **The Drakensberg "Amphitheatre"** is one of South Africa's natural wonders, a 5km long (3 mile) vertical cliff face.

THE DISTILLERIES

Founded in 1886, the James Sedgwick distillery began making single malt whisky in 1991.

This was when Yorkshire-born Andy Watts became distillery manager. Since then, it has become a self-contained Scotch-style facility, carrying out every process on-site, bar malting. Its pot and column stills produce both malt and grain whiskies. Its production capacity is greater than all of Australia's whisky distilleries combined. Following Sedgwick's lead, Drayman's in eastern Pretoria and Calitzdorp's Boplaas now make whisky, too.

▲ **James Sedgwick Distillery** is based in Wellington, in the heart of South Africa's Cape Winelands region.

BACKGROUND

South Africa's first licensed whisky distillery was *De Eerste Fabrieken* (The First Factory).

It opened in 1883, making un-aged "whisky" for Pretoria's miners. In the mid-1960s, a modern grain whisky distillery was built in Stellenbosch: the R&B Distillery. It was later bought by the Stellenbosch Farmers' Winery (SFW) group and became the birthplace of Three Ships whisky. Demand soon outstripped supply and production moved to the James Sedgwick Distillery, which had been making brandy and other spirits since 1886.

TASTING 17/20

SOUTHERN HEMISPHERE WHISKY

BAIN'S CAPE WHISKY

SINGLE GRAIN WHISKY

WELLINGTON, SOUTH AFRICA
40% ABV

Here we take three Australian whiskies and one South African whisky to see the quality of the liquid being made in the southern hemisphere – one of the world's most vibrant whisky regions.

IF YOU CAN'T FIND THIS use Kilbeggan 8YO Single Grain

WEIGHT 1	The only single grain whisky from the only commercial South African distillery.

HOW IT WORKS

Most Australian and South African whiskies are single malt or Scotch-style blends. Bourbon-style whiskies and ryes are popular, too, such as the Tiger Snake included here. Add in an aperitif-style South African single grain and two single malts, one of them peated, and here you have an interesting picture of tasty southern hemisphere whiskies.

THE LESSON...

As for any areas with a "younger" distilling scene, this tasting will have shown you that centuries of distilling history are not a prerequisite when it comes to making interesting, innovative whiskies. All four whiskies are made in climates that encourage faster maturation, making the age statements on their labels not as relevant as they would be in Scotland, for example.

HERE YOU HAVE AN INTERESTING PICTURE OF TASTY SOUTHERN HEMISPHERE WHISKIES

 RICH GOLD

 SOFT MARSHMALLOWS and candyfloss, with a squeeze of lemon zest

 LEMON DRIZZLE CAKE; palate-soothing vanilla and lemon sorbet

LONG, SWEET, TANGY; fresh vanilla spice and menthol

FLAVOUR MAP

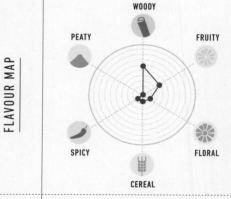

WOODY
PEATY
FRUITY
SPICY
FLORAL
CEREAL

LIKE THIS? Try Teeling Single Grain

TIGER SNAKE

SINGLE GRAIN WHISKY

ALBANY, WESTERN AUSTRALIA
43% ABV

IF YOU CAN'T FIND THIS use
Jim Beam Old Grand-Dad

WEIGHT **3**	A Western Australian take on a classic Tennessee or Bourbon sour mash.

PALE AMBER

SWEET, LIGHTLY SPICED MARZIPAN; fresh cut flowers; mouth-watering toffee

FRESH SPICE; ripe fruit; fresh, fragrant herbs; a hint of peppery caramel

LONG FINISH; a lively citrus tang

LIKE THIS? Try Woodford Reserve

STARWARD NOVA

SINGLE MALT WHISKY

MELBOURNE, VICTORIA
41% ABV

IF YOU CAN'T FIND THIS use
The Lakes Distiller's Reserve

WEIGHT **4**	Melbourne's Starward matures its whisky in ex-red wine casks.

RICH AMBER

STEWED APPLES and rhubarb. Tropical fruit, vanilla; savoury, meaty notes

TANGY STRAWBERRY JELLY, zesty pink grapefruit, warming cinnamon, caramel

VELVETY, but mouth-watering acidity and light vanilla

LIKE THIS? Try Kavalan Conductor

HELLYERS ROAD PEATED

SINGLE MALT WHISKY

HAVENVIEW, TASMANIA
46.2% ABV

IF YOU CAN'T FIND THIS use
Bakery Hill Peated

WEIGHT **4**	From Australia's "whisky isle" of Tasmania, with its nine distilleries.

PALE GOLD

BURNING GRASS and bracken; oily smoke; linseed, seared lime, coal tar

SMOULDERING BONFIRE; cigarette smoke, burnt pineapple; pepper; spice

DRY, LONG FINISH; a bonfire's glowing embers

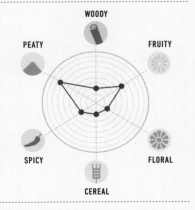

LIKE THIS? Try Connemara Turf Mor

EUROPE

LARGELY INSPIRED BY the craft and micro-distilling movements, Europe is becoming something of a whisky-making hotspot. Motivated by a genuine love and respect for this most venerable of spirits, the region's whisky distillers have been embarking on whisky-making projects like never before.

This section begins in England (left, the Derbyshire Peak District) and Wales, two relatively new whisky-making nations emerging from the shadow of their mighty northern distilling neighbour, Scotland. After that, there's a "grand tour" of Europe, venturing as far north as Scandinavia, down through the Low Countries and further south to France, Spain, and Italy, before exploring the Alpine regions of Germany, Switzerland, and Austria.

The sheer variety of whiskies produced in all of these areas is an education in what "new" whisky-making regions are capable of. It also shows how accidents of climate and history in particular play important roles in deciding what style of whisky different countries choose to make – and how they prefer to do it.

ENGLAND AND WALES

Given their proximity to Scotland and Ireland, why don't these two countries have more established whisky industries? And what are they doing to change that?

FIRST WHISKY PRODUCTION
Late 1800s

MAIN WHISKY STYLES Single malt, rye, grain

KEY DISTILLERIES
- Penderyn, Brecon Beacons, Wales
- St George's Distillery, Norfolk, England
- The Lakes Distillery, Cumbria, England
- The Cotswolds Distillery, England
- The London Distillery Co., England

NUMBER OF DISTILLERIES
Approx. 18

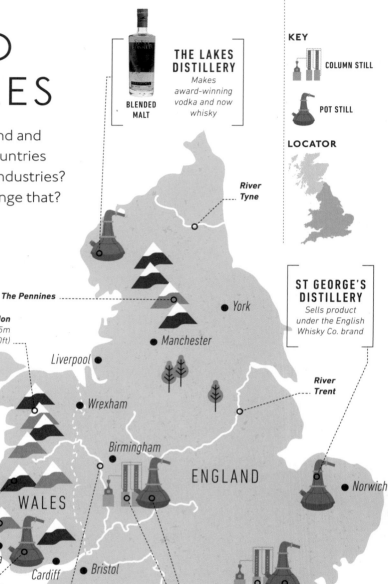

KEY

COLUMN STILL

POT STILL

LOCATOR

THE LAKES DISTILLERY
Makes award-winning vodka and now whisky

BLENDED MALT

River Tyne

ST GEORGE'S DISTILLERY
Sells product under the English Whisky Co. brand

River Trent

The Pennines

Snowdon
1,085m
(3,560ft)

York

Manchester

Liverpool

Wrexham

Birmingham

ENGLAND

Norwich

WALES

Cambrian Mts

Brecon Beacons

Swansea

Cardiff

Bristol

London

SINGLE MALT

PENDERYN
The oldest whisky distillery in Wales, founded in 2004

River Severn

SINGLE MALT

THE COTSWOLDS DISTILLERY
First whisky casks laid down in 2014

River Thames

THE LONDON DISTILLERY CO.
Makes vodka and gin, as well as rye whisky

LOCATION

England and Wales are part of the United Kingdom, a country separated from mainland Europe by a narrow channel.

Both countries are abundant in woods and agricultural land. England's south-east and the former industrial centres of the north are the most heavily urbanized areas, as is south Wales' ex-coal mining heartland. Wheat, rye, and barley, all good whisky-making crops, are widely grown. The English and Welsh climate is temperate, with mild winters, warm summers and, famously, plenty of rain. The distilleries of both countries are mostly situated in cities or in rural areas.

▶ **The River Wye** forms part of the border between England and Wales. The Wye Valley is also wine-making country.

THE DISTILLERIES

In 2000, Penderyn became the first distillery for a century to make Welsh whisky.

They were helped in their endeavour by whisky guru, Jim Swan. Four years later, Healeys in Cornwall began distilling English whisky. The English Whisky Co. (or St George's), in Norfolk, opened in 2006, and was England's first purpose-built whisky distillery for 100 years. Today, the English and Welsh whisky industries are gathering strength, with new producers starting up in Yorkshire, North Wales, and other locations to indicate a healthy future.

▲ **Healeys, best known** for its cider, is also England's longest established whisky maker, and began distilling in 2004.

BACKGROUND

The landscape, climate, and access to barley make England and Wales "natural" whisky-making locations.

However, England was always more gin focused. Plus, with Scotland's whisky industry close by, England and Wales could not compete. The few original distillers all failed, the last closing around 1905. Arguably, the first wave of new distillers, such as Penderyn and St George's, pioneered the global craft whisky movement – though, along with newer makers such as London Distillery Co. and the Lakes Distillery, they don't label themselves as such.

TASTING 18 / 20

ENGLISH AND WELSH WHISKY

Not long ago these pages would have been blank. The three English whiskies and one Welsh whisky here represent the growth of distilling in the two nations, and the quality of product being made.

HOW IT WORKS

English and Welsh whisky have had a good new millennium. Since Norfolk's The English Whisky Co. started production in 2006, the floodgates have opened. New distilleries have popped up across England with satisfying regularity ever since. Two post-2017 additions have tripled the roster of Welsh distilleries. So, how does their product taste?

THE LESSON...

The Norfolk whisky is single grain using a top secret mash bill of eight grains. The Penderyn distillery uses a rare Faraday still and Madeira casks for its single malt. Then we have two of the newest English distilleries, The Cotswolds and The Lakes, showing what they can do with single malt. Did you taste the differences between them all? Which did you prefer?

ENGLISH AND WELSH WHISKY HAVE HAD A GOOD NEW MILLENNIUM

THE NORFOLK FARMERS BLEND

SINGLE GRAIN WHISKY

NORFOLK, ENGLAND
45% ABV

IF YOU CAN'T FIND THIS use
The Norfolk - Parched

| WEIGHT 2 | Unusual grain whisky from the first purpose-built English distillery for over 100 years. |

GOLDEN STRAW

SUBTLY SAVOURY notes, like salted crisps; sweet citrus and vanilla

DRIED HERBS and lemon curd. Sweet apricots and peaches in tangy syrup

QUITE SWEET, supple and medium length

FLAVOUR MAP

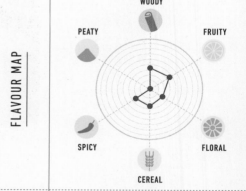

LIKE THIS? Try Nikka Coffey Grain Whisky

PENDERYN MADEIRA CASK

SINGLE MALT WHISKY

BRECON BEACONS, WALES
40% ABV

IF YOU CAN'T FIND THIS use Jura 12YO

WEIGHT **2**	Welsh distillery developed with the help of the legendary Jim Swan.

GOLDEN STRAW

GINGERBREAD, honeysuckle; lightly spiced vanilla fudge

SUGARED SHORTBREAD, sweet-crust pastry, rice-pudding; raisins, marzipan

SWEET, QUITE LONG, subtle and fresh

THE COTSWOLDS 2014 ODYSSEY

SINGLE MALT WHISKY

COTSWOLDS, ENGLAND
46% ABV

IF YOU CAN'T FIND THIS use Cotswolds Founder's Choice

WEIGHT **3**	This English distillery uses mainly ex-Bourbon and red wine casks for maturation.

PALE GOLD

STRAWBERRY JAM; honeyed biscuits and cinnamon

TANGY APRICOT tart with clotted cream and a sprinkle of sea salt

LIGHT MEDIUM-LENGTH finish with citrus

THE LAKES WHISKYMAKER'S RESERVE NO.1

SINGLE MALT WHISKY

CUMBRIA, ENGLAND
61% ABV

IF YOU CAN'T FIND THIS use Adnams Southwold

WEIGHT **4**	An English whisky still maturing at time of writing. Its ABV will be lower when released.

RICH AMBER

BIG HIT of ginger cake and oaky spices. Sublte clove, cinnamon, and citrus

TART APPLE CRUMBLE and custard. Grapefruit sprinkled with brown sugar

LONG, SPICY FINISH; slightly refreshing tang

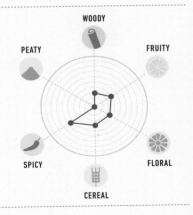

LIKE THIS? Try Balvenie Doublewood

LIKE THIS? Try Oban 14YO

LIKE THIS? Try Starward Wine Cask

KEY

COLUMN STILL

POT STILL

LOCATOR

Scandinavian Mts

MACK

SINGLE MALT

MACKMYRA
*Swedish
self-styled
"explorers in
whisky"*

FINLAND

Helsinki

TEERENPELI
*Finland's largest
distillery,
established 2002*

Stockholm

SWEDEN

Gothenburg

FIRST WHISKY PRODUCTION 1970s

MAIN WHISKY STYLES
Single malt, rye

KEY DISTILLERIES
- Belgian Owl, Belgium
- Mackmyra, Sweden
- Millstone, Netherlands
- Stauning, Denmark
- Teerenpeli, Finland

NUMBER OF DISTILLERIES
Approx. 25

"KAOS" BLENDED

STAUNING
*Began as a
"hobby" start-up
in 2004*

DENMARK

Copenhagen   *Malmo*

Swedish oak
*grown here is used
by the Mackmyra
distillery*

Oresund Bridge
*connects Sweden
and Denmark*

Amsterdam

Rotterdam NETHERLANDS

MILLSTONE
100 RYE

RYE WHISKY

MILLSTONE
*Makes rye, malt
and peated
whiskies*

BELGIUM

Brussels

**BELGIAN
OWL**
*Award-winning
single malt
whisky producer*

WHISKY

SINGLE MALT

NORTHERN
EUROPE

There's some interesting whisky making going
on in the top-left corner of Europe. Here is a
look at what is happening in Sweden, Finland,
Denmark, the Netherlands, and Belgium.

LOCATION

Bounded by the North Sea, the North Atlantic, and the Baltic, this part of Europe is wet, cool, and cold, especially in the north.

Denmark, Belgium, and, especially, the Netherlands are very low-lying and more temperate in climate, and are more "natural" Scottish-style whisky making areas. Large areas of western Holland are actually below sea level, having been reclaimed from the North Sea and protected from re-flooding by that country's famous dykes. Sweden and Finland are heavily forested and, in their northern areas, mountainous, with good, clean water for making spirit – especially where the two nations share a border up towards the Arctic Circle.

▶ **The Oresund Bridge** is an 8km-long (5 mile) engineering marvel connecting Sweden and Denmark.

THE DISTILLERIES

The Netherlands' Zuidam Distillery has been producing whisky since the 1990s.

Perhaps the best-known regional distillery is Mackmyra, founded in 1999, near Gavle in south-east Sweden, with its innovative 35m-high (115ft) "gravity" distillery. Across the Gulf of Bothnia, Sweden's neighbour Finland is also producing interesting whisky. Denmark's Stauning, having opened in 2006, and the Box distillery in central Sweden, from 2010 followed the Scandinavian whisky path opened by Mackmyra, making this a vibrant whisky region.

▲ **Sweden's Mackmyra** produces a range of whiskies at its distillery around 100km (62 miles) north of the capital, Stockholm.

BACKGROUND

None of these countries has a whisky-making tradition. Gin was the most common regional spirit.

This was certainly the case in Belgium and the Netherlands. In Scandinavia, vodka enjoys more popularity, as does aquavit, which is distilled from potatoes, or grain seasoned with herbs. But whisky consumption is popular regionally. This interest in drinking whisky has morphed into a desire to distil it, using, as Mackmyra's state-of-the-art distillery shows – and with Stauning planning an equally eye-catching new facility – a stylish and clever approach.

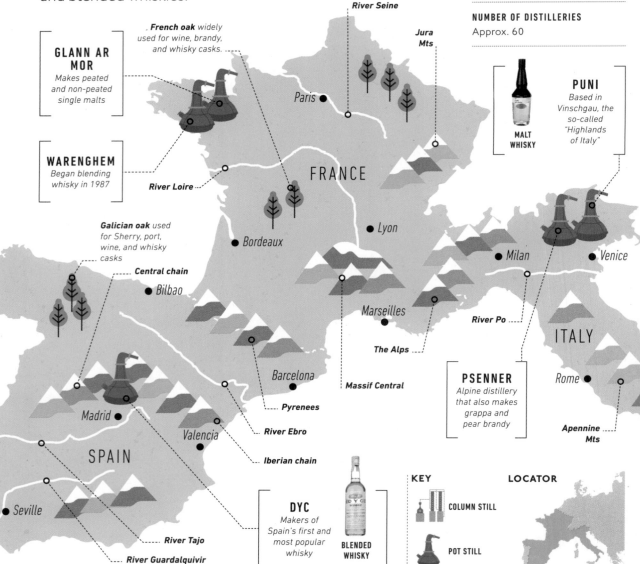

WESTERN EUROPE

France, Spain, and Italy are among the world's biggest consumers of Scotch whisky. But they also make the spirit, especially single malts and blended whiskies.

FIRST WHISKY PRODUCTION 1959

MAIN WHISKY STYLES Single malt, blended whisky

KEY DISTILLERIES
- Glann ar Mor, France
- Warenghem, France
- Puni, Italy
- Psenner, Italy
- DYC, Spain

NUMBER OF DISTILLERIES
Approx. 60

River Seine

Jura Mts

GLANN AR MOR
Makes peated and non-peated single malts

French oak widely used for wine, brandy, and whisky casks.

WARENGHEM
Began blending whisky in 1987

River Loire

Paris

FRANCE

PUNI
Based in Vinschgau, the so-called "Highlands of Italy"

MALT WHISKY

Galician oak used for Sherry, port, wine, and whisky casks

Central chain

Bilbao

Bordeaux

Lyon

Milan

Venice

Marseilles

River Po

ITALY

The Alps

Rome

PSENNER
Alpine distillery that also makes grappa and pear brandy

Barcelona

Madrid

Pyrenees

River Ebro

Valencia

Iberian chain

Apennine Mts

Massif Central

SPAIN

Seville

River Tajo

River Guardalquivir

DYC
Makers of Spain's first and most popular whisky

BLENDED WHISKY

KEY

COLUMN STILL

POT STILL

LOCATOR

LOCATION

Italy and Spain enjoy a warm, Mediterranean climate, as does the south of France.

The rest of France is more temperate. The landscapes of all three territories are quite varied. The French and Spanish border is demarcated by the Pyrenees, while the Alps separate parts of southeast Italy and northern Italy, whose "spine" is formed by the Apennine Mountains. France is still a highly rural, agricultural nation. All three countries have wine-producing industries, and Spain and Italy also grow olives for domestic use and export. Fermenting and distilling alcohol is part of the culture, though making whisky there is a relatively new concept.

THE DISTILLERIES

France's best-known distillery is Warenghem, in Brittany, a single malt whisky producer since 1987.

It introduced its Armorik brand in 1997. Glann ar Mor, also in Brittany, has been distilling peated and unpeated malts since 2005. Puni, in Italy, houses new Forsyth stills in an innovative cube-shaped building. Psenner has been making Italy's first single malt whisky since 2013, using ex-grappa barrels. The large DYC distillery in Madrid has an annual capacity of 20 million litres. It has since 2009 produced a 10-year-old single malt, although most of its output is a more basic whisky intended to be drunk with cola and ice – a favourite drink in Spain.

▲ **Italy's Puni distillery** produces malt whisky in traditional copper pot stills, housed in a stylish "latticed" cement cube.

▲ **Vinschgau, also known** as Val Venosta, in the alpine South Tyrol is a hub of the region's growing distilling industry.

BACKGROUND

France, Spain, and Italy have long distilling backgrounds, in Cognac and Armagnac, brandy and grappa respectively.

All three are among the top 20 importers of Scotch whisky, with France at number one worldwide in terms of volume. It makes perfect sense, then, that local whisky fans have turned their attentions to making the spirit themselves. What is perhaps surprising is that the first whisky production only began in 1959, at Spain's DYC distillery. More distilleries are now planned in the three territories and there is a growing craft whisky movement in France and Italy particularly. Whisky making culture is firmly embedding itself in the region.

▲ **Brandy, Armagnac** and grappa production have much longer histories in this region than whisky.

ALPINE EUROPE

The boom in whisky-making in central Europe, particularly in and around the Alps, is a testament to the spirit's growing popularity in Germany, Austria, and Switzerland.

FIRST WHISKY PRODUCTION
Early 1980s

MAIN WHISKY STYLES Single malt whisky, rye whisky

KEY DISTILLERIES
- Blaue Maus, Germany
- Stork Club, Germany
- Waldviertel Distillery, Austria
- Locher Distillery, Switzerland

NUMBER OF DISTILLERIES
Approx. 300

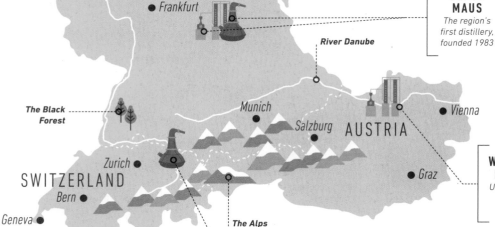

River Elbe ·········· Hamburg

Berlin

GERMANY

River Rhine ·········· Frankfurt

River Danube

STORK CLUB
Made at the Spreewood distillery, close to Berlin

STRAIGHT RYE

BLAUE MAUS
The region's first distillery, founded 1983

The Black Forest

Munich

Salzburg

AUSTRIA

Vienna

WALDVIERTEL DISTILLERY
Uses locally grown rye for its whiskies

Zurich

SWITZERLAND

Bern

Graz

Geneva

The Alps

LOCHER DISTILLERY
Switzerland's first whisky distillery

SINGLE MALT

KEY

 COLUMN STILL

POT STILL

LOCATOR

LOCATION

We have classed these three whisky-making regions as "Alpine" as many of their most notable distilleries are located in the Alps.

This mountain range the forms a large part of southern Germany, central and southern Switzerland, and much of Austria. Germany, the largest of the three countries, is bisected by mighty waterways such as the Rhine, Elbe, and Danube rivers, and is heavily forested in its heartland. Winters are cold and summers warm. Switzerland and Austria are more mountainous in general, with generally sub-arctic and "oceanic" climates with very cold, snow-heavy winters and short, but warm, summers.

▶ **The Alpine** climate and topography, not unlike those of the Scottish Highlands, make for ideal whisky-making territory.

THE DISTILLERIES

The oldest regional distillery is Blaue Maus, in Germany, founded in the early 1980s.

The Spreewood distillery, 60km (37 miles) from Berlin, specializes in rye whiskies. The Waldviertel distillery in Roggenreith was Austria's first whisky distillery, established in 1995. Like many "Alpine" distilleries, it produces a variety of styles, including single malt, rye, and malted rye. In Switzerland, the Locher family has been distilling since 1886, from their Alpine base in Appenzell. The first bottlings of Swiss single malt whisky emerged in 2002.

▲ **Säntis single malt,** from Switzerland's Locher Distillery, an example of what its maker calls "the Alpine whisky".

BACKGROUND

Germany and Austria have Continental Europe's longest whisky-making lineages.

By the 1980s, they already had good distilling infrastructures, due to their production of brandy and schnapps, for example. Whisky making in Switzerland began after anti grain-distilling legislation was lifted in the 1990s. Many makers favour rye whisky, partly because this hardy grain grows well in the area's cold conditions. "Alpine" rye is actually highly sought-after beyond the region, with Kentucky distillers Wild Turkey importing it for use in their rye whiskies.

TASTING 19 / 20

MAINLAND EUROPEAN WHISKY

This tasting highlights some of the gems being produced across Europe's growing whisky-making scene, with a focus on the north of the Continent and its cooler, "Scottish"-style climate.

HOW IT WORKS

As befits the continent's size, Europe's whiskies are varied. They are well worth exploring, and the four selected here represent the variety of styles on offer. They should all be available from your local whisky specialist, too. Taste from left to right.

THE LESSON...

Did you notice the differences between the malted rye from Finland and the German unmalted rye? What about the two single malts? You will have tried several Scottish peated single malts by now, so compare the French example here against them. That's the takeaway from this tasting: good whisky is being produced everywhere, and provenance is no longer a barrier to quality of product.

AS BEFITS ITS VAST SIZE, EUROPE'S WHISKIES ARE VARIED. THEY ARE WELL WORTH EXPLORING

MACKMYRA BRUKSWHISKY

SINGLE MALT WHISKY

GÄVLE, SWEDEN
41.4% ABV

IF YOU CAN'T FIND THIS use Box Single Malt

WEIGHT 2	From this Swedish maker's eye-catching "gravity" distillery, opened in 2011.

PALE STRAW

SOFT, SWEET CITRUS; herbal hints; strawberry sweets; mint

LEMON BOILED SWEETS; warming spice and fresh herbs, maybe thyme

LONG, DELICATE and aromatic finish

FLAVOUR MAP

WOODY

PEATY

FRUITY

SPICY

FLORAL

CEREAL

LIKE THIS? Try Glenkinchie 12YO

KORNOG ROC'H HIR

SINGLE MALT WHISKY

**BRITTANY, FRANCE
46% ABV**

IF YOU CAN'T FIND THIS use
Armorik Triagoz

WEIGHT 3	Brittany-based distillery using rare, directly-fired stills.

PALE STRAW

UPFRONT, ZESTY peat smoke, with plenty of sweetness behind it

SMOKY SWEETNESS; unripe pear and seared lemon. Nettles and ferns

QUITE GENTLE, long-lasting finish

LIKE THIS? Try Westland Peated

STORK CLUB RYE

RYE WHISKY

**SCHLEPZIG, GERMANY
55% ABV**

IF YOU CAN'T FIND THIS use
Millstone 100 Rye

WEIGHT 3	Made at Spreewald, Germany's first rye distillery, which opened in 2016.

PALE AMBER

RICH, BURNT TREACLE; cured meats, fresh thyme; sweet and sour sauce

CARAMEL and sticky toffee pudding heaped with cinnamon-infused custard

LONG, SWEET, luxuriously oily finish

LIKE THIS? Try Rittenhouse Rye

KYRO RYE

RYE WHISKY

**TAIPALE, FINLAND
47.8% ABV**

IF YOU CAN'T FIND THIS use
Hudson Manhattan Rye

WEIGHT 4	The only Finnish distillery to focus solely on rye whisky.

GOLDEN AMBER

CLASSIC RYE characteristics of smoked bacon, capsicum and pepper

MORE MELLOW than the nose indicates. Fleshy red fruit; spicy but gentle vanilla

VELVETY MOUTHFEEL with soft citrus and spice

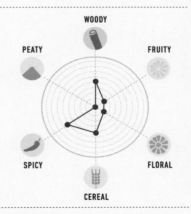

LIKE THIS? Try Koval Rye

CHAPTER | 5

WHISKY KNOW-HOW

DISCOVERING WHAT WHISKY IS, where it comes from, and how it's made are vital. As is knowing how to taste it. But the final piece of the puzzle is *applying* that knowledge. Whisky is not meant to be enjoyed in a vacuum. It is a social drink, something to be enjoyed in company (or occasionally alone), perhaps with food, or in a cocktail or with mixers. And, discovering the best environments in which to drink whisky, whether how much you pay for it matters, or how to keep it, are just as important.

▲ **The Nihon whisky bar** in San Francisco makes hard-to-find Japanese malts available and accessible to Californian drinkers.

WHERE TO TASTE

It's well established that *where* you eat and drink influences how you taste and enjoy the experience. Where is the ideal place to enjoy whisky? At home? In a bar? What about a tasting event?

A PUB OR BAR

On paper, a good idea. But beware: buying whisky in a pub or bar can be an expensive experience, with prices generally and necessarily marked up. Presentation is key, too, so if your whisky is handed to you in an inelegant Highball glass or a much-used and chipped tumbler, request something more acceptable.

Luckily, there are specialist whisky bars around the world that cater for those who want to drink whisky without it costing too much, and in a suitably whisky-friendly setting. Search them out. They are usually run by whisky enthusiasts, and the best will have whisky-specialist staff offering help and advice.

AT HOME

The obvious choice for many. It is where your whisky is, plus you can control the environment. You can choose the company, the music, the glassware, and the amount of whisky you pour. You may lose

GOOD WHISKY SHOULD TASTE GOOD EVERYWHERE. BUT THERE IS ONE PLACE WHERE IT OFTEN TASTES BEST OF ALL: WHERE IT WAS MADE

some of the atmosphere of a great bar but it is relatively risk-free and much cheaper.

A WHISKY TASTING OR FESTIVAL

If you are either in sociable or "explorer" mode, a public tasting event can be just the ticket. If you're looking for new favourites or a chat with like-minded others, this could be for you. There are whisky-tasting events run all over the world catering for all levels of enthusiast. Look out for one near you. You may find whiskies – and new friends – for life.

THE ABSOLUTE BEST

Good whisky should taste good everywhere. But there is one place where it often tastes best of all: where it was made.

There is nothing like visiting Islay, for example, touring your favourite distillery, and rounding things off with a tasting. Great whisky speaks of its place, its ingredients, and the people who made it, and vice versa. Start locally and work your way out, making the pilgrimage to distilleries big and small. Many distilleries are visitor-friendly and are fascinating places to explore.

NOT WHERE, WHO

Tasting great whisky on your own is fine. But your feelings towards it are magnified when you share it and taste it with friends.

You can bounce ideas off each other, reminisce about past whiskies you've tried, plan distillery trips or just enjoy the whisky in your hand. You will each find different flavours and dimensions to the whisky. You may even disagree over the taste or quality of your drink. It doesn't matter. What matters is that you are talking about it.

▼ **Visitors at Sullivans Cove** distillery, in Tasmania. On-site tastings are a great way to both try and learn more about whiskies.

INDEPENDENT BOTTLERS

Ever seen a bottle of your favourite single malt whose label bears no resemblance to the branding you are used to? There is every chance this is an independent bottling.

▲ **Cadenhead's Small Batch** whiskies display their contents' provenance on the label – in this case, Islay's Caol Ila distillery, known for its peaty product.

WHAT ARE THEY?

An independent (or "Indie") bottler is a business that buys casks of whisky from distillers and whisky brokers, and then bottles under their own label. Most, but certainly not all, indie bottlers are Scottish companies with close ties to the distilling industry, but who do not necessarily own a distillery.

Examples of Indie bottlers include Gordon & MacPhail, Cadenhead's, Berry Brothers and Rudd, Douglas Laing, Murray McDavid, and Wemyss. Bottlers come in all shapes and sizes. Some have tiny portfolios, selling one or two whiskies a year; others have hundreds, or thousands, of casks in their inventory.

WHY DO IT?

At their best, Indie bottlings are a great opportunity to taste liquid that might otherwise cost you a lot more. Most Indie bottlers don't have the overheads and marketing responsibilities of the larger whisky-making businesses. Until recently, the packaging was, generally, less expensive and elaborate – in the case of older bottlings – with the liquid being the main emphasis. Many of their bottlings will be "single cask", meaning that the whisky has been drawn from one cask.

When buying from independent bottlers, as with any whisky, it's best to try before you buy. No two casks are the same, so you are putting your taste-buds in the hands of whoever has bottled your whisky. This is usually the role of one person, such as Douglas McIvor of Berry Brothers, or Mark Watt of Cadenhead's, two of the UK's best-known and highly-skilled bottling experts, with decades of experience between them.

PIONEERING SPIRITS

Independent bottlers have had a huge influence on the modern whisky industry. In Scotland, until the 1960s just a handful of whisky-makers bottled single malts. The industry then was almost entirely focused on creating blended Scotch whiskies, and single malts were just there to help facilitate this.

Gordon & MacPhail changed all that. An Elgin-based grocery store sounds like an unlikely base for shifting the way the world perceived single malt whisky, but it did.

In 1968 they released their "Connoisseurs Choice" range of single malts from all over Scotland, bringing a new world of whiskies to the likes of the UK, the USA, France, and Holland initially. Without this catalyst, it is arguable we would not have the same rich kaleidoscope of whisky choice we now enjoy today.

IN SCOTLAND, UNTIL THE 1960S JUST A HANDFUL OF WHISKY-MAKERS BOTTLED SINGLE MALTS

▼ **Founded in 1895,** Gordon & MacPhail's shop, which is still in Elgin, Scotland, offers more than 1,000 malt whiskies for sale.

WHAT IS WHISKY'S "IDEAL" AGE?

Does old whisky mean good whisky and young whisky mean bad? It depends on where it's from and how it was made. In terms of taste, there's a lot to be said for both "old" and "young" whiskies.

WHY AGE WHISKY?

Whisky is almost always aged in oak casks, and it is during its time in the wood where the spirit receives most of its flavour.

This is a good thing. But it's important to know how long the whisky should stay in the cask for. How long is enough, and, conversely, how much time is too much time? And what does this do to the final taste? These are all good questions, and we will try to tackle them here.

WHAT'S A GOOD AGE

One key thing to remember is that whisky matures differently in different cask types and in different climates. There's also the fact that each distillery has its own production regime that it employs prior to maturation and this has an impact, too.

With those factors in mind, you'll see it's almost impossible to state what a "good" age is for whisky. With every distillery in every country or region doing

things differently from each other, there are almost limitless possibilities on offer.

IS THERE AN OPTIMUM WHISKY AGE?

Each distillery has an optimum age at which they release their flagship bottling. Ten years old for Glenmorangie, for example, or 16 years for Lagavulin. These timescales are the result of years of trial and error and fine-tuning. What happens beyond these

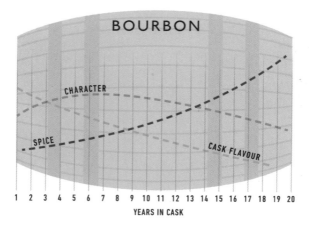

▲ BOURBON
The number of years in a cask affects how oaky, spicy, and characterful a Bourbon is. Bourbon can only be aged in new, charred oak casks, and this too affects the flavour as compared to Scotch, for example.

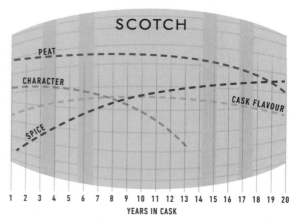

▲ SCOTCH
As it is matured in used, often ex-Bourbon casks, Scotch-style whiskies have a different age/flavour profile to Bourbons. The cask flavour holds up better, for example, and the rise in spiciness is not as dramatic.

◀ **The role of the cask** should never be underestimated. This is where the alchemy of maturation takes place, and where flavour and character develop and change.

timescales is the continuation of two things: the oak influence creeps upwards, and the original spirit character diminishes.

That's one reason why, for example, a 16-year-old Lagavulin, doesn't taste the same as an older or younger Lagavulin.

IS OLDER BETTER?

In short, no. It is simply older. And "oakier". And more expensive. What is more important than age is the cask. A whisky can spend ten or 15 years in a cask but, if that cask has been previously used too much – or not enough – the whisky within it will suffer.

A truly great older whisky is one that has been aged in a cask that has just the right amount of character, that has not been under-used or over-used.

Of course, business concerns are important, too. Many distillers and bottlers need to have 18, 21, 25, 30, and 40 year-old whiskies on their inventories in order to hit key anniversaries or commemorative events that generate sales. This does not mean that all of these whiskies are necessarily good.

CLIMATE CHANGE

With the advent of so many new distilleries around the world, the Holy Grail for many of them is working out how to accelerate the maturation process, to make their whiskies ready sooner.

Countries with warmer climates, such as Taiwan and India, have an almost unfair advantage. In these places, whiskies matured in standard-sized barrels, or hogsheads, can reach their optimum in just over three years. In cooler climates, such as Scotland and Ireland, it takes longer for the cask's wood to do its thing. Some makers have been experimenting, with a degree of success, with using smaller, fresher casks to speed up maturation.

So, age is and isn't important. Just taste whisky. If you like it, buy it. Regardless of age.

THE WORLD'S OLDEST

Older whiskies can be a good investment – if you can afford to buy one.

MORTLACH 70YO

This Speyside whisky was casked in 1938 – and only bottled in 2008. Just 54 full-sized bottles were produced, each one retailing for £10,000. A further 162 smaller bottles were also made available, at "just" £2,500 each.

ZAGATTI'S UNKNOWN WHISKY

Among the Zagatti Collection in the Netherlands is a bottle marked as being from 1843. Unfortunately very little is known about this ancient bottle.

WHAT SHOULD I PAY FOR WHISKY?

It is easy to assume that the more you pay for whisky the "better" it is. Price is definitely an important indicator of a whisky's quality, but it's not the only factor to bear in mind when you buy it.

WHY IS WHISKY EXPENSIVE?

Whisky tends to cost more than clear spirits such as vodka and gin. This is mainly due to the fact that whisky can, and usually does, take several years to mature and therefore must be stored.

In addition, the apparently insatiable worldwide thirst for older whiskies means that prices have risen dramatically. This has caused a dent in aged stock in Scotland and Japan in particular, with the market price for the remaining stock rising accordingly.

Distillers are now ramping up production. Plus, since the millennium, there has been a massive boom in craft- and micro-distilling globally, all in an effort to satisfy demand.

This could lead to price problems later for whisky-makers, when all this new whisky matures. If demand for whisky slows, as it has at various times in history, a surplus of product could lead to prices falling.

IS CHEAP WHISKY BAD?

Not necessarily. For example, whiskies released by independent bottlers or supermarket-branded spirits can offer good value. But the quality can also vary massively, so check any reviews if available.

Ultimately, you need to recognize that whisky is a luxury and decide what you are happy to pay for it. Doing some research

◀ **Macallan's distillery** produces renowned mid- to high-priced whiskies and is the world's third best-selling single malt brand.

◄ **Edinburgh's Royal Mile** specialist whisky shop is one of the world's best-known, famed for the range of its whiskies and its well-informed staff.

into whisky prices in your region will give you a good benchmark on what to budget for.

WHERE SHOULD I BUY IT?

Aside from areas with legal or religious prohibitions, whisky is widely available. From supermarkets to the internet, airports, and wine and spirit retailers, there is no excuse for not locating decent whisky in most parts of the world.

However, there is no substitute for going to a specialist spirit or whisky shop, where you will get good advice from a fellow enthusiast, a warm welcome, and, potentially, be able to taste the stuff on-site.

You may occasionally (but not always) pay a little more for the product, but for the service, the valuable insights, and the banter you might get, surely it is worth it. You will be supporting a local business as well.

THE STATE'S SHARE

One important factor in the price you pay for whisky is tax. It varies from country to country, and even territory to territory, but it is rare to find a bottle of whisky that has not incurred an excise payment, a duty cost, or a tax at some point during its manufacture or sale.

Unsurprisingly, it's something that is not wholly popular with distillers and customers alike. In the UK, for example, a 3.9 per cent increase in the sales tax for Scotch whisky in 2017 resulted in a 2.6 per cent drop in sales.

In 2018, the EU imposed a 25 per cent tariff on US whiskey and Bourbon imported into the European Union, largely in response to an imported steel tax levied by President Trump.

Whatever the reason, it is almost always the case that tax increases on "non-essential" goods, such as whisky, leads to a rise in their price in store.

THE AIRPORT TEMPTATION

We've all been there. You are passing through an airport and you spot a whisky you have never seen before from a distillery you like.

You reach for your credit card, ready to hand over your hard-earned cash that airport retail units absorb so efficiently. Beware: these airport-based "travel exclusives" are not always as exciting to taste as they are to look at. There is usually someone on hand to offer you a sample, so always try before you buy if at all possible.

WHISKY AND TEMPERATURE

Is there a "right" temperature at which to drink whisky? It's a much-debated subject that excites strong opinions. More importantly, what does tasting it at different levels of heat do to its flavour?

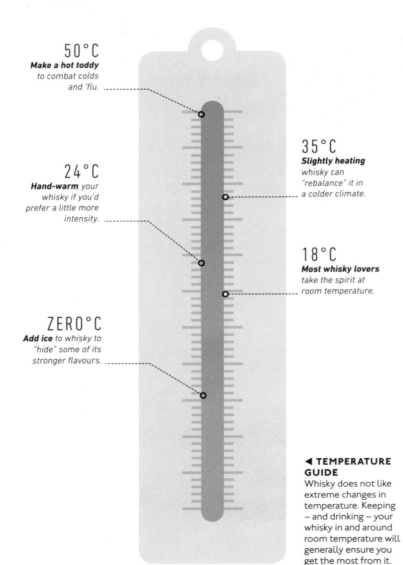

50°C
Make a hot toddy
*to combat colds
and 'flu.*

24°C
Hand-warm *your
whisky if you'd
prefer a little more
intensity.*

ZERO°C
Add ice *to whisky to
"hide" some of its
stronger flavours.*

35°C
Slightly heating
*whisky can
"rebalance" it in
a colder climate.*

18°C
Most whisky lovers
*take the spirit at
room temperature.*

◀ **TEMPERATURE
GUIDE**
Whisky does not like
extreme changes in
temperature. Keeping
– and drinking – your
whisky in and around
room temperature will
generally ensure you
get the most from it.

WHAT IS THE IDEAL TEMPERATURE?

There is no correct answer to this question as it's such a subjective topic.

But with that in mind, there are a few considerations you should make before you try taking your whiskies at different temperatures. Whisky too good a drink – and too expensive an investment – to experiment with indiscriminately.

First off, to get the most detail and information from your whisky, you should taste it at room temperature. This is what the experts do: the master distillers, blenders, and spirit judges. It is where the whisky reveals its taste most openly.

Occasionally, when you pour your whisky, you may find that it is a little cooler than you'd like. If this is the case, simply hold the whisky glass in your hand for a short while, cupping it and allowing your natural body warmth to bring it up to the desired temperature.

ICE AND "THE NORTH SEA EFFECT"

One respected Scottish whisky expert has memorably put forward a vivid – but effective – analogy to

◄ **Drinking "on the rocks"** will restrain the spirit's flavours, but as the ice melts it will, slowy, release those flavours back into the whisky.

TO GET THE MOST INFORMATION AND DETAIL FROM YOUR WHISKY YOU SHOULD TASTE IT AT ROOM TEMPERATURE

describe the effect of ice on whisky. Imagine, he posited, walking into an Alpine lake, naked, on a winter's day. What, he asked, would be the effect on certain sensitive areas of your body?

The point he was making is that whisky "closes up" when it is too cold, hiding much, if not most, of its flavours. Ice also numbs the palate, making it harder to discern the whisky's essence. The fact that our expert put it the way he did shows what strong opinions the "ice effect" excites. That's not to say don't add ice. It's your choice. But if you do, brace yourself.

SOME LIKE IT HOT

Conversely, drinking whisky too warm, or even hot, does not bring out the best in it either. It is perhaps not quite as dramatic a difference as the ice effect, but you are still denying yourself the full high-density picture by heating it.

Possibly the only time you should warm up whisky, apart from making a hot toddy, is if you are drinking it in a very cold climate (perhaps before taking that naked dip in an Alpine lake). Warming a cold whisky will help to "rebalance" its flavour.

THE HOT TODDY

This traditional remedy for colds and 'flu can make you feel better. Honest.

This is not least due to the antiseptic qualities of the whisky's high alcohol content and the mucus-generating effect of the heat and the drink's sweet and sour flavours. There are many hot toddy recipes, but here is a simple one to get you started: take 50ml/I ¾fl oz (at least) of your least treasured whisky, add the juice of one lemon, a lemon slice pitted with cloves, a teaspoon of honey and top up with hot water.

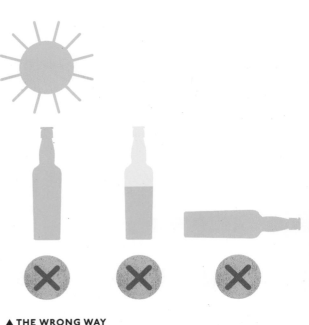

▲ THE RIGHT WAY
Make sure your whisky bottle is upright, kept
in a cool environment and, once opened,
decanted if at all possible.

▲ THE WRONG WAY
Store whisky out of direct sunlight. Don't
keep it in the bottle once you have drunk a
significant amount, and don't lay it on its side.

HOW TO KEEP WHISKY

Once you know which whiskies you like, and have
discovered where they are from and how they are made,
the next step is learning how to keep the whiskies you
have bought in optimum condition.

STORAGE

It is common sense, really. Keep
your whiskies away from direct
sunlight and in cool or room-
temperature conditions.

Whisky, if you keep it in the
bottle, should be stored upright,
not laid down, like wine, which
requires the liquid to stay in
contact with the cork to stop it
shrinking and letting in air. Most
"good" whisky producers use corks,
not screw-caps, so this is an issue
you should bear in mind.

The reason why wine bottles
with corks should be laid down but
whisky bottles with corks should
not is because whisky's alcohol
content is much higher. This will
cause the whisky bottle's cork to
disintegrate over time. As regards
where to house your bottles, a
drinks cabinet, once a feature of
many homes, may be worth
investing in if you want to build
up a collection of whiskies.

DECANTING

Remember those heavy crystal
decanters that were so popular
way back when? Perhaps you or

your family had one, or you've seen them on television or in old movies, a convenient shorthand to show how our whisky-drinking hero is debonair and worldly-wise.

However, decanters, and the process of decanting, actually have a crucial role, when it comes to looking after a precious whisky that you want to protect.

You know the one: a bottle you either bought for yourself or was bought for you for a special occasion. A bottle that you would like to savour over the course of months or even years. If you do this, and keep it in the bottle, you

WHISKY, IF YOU KEEP IT IN THE BOTTLE, SHOULD BE STORED UPRIGHT, NOT LAID DOWN, LIKE WINE

risk the whisky losing its "power" to the oxygen slowly taking over the bottle space. To stop this, the best thing to do is buy a set of increasingly smaller bottles, from 35cl down. When your beloved bottle hits less then half full transfer it into the 35cl bottle.

When it hits less than 20cl, put it into a 20cl bottle. By all means keep the original bottle for sentimental value – and to help you remember what is was – but keeping the whisky in peak condition is paramount.

DOES WHISKY AGE IN THE BOTTLE?

No. Or yes. Maybe. The common belief, and the official scientific answer, is that there is nothing going on in a sealed, full bottle. Once the bottle has been sealed, the chemical experts say, the liquid within does not – indeed, cannot – change.

But, there are those working in the distilling industry who believe that something may be going on after all, albeit at a slow rate.

They call it the "Old Bottle Effect", but this is mainly restricted to blended whiskies bottled decades ago. If you are interested, and of a technical turn of mind, it is something worth reading up on.

So, while it is convenient to say that no chemical processes take place inside a sealed bottle of whisky, this may, in time, prove to be too simplistic a statement. Research, as they say, is ongoing.

◄ **Decanters were once** made from lead crystal, a form of glass containing lead oxide that gave a clearer finish. Today, decanters are more generally made from lead-free crystal.

ADDING MIXERS

There is a big debate among the whisky-drinking community about adding mixers. Some do it, some don't. You will only know if you are a "mixer" or not once you have tried a few yourself.

MIXING IT UP

Few things excite more passion with the whisky world than the question of whether it is permissable to add other liquids into it. For some purists, whisky should be drunk "straight" only, or with a little water added at best. While this is not the majority view, it does represent an influential school of thought.

It's important to remember, then, that mixers have been added to whisky for centuries.

There was even a time when whisky would have been undrinkable without something mixed in to take the edge off its rough-hewn taste. Today, whisky is more refined. Sophisticated production techniques have ensured that modern whiskies can be drunk straight, if that's your thing. There's no reason anymore to add anything to whisky to make it palatable.

But that does not mean that you shouldn't. We are not talking here about enhancing whisky, as such. Rather, the aim is to make an enjoyable and refreshing beverage where a neat dram may not somehow be appropriate.

TAKE YOUR PICK

You can add whatever you like to whisky. There are, of course, classic whisky-mixer combinations, but in the end it is about finding a concoction that works for you. However, narrowing things down to find out which flavours best match different whisky styles is well worth the effort. That's what we are doing here.

Peatier Scotch whiskies, for example, work well with cola. That's why some call this combination a "Smoky Cokey". Try it. The sweet maltiness of the cola combines nicely with the whisky's smokiness. Then, of course, there's the "Jack and Coke", a drink that needs no further comment, such is its global renown.

At the less-sweet end of the taste spectrum, ginger ale works with fruitier, spicier Speyside single malts as well as with blended Scotch whiskies. It brings a sharper edge that grabs the attention.

◀ **Mixers can "lighten"** a whisky, turning it into a refreshing drink. Whisky and ginger, with a twist of lime, is a classic combination.

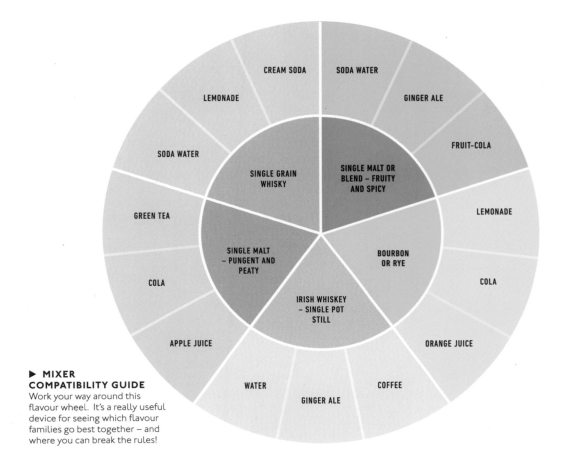

CREAM SODA
SODA WATER
LEMONADE
GINGER ALE
SODA WATER
FRUIT-COLA
SINGLE GRAIN WHISKY
SINGLE MALT OR BLEND – FRUITY AND SPICY
GREEN TEA
LEMONADE
SINGLE MALT – PUNGENT AND PEATY
BOURBON OR RYE
COLA
COLA
IRISH WHISKEY – SINGLE POT STILL
APPLE JUICE
ORANGE JUICE
WATER
COFFEE
GINGER ALE

▶ **MIXER COMPATIBILITY GUIDE**
Work your way around this flavour wheel. It's a really useful device for seeing which flavour families go best together – and where you can break the rules!

And what about lemonade, orange juice, or even cider? There are no rules, so by all means experiment until you find your favourite mixer. That's part of the fun. As you do so, you will learn more about different whiskies: their complexities of taste and the families of flavours they are part of.

The image above, for example, while a useful at-a-glance guide to matching the main whisky styles with their most compatible mixers, is not definitive. Use it as a jumping-off point for you to begin your own whisky-mixing investigations. Everyone has different tastes, after all.

THE HIGHBALL

This combination of whisky and soda water over a glassful of ice is something of a national drink in Japan. And this is a nation that takes whisky making and drinking very seriously.

Invented in the 1950s, it was popularized by Suntory, Japan's first whisky maker, under the Kakubin Highball brand. Highballs are taken with the evening meal instead of wine in many Japanese households and have also become fashionable with Japan's younger drinkers. You can even buy them from on-street vending machines.

THERE ARE NO RULES, SO BY ALL MEANS EXPERIMENT UNTIL YOU FIND YOUR FAVOURITE MIXER. THAT'S PART OF THE FUN

WHAT WHISKY, WHEN?

Drinking the wrong whisky at the wrong time can be a disappointment. While it's not strictly speaking a "seasonal" spirit, it is true that different styles of whisky work best in different situations.

A WHISKY FOR ALL SEASONS

There are no hard and fast rules as to what you should drink and when you should drink it, but it should be clear by this stage that some whiskies will taste better at certain times or seasons, or indeed in different situations.

Lighter whiskies, with a more citrussy and tangy flavour, suit the summer months, for example. As the year moves on and temperatures fall, so heavier, more peaty or spicy whiskies begin to suit the changing seasons.

"MOOD" WHISKIES

This may sound frivolous, but you should never drink whisky when you are angry. It's simply a waste of good spirit – and it will not improve your bad mood.

Apart from that, in the same way you can match whiskies to

SPRING

TRY:
LOCH LOMOND
BAIN'S
MELLOW CORN
AUCHENTOSHAN

SUMMER

TRY:
ARRAN
LARCENY
GREEN SPOT
STARWARD

AUTUMN

TRY:
SPRINGBANK
STORK CLUB
REDBREAST
FEW

WINTER

TRY:
KILCHOMAN
KOVAL
AMRUT
CONNEMARA

the seasons, you can also match them to your mood. Generally, like the seasons, if you are feeling light and happy, you may reach for a whisky of a similar nature. If you

▲ **SEASONAL WHISKIES**
Matching whisky to the time of year can be rewarding, with "heavier" or "lighter" flavours complementing the changing seasons.

are in a more reflective frame of mind, something more complex and challenging is perhaps more appropriate. Once you've developed your collection, you will know which whiskies work best for you, in terms of both complementing your mood or lifting your spirits.

IN THE SAME WAY YOU CAN MATCH WHISKIES TO THE SEASONS, YOU CAN ALSO MATCH THEM TO YOUR MOOD

▶ **A shared enthusiasm** can greatly enhance the tasting experience, meaning you can share notes with like-minded whisky-lovers.

DRINKING WITH OTHERS

Whisky is best shared with friends. Most of the time. Experience shows that your fellow drinkers will almost always fall into one of three categories:

1. The Whisky-Hater

You may see it as your responsibility to convert this person to the cause. Win them over at first with mixers, before moving them on to whisky on its own. If that doesn't work, give them a gin and tonic and keep the good stuff for yourself!

Whisky-hater drinks:
• Smoky Cokey
• Whisky and ginger
• Manhattan

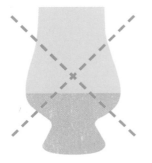

2. The Whisky-Curious

This is the friend who has perhaps tasted a whisky or two and is ready to go all in. Don't destroy their burgeoning interest and enthusiasm by firing a peaty Laphroaig or a spicy Koval Rye at them from ten paces. Break them in gently and watch their flower grow.

Whisky-curious drinks:
• Redbreast 12YO
• Glenlivet 12YO
• Kavalan Classic
• Woodford Reserve Bourbon

3. The Whisky-Lover

This is where things get interesting. You are looking for a kindred spirit here, not a one-upping whisky bore. This should be the person that you most enjoy exploring new whiskies and producers with. Someone who shares your passion and is deserving of your best drams.

Whisky-lover drams:
• You choose. It's time to use everything you have learned so far and stretch your wings…

TASTING
20 / 20

AGE IN SINGLE MALTS

This final tasting looks at two distinguished distilleries, comparing two age variants of their single malts in order to see what occurs to the "same" whiskies over time.

HOW IT WORKS

We look here at two whiskies from two distilleries at different ages, to see how they develop over time. Taking them in pairs, nose between them intensively before tasting them. What differences do you discern? What changes have occurred in the whisky over time? Remember, each bottle's label displays the age of the youngest whisky in the batch it came from. However, there should not be anything in each bottle much older than the age of that youngest whisky.

THE LESSON...

Hopefully you spotted a good deal of development in the older whiskies versus their younger selves, and you now have a better understanding of what flavours develop over time. The older whiskies, with those extra years in the wood, will contain spicier, oaky tones. None is "better" than the other. The important thing is what you taste, and how you enjoy the experience.

YOU NOW HAVE A BETTER UNDERTANDING OF WHAT FLAVOURS DEVELOP OVER TIME

OLD PULTENEY 12YO

SINGLE MALT WHISKY
WICK, HIGHLANDS
40% ABV

IF YOU CAN'T FIND THIS use Clynelish 14YO

WEIGHT 3	Wick-based distillery whose unusual wash still uses a lyne arm with no "swan neck".

 PALE GOLD

 PRICKLES like a struck match; pineapple and grapefruit; lemon peel and honey

 SPICED PEARS and peaches. Slightly peppery; creamy toffee and vanilla

 PALATE-DRYING PEPPER; medium-length finish

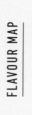 FLAVOUR MAP

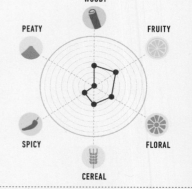

 LIKE THIS? Try Tomatin 12YO

OLD PULTENEY 18YO

SINGLE MALT WHISKY
WICK, HIGHLANDS
46% ABV

IF YOU CAN'T FIND THIS use
Glencadam 18YO

WEIGHT **3**	The distillery closed for 21 years in 1930 due to local parish prohibition laws.

RICH GOLD

HINT OF SULPHUR, dark chocolate, oaky spice, toasty vanilla, crème caramel

SPICY baked apples sprinkled with cinnamon and brown sugar

DRY, LAVENDER and subtle fruit. Fades slowly

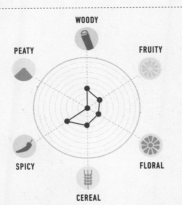

LIKE THIS? Try Glen Moray 18YO

TALISKER 10YO

SINGLE MALT WHISKY
SKYE, HIGHLANDS
45.8% ABV

IF YOU CAN'T FIND THIS use
Bowmore 12YO

WEIGHT **4**	Talisker was *Treasure Island* writer Robert Louis Stevenson's favourite whisky.

RICH GOLD

PEAT-INFUSED marmalade; candied citrus fruit; slight BBQ sauce; salty ribs

SOFT AND SUPPLE FRUIT, followed by spice, peat, then fiery pepper

THE PEPPER GIVES WAY to the peat, then to the fruit

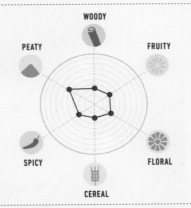

LIKE THIS? Try Inchmoan 12YO

TALISKER 18YO

SINGLE MALT WHISKY
SKYE, HIGHLANDS
45.8% ABV

IF YOU CAN'T FIND THIS use
Bowmore 18YO

WEIGHT **4**	Both Taliskers were matured in ex-Bourbon American oak casks.

PALE AMBER

FRAGRANT DRIED HERBS; seared apricot tart. A hint of leather and cigars

SPICY APRICOT and mandarin. Background pepper and peat

THE PEPPER and peat emerge, in a long, oily finish

LIKE THIS? Try Highland Park 18YO

CLASSIC WHISKY COCKTAILS

Whisky is a complex spirit and it can be used to make equally complex cocktails. The three cocktails here are all robust recipes designed for those who like their whisky cocktails to pack a punch.

WHAT IS A COCKTAIL?

Put simply, it is a spirit-based drink flavoured with liqueurs and/or juices or other liquids, such as bitters. Of course, there's a lot more to it than that.

Making cocktails is a craft, some say an art, requiring skill and a genuine appreciation for the ingredients at hand.

Cocktails may seem like a modern phenomenon, but in fact they have a very long lineage. The earliest distilled spirits were quite basic, so adding something softer to mask the rough flavour was more a necessity than a luxury. From these very rudimentary beginnings, the cocktail was born.

THE COCKTAIL'S ROLE

Cocktails have several functions. One way to group them is to say that some cocktails are used to emphasize the "blending" element of mixing drinks together, to create an ensemble piece greater than the sum of its parts. Other cocktails, such as those featured here, serve more to highlight the flavour and influence of their star spirit.

WHY WHISKY?

As a spirit, whisky, in contrast to vodka or gin, likes to make its presence felt. Put it in a cocktail and you can't miss it – so why not make sure you *really* can't miss it.

The Rob Roy – and its American cousin the Manhattan – follows that line of thinking precisely.

Comprising just a few ingredients it's full of character that make it a timeless favourite.

The Old Fashioned is even more simple but no less delicious. The trick to making it correctly is to use the "right" Bourbon or rye. Right, that is, for you.

Finally, there's the Sazerac. Created in pleasure-loving New Orleans, where they take their fun seriously, the Sazerac reflects that city's hard-playing attitude. The spicy rye whiskey, the punchy bitters, and the powerful absinthe combine in a cocktail that's definitely not for the faint-hearted.

Note also, the whiskies chosen here should all be widely available for you buy – as well, of course, as working well in these cocktails.

► **Cocktails are best** enjoyed in a bar. The best cocktail "mixologists" will talk you through the cocktail-making process and show you how it's done.

ROB ROY

The Scotch whisky version of the Bourbon-based Manhattan. Perfect for autumn.

INGREDIENTS

50ml (1 ¾fl oz) Scotch whisky, possibly a Glenfarclas, or a blend such as Great King Street

25ml (⅘fl oz) sweet vermouth

Angostura bitters

METHOD

Fill a mixing glass with ice, add the whisky and the vermouth and 2–3 dashes of bitters.

Stir gently for 30 seconds. Strain into a cocktail glass and garnish with a maraschino cherry.

Note: Use dry vermouth for a less sweet version. Use Bourbon or rye for a Manhattan. For the Rob Roy, as for many other cocktails, the ingredients across different recipes may vary (apart from the main components, that is). Some Rob Roy recipes, for example, recommend a twist of lemon as an alternative to the maraschino cherry in order to create a drier version.

OLD FASHIONED

A simple but effective classic. It takes time to make, but is worth it. A perfect "anytime" cocktail.

INGREDIENTS

50ml (1 ¾fl oz) rye or Bourbon whiskey, such as Rittenhouse or Koval

Angostura or Peychaud's bitters

3 large ice cubes

1 brown sugar cube or sugar/simple syrup

Orange peel strip

METHOD

Put the sugar cube in a heavy tumbler. Add 2–3 dashes of the bitters. Mix with a spoon, maybe adding a splash of water. Next, add a third of the whiskey and one ice cube. Stir gently.

After around half a minute add more whiskey and another ice cube, still stirring. Add the rest of the whiskey and the last ice cube. Twist the orange peel over the glass, then place it in the liquid.

Note: The key is to keep stirring throughout the process so that the flavours combine.

SAZERAC

Sweet, spicy, and herbal, this drink was designated New Orleans' official cocktail in 2008.

INGREDIENTS

75ml (2 ½fl oz) rye whiskey – preferably Sazerac Rye

1 sugar cube

A handful of ice cubes

Angostura or Peychaud's bitters

Absinthe

Lemon peel

METHOD

Put the sugar cube and a few drops of water in a tumbler. Add the ice, then the whiskey and two dashes of Peychaud's and one dash of Angostura bitters. Stir.

Coat the walls of a second tumbler with absinthe then add the contents of the first glass. Garnish with the lemon peel.

Note: Although absinthe is famed – and is notorious even – for its strength, the whisky is still the "star" of this cocktail. The absinthe, being used to coat the glass, is here more of an accent flavour.

LIGHTER WHISKY COCKTAILS

Although whisky cocktails can be enjoyed at any time, you may find "lighter" options more palatable in warmer weather, the mix of zesty and refreshing ingredients and interesting whiskies matching well.

GETTING STARTED

The cocktail recipes here are all tried and tested members of the whisky cocktail hall of fame – but with the occasional twist.

That's something to always consider when you come to make cocktails for yourself: you should never be afraid to play around with ingredients once you've mastered the basics.

Begin with these simple recipes, adjusting the components to your tastes where necessary. After a few attempts you'll soon be creating your own versions that better match your tastes.

It's important to remember also that making cocktails is a technique, a skill or a craft to be mastered. The combining of flavours is an almost alchemical process that goes beyond the mere mechanics of mixing different ingredients together. Your first few attempts at making cocktails may not quite work. Keep trying.

MIX AND MATCH

The three examples chosen here are all well-suited to cocktail enthusiasts that prefer their drink to have a "milder" taste. The whisky is still very much present in all of

them, though, and you will absolutely taste its personality and character in each one.

To show it's possible to play around with conventional cocktail wisdom, the Blood and Sand here has been made with a smoky, peated single malt. If that's not to your taste, try unpeated instead.

The same goes for the Whisky Sour. We've given you some options, but there are many other whiskies you can make it with.

And while a Mint Julep is usually made with Bourbon, you can substitute it with a rye whiskey, something like a Michter's Single Barrel or a Bulleit Small Batch.

Finally, while we suggest this trio as ideal for spring or summer, if you like them, drink them any time.

EXPLORE MORE

Make the cocktails here and you will have gained great "hands on" experience of making flavour combinations work.

▼ **Cocktails have a wide appeal.** Even those who profess not to like whisky will often happily drink it when blended with other flavours.

WHISKY SOUR

Hailing from 1860s America, this drink's refreshing citrus zing makes it an abiding favourite.

INGREDIENTS

60ml (2fl oz) Bourbon,

maybe a Four Roses, or a Buffalo Trace. For variety, why not try a rye whiskey, such as Templeton Rye

25ml (4/5fl oz) fresh lemon juice

15ml (1/2fl oz) simple/sugar syrup

Ice

Angostura bitters

Egg white (optional)

METHOD

Add all of the ingredients, except the bitters and egg white, into a cocktail shaker and shake vigorously. Then strain the mix into an ice-filled rocks glass. Garnish with three dashes of the bitters.

Note: Adding the egg white to the cocktail mixture adds a creamy smoothness to the drink that would be lacking without it. A whisky sour containing egg white is sometimes called a Boston Sour.

MINT JULEP

A refreshing Bourbon-based summer cocktail from America's Deep South.

INGREDIENTS

50ml (1 ¾fl oz) Bourbon. Something lighter like a Sonoma or Woodford

5ml (⅕fl oz) simple/sugar syrup

Fresh mint

Crushed ice

Angostura or Peychaud's bitters (optional)

METHOD

Take a Julep cup (if you have one) or a heavy tumbler. Muddle the mint leaves and syrup, add the Bourbon then fill to the brim with crushed ice.

Stir gently as the glass frosts over, then add more ice to form a dome. Add a sprig of mint and an optional dash of bitters to finish.

Note: This is one of the American south's most iconic drinks. It was created in the 18th century. Today, it is strongly linked with the Kentucky Derby, being the race's officially promoted drink.

BLOOD AND SAND

A twist on a classic. Can be made with unpeated whisky if this version is not to your taste.

INGREDIENTS

20ml (¾fl oz) blended Scotch whisky. Chivas Mizunara works well

10ml (⅓fl oz) peated single malt. Lagavulin or Ardbeg.

20ml (¾fl oz) cherry brandy. Heering has good natural cherry flavouring

20ml (¾fl oz) sweet vermouth

30ml (1fl oz) orange juice, preferably freshly squeezed

METHOD

Fill your cocktail shaker with ice and pour in all of the ingredients. Cover and shake for 30 seconds.

Strain into a cocktail glass. Garnish with orange peel or a cherry.

Note: This drink hails from the 1920s, the golden age of cocktail creation. It was actually named after the 1922 film of the same name, starring Rudolph Valentino and was originally made with the red juice of a blood orange.

▲ **Pairing food and whisky** is gaining in popularity, offering different perspectives on both than, say, wine will offer.

WHISKY AND FOOD

There's a lot to think about when pairing whisky with food. Not all whisky styles go with every type of food. It can take some unravelling, but when you get it right, matching whisky and food can really hit the mark.

The pairings of and whisky and food suggestions that follow are just that – suggestions. Hopefully, though, these will give you a good idea of which food flavour groups go best with different whiskies. With this is mind, you'll then be able to make your own matches.

AN APERITIF

One way in which whisky can help enhance your culinary experiences is as an aperitif.

A refreshing whisky, such as a light and citrussy single grain, for example, like the Bain's Cape

Whisky, can help to warm up your palate for what's to come and stimulate your taste buds.

Alternatively, if you think starting off with a "full" whisky is more than you'd like, you can try a cocktail, something refreshing such as a Blood and Sand.

STARTERS

If you're having cold cuts to start there are a few ways to go. Salami and cured pork, being creamy and salty, will match with sweeter single malts, such as a Balvenie.

Spicier meats, such as paprika-rich chorizo, can be offset nicely by a sweet Bourbon.

For fish lovers, smoked salmon likes single malt, too, so a "briny" Old Pulteney 12YO would be a good partner here.

MAINS

The ideal whisky match for a main course depends on what you are planning to eat, of course. As a rough guide, lighter bites, creamy pastas or fish, for example, match well with "lighter" whiskies – perhaps a single grain or a more delicate single malt.

For richer meals, perhaps involving sauces and/or red meat, a higher-proof and fuller-bodied single malt will pair nicely. A full meal if ever there was one, though a satisfying one nonetheless.

Whisky goes well with shellfish, so if you are having lobster, langoustine, prawns, or crab select a peaty Islay whisky. Saline, but sweet and aromatic shellfish, paired with the medium-peated and zesty Caol Ila 12YO, for example, is a really beautiful, briny, and heady flavour combination.

DESSERT OR CHEESE

All whiskies, even peaty ones, have some element of sweetness to them. This makes them particularly suited to pairing with desserts. A match well worth trying is crème brûlée with a single pot still Redbreast 12YO Irish whiskey. The sweet, spicy vanilla and mocha tones of the Redbreast work perfectly with the creamy vanilla and caramel of the dessert.

As an added bonus, the creamy texture of the crème brûlée only serves to emphasize the synergy between the two.

For cheese lovers, fortunately most hard cheeses pair well with most whisky, so why not experiment to see what works best for you? Softer cheeses such as brie or dolcelatte, like the crème brûlée above, are well-suited to single pot still Irish whiskeys.

More robust soft cheeses, for example a salty, tangy Roquefort, can be contrasted nicely with a muscular, peated single malt, such as a Lagavulin 16YO.

A DIGESTIF

Whisky's high alcohol content makes it useful as a digestif. It stimulates the stomach's enzymes, which break down food.

Avoid sweeter whisky in this regard and opt maybe for single malts instead.

THE WHISKY CHALLENGE

For some foodstuffs, finding a whisky to pair with can be more of a challenge – but it's still possible and definitely worth trying.

GARLIC, CHILLI, WASABI

Pungent garlic, and spicy chilli and wasabi are all at the stronger end of the flavour spectrum and can suppress your taste receptors. If you take them with whisky, try to use them in moderation.

GOATS' CHEESE

Tart and gamey (in a good way) this dairy product will "battle" whisky for control of your taste receptors. A corn-based or wheat whiskey could be your best option here.

RED MEAT

With grilled and roasted red meat, think of the sauces and marinades involved. Barbeque beef and Bourbon, for instance, could be a marriage made in heaven.

WHISKY CAN MAKE A GREAT APERITIF. SPICY RYE WHISKIES IN PARTICULAR CAN HELP TO STIMULATE THE PALATE

WHISKY AND CHOCOLATE

You may not think of whisky and chocolate as obvious bedfellows. Maybe it's time to think again. They are both luxury indulgences, so perhaps they were made for each other after all.

WHY CHOCOLATE?

Why not? It's chocolate, after all. Better still, chocolate does something special to whisky; when matched correctly it can do something *really* special.

Also, whisky and chocolate actually share production and flavour similarities that make them compatible. Where they do contrast with each other, those contrasts are often both pleasing and interesting.

WHICH CHOCOLATE?

The thing to look for is balance. If the chocolate is too sweet, its flavour will be lost against the whisky; go too bitter with the chocolate and the whisky will struggle to break through. It may take several attempts to find that balance, but it will be fun trying.

In general, dark chocolate is a better partner for whisky. There are a number of "grades" of dark chocolate, with around 50 per cent cocoa solids being quite sweet to 90 per cent cocoa solids being very bitter. This offers a range of pairing possibilities up and down the cocoa-solids scale.

Milk chocolate can work, but needs to be very good quality. Flavoured truffles are a great option, and their silky texture is an added sensory delight. The key, as always, is to taste and taste again.

◄ **Whisky and chocolate** share similar chemical compositions that make them very compatible – in moderation, of course.

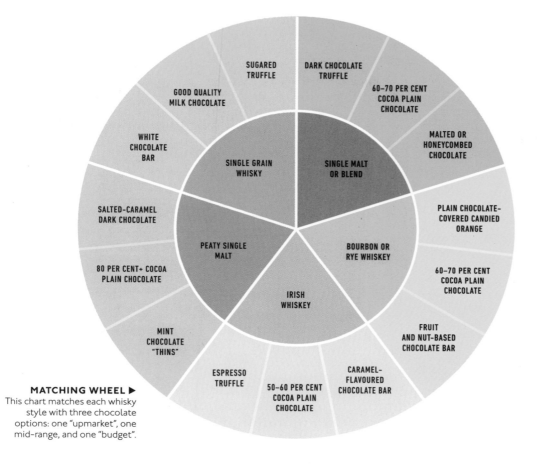

SUGARED TRUFFLE

DARK CHOCOLATE TRUFFLE

GOOD QUALITY MILK CHOCOLATE

60–70 PER CENT COCOA PLAIN CHOCOLATE

WHITE CHOCOLATE BAR

MALTED OR HONEYCOMBED CHOCOLATE

SINGLE GRAIN WHISKY

SINGLE MALT OR BLEND

SALTED-CARAMEL DARK CHOCOLATE

PLAIN CHOCOLATE-COVERED CANDIED ORANGE

PEATY SINGLE MALT

BOURBON OR RYE WHISKEY

80 PER CENT+ COCOA PLAIN CHOCOLATE

60–70 PER CENT COCOA PLAIN CHOCOLATE

IRISH WHISKEY

MINT CHOCOLATE "THINS"

FRUIT AND NUT-BASED CHOCOLATE BAR

ESPRESSO TRUFFLE

50–60 PER CENT COCOA PLAIN CHOCOLATE

CARAMEL-FLAVOURED CHOCOLATE BAR

MATCHING WHEEL ▶
This chart matches each whisky style with three chocolate options: one "upmarket", one mid-range, and one "budget".

METHOD

Here is the best way to taste whisky and chocolate. First take a small sip of the whisky. Spread the whisky around the inside of your mouth, coating every area, and swallow a little of it.

With a small amount still in your mouth, put a little (but not too much) chocolate in your mouth and allow it to mingle with the whisky. As the chocolate slowly softens and melts its flavours will start to release, mingling seductively with the whisky. Savour the moment, but don't hold onto the mixture for too long.

When you are ready, swallow the mashed-up, gooey, and very delicious mess.

THE OAK EFFECT

As with much else concerning whisky, oak has an important role to play in ensuring these two consumables get on well.

The oak casks that most whisky is matured in contain vanillin compounds, which are intensified when the cask has been charred. As the name implies, these impart vanilla notes into the whisky that is chocolate's best friend – milk chocolate especially, but dark chocolate, too.

CHECK THE CHART

This chart shows you which whiskies go best with a range of chocolates. Work your way around the "wheel" and it will become apparent how different whisky styles pair best with particular types of chocolate. See how peaty whiskies "like" salty or high cocoa-solid examples, while sweeter Speyside malts go well with honeycomb-coated chocolates. Other combinations are not so obvious, being contrasting rather than complementary. Try them.

One you have done that, think about inventing your own pairings based on what you've learned here.

GLOSSARY

ABV Alcohol by volume. The strength of alcohol, expressed as a percentage. Scotch whisky must be bottled at a minimum of 40% ABV.

Active cask A cask that is generally "fresher" and more likely to give more flavour and colour to the whisky.

Age statement Label information showing how old the youngest whisky in the bottle is. Most whiskies are "vatted" from many casks, all of varying age.

Angel's share The volume of whisky lost through evaporation whilst maturing in the cask. Varies from 1 per cent in cooler climates to 15 per cent+ in hotter areas.

Aqua vitae Latin for "water of life". Its Gaelic translation, *"uisge beatha"*, became the word "whisky".

ASB American Standard Barrel. 200 litre cask used for maturing Bourbon and US- style whiskies before being utilized by Scotch and scotch-style producers.

Barley Common cereal type found all around the world. Biological name, *Hordeum vulgare*.

Beer Alcoholic beverage fermented from a cereal mash, usually barley.

Blended whisky Usually a blend of malt and grain whiskies.

Blended malt whisky A blend of two or more single malts. Once called "Vatted Malt" or "Pure Malt".

Blended Scotch whisky A blend of one or more single malts with one or more single grain whiskies.

Body The "weight" or mouthfeel of the whisky.

Bourbon A US whiskey-style distilled from a corn-dominant mash bill and aged in brand-new charred oak casks.

Bung A normally wooden stopper (usually poplar) inserted in a hole in the cask.

Butt A cask used for maturing sherry. Normally around 500 litres.

Cask Wooden container used for storing and maturing whisky. Usually oak.

Cask strength A whisky that has not had water added to it prior to bottling.

Charring The burning of the inside of a cask to produce a carbon layer that removes undesirable sulphur-containing compounds from the spirit.

Chill-filtering Process of filtering out long-chain fatty acids (hexadecanoate) that would otherwise make whisky cloudy when chilled or after the addition of water.

Column/Coffey still Tall still using continuous distillation. Used mainly for grain and US whiskeys.

Condenser Part of the distilling equipment that cools alcohol vapours in the still and converts them into liquid.

Continuous distillation See Column/Coffey Still.

Cooper A skilled craftsman responsible for building and maintaining whisky casks. Normally works in a cooperage.

Corn/Maize A common harvested vegetable from which kernels are extracted and used for whisky-making. Biological name, *Zea mays*.

De-char, Re-char The process of rejuvenating a cask that has been used a number of times. The inside of the cask is stripped and the freshly exposed oak re-charred.

Distilling The process of turning low-alcohol wash, or beer, into highly alcoholic spirit.

Distillery Production facility where alcoholic spirits are made.

Double distillation The description of a distillery that carries out two distillations. This is usually the minimum number of distillations for a single malt whisky.

Doubler A simple pot still employed by some US distillers to encourage further flavour development, after column distillation has taken place.

Draff Residue left from the mashing process. Often dried, compressed and turned into animal feed.

Dram Traditional Scottish term for a normal measure of whisky. "A wee dram!"

Drum malting Modern method of turning the barley in a large metal drum to ensure an even germination among the grains.

Dunnage warehouse A traditional single-floored warehouse for maturing whisky in the cask.

Enzymes Proteins which act as biological catalysts. They play an important role in the reactions that occur during germination (malting), mashing, and fermentation.

Feints/Tails The last portion of liquid collected from pot still distillation, which contains undesirable and unwanted compounds and elements.

Fermentation The process of turning sugar into alcohol, catalysed by adding yeast to the wort.

Finish Flavours found as the whisky is swallowed.

First fill, Second fill etc. First fill = the first time whisky is filled into a second-hand cask. Second fill = the second time, and so on. After several fills a cask may be re-charred, to "reactivate" it.

Flavour wheel Visual device for identifying and describing flavour.

Flight A group of whiskies served and tasted successively.

Floor malting Traditional method of spreading water-soaked barley on a stone floor and turning it by hand to allow for even germination. It is a process rarely used nowadays.

Foreshots/Heads The first liquid that passes from the spirit still through the spirit safe. Highly alcoholic and unusable for use in the final spirit.

Germination The process of natural growth and development in a plant seed.

Grains For whisky-making purposes, the main grains used are barley, corn, rye, and wheat.

Grain whisky Whisky made from predominantly corn or wheat using patent or continuous stills.

Grist Malted barley is milled/ground into a coarse grist before hot water is added.

Highball Drink of whisky, ice, and soda water very popular in Japan.

Hogshead A 250 litre cask fabricated from staves re-used from smaller casks for use in the whisky industry.

Hydrometer Device used for measuring alcoholic strength based on density.

Kiln Heated room where barley is placed to halt the germination process. Traditionally heated by a peat fire, but now usually by coal or oil.

Low wines The alcohol created during the first phase of distillation at around 22–25% ABV.

Lyne arm Part of the still that transports spirit vapour to be condensed back into liquid.

Madeira drum A cask previously used for maturing Madeira wine.

Malt or Malted barley Barley grains that have been through the malting process.

Malting The processing of raw barley into malted barley (or malt). Enzymes are produced that make the starch accessible, and which will convert the starch to sugar during mashing.

Mash bill The cereal recipe for each individual distillery. May describe the percentage of corn vs rye vs wheat, etc in US whiskies.

Mashing Process of enzymatic conversion of starch to sugar and extraction of soluble sugars as "wort" from the malt grist, by the adding of ever-hotter water to it in a mash tun.

Mash tun Large vessel (normally stainless steel) where mashing takes place.

Master blender The skilled professional that mixes and blends whiskies of different ages, styles or provenance to create a whisky maker's preferred flavour profile.

Maturation The process of the ageing of whisky in wooden casks.

Middle/Spirit cut The spirit left once it has been separated from the undesirable foreshots and feints and destined to become whisky.

Milling The process where dried malted barley is ground into grist.

Mizunara Japanese oak, highly sought after and used sparingly for whisky maturation due to its rarity.

Mouthfeel Description of the sensation of the feel of the whisky in your mouth.

Neck Section of a pot still between the main body and the lyne arm. The width and height dictates the volume and flow of alcohol vapours that will be condensed into liquid spirit.

New-make (spirit) The final spirit cut, straight from the still, unaged in wood.

Nosing The act of smelling whisky to assess its aroma.

Pagoda Traditional pyramid-shaped roof offering ventilation from the kiln where malted barley would have been dried. Mainly for decorative purposes nowadays, as malting takes place off-site more often than not.

Palate How the whisky tastes.

Patent still See Column/Coffey still.

Peat Decomposed and compressed vegetation. A traditional fuel source, when used to dry malted barley it imparts a pungent, smoky flavour.

Peated Usually a reference to a whisky that has been made using peated malted barley. May vary from slightly smoky (lightly peated) to powerful and medicinal (heavily peated).

Phenols A diverse group of aromatic chemical compounds found in peat smoke. Measurement of the level of phenols in barley indicate how intensely smoky the whisky might be.

Polymers Molecules made up of two or more repeating chemical units. For example: cellulose, hemicellulose, and lignin, which make up oak wood. Polymers are important for flavour development in maturation.

Port pipe A cask previously used for maturing port.

Pot still Type of still most commonly used for making single malt whisky, consisting of pot, neck, and lyne arm. Made of copper due to that metal's ability to efficiently conduct heat and remove sulphurs from the liquid.

Poteen The Irish word describing new-make spirit or spirit straight off the still.

Proof A traditional method of measuring alcohol. Mainly used now in the US, where the proof measurement is double the %ABV. So 50% ABV is 100 US proof, for example.

Purifier A device connected to the lyne arm in a few distilleries that re-directs very heavy alcohol vapours back into the still for re-distillation.

Quaich Traditional Scottish whisky-drinking cup with a short handle on either side. Share a drink with someone from a Quaich and you will be friends forever!

Reflux Description of the process whereby spirit vapour condenses in the neck of the still, lyne arm, or purifier before reaching the condenser. The liquid falls back into the pot and is re-distilled.

Rye A hardy and tough cereal grown in Northern Europe and cooler parts of the US. Biological name: *Secale cereale*.

Shell and tube condenser Network of small, cold-water filled copper tubes, which convert alcohol vapours back into liquid upon contact.

Single barrel/Single cask whisky Usually a single malt or Bourbon, bottled from one "single" cask.

Single malt Whisky made from 100 per cent malted barley from a single distillery. Can be, and normally is, blended from several casks from the same distillery.

Spirit safe A device in which the stillman will decide when to separate the spirit cut from the foreshots and feints, using sensory analysis and hydrometers.

Spirit still The second set of stills, where the low wines are re-distilled to further purify and concentrate the alcohol.

Still Apparatus for the making of distilled liquids.

Stillman Person who operates the stills and has charge over the spirit output from them.

Sulfur American spelling of sulphur.

Sulphur A chemical element responsible for both desirable ("meaty") and undesirable (vegetable, rotten eggs) aromas in new-make spirit. Removed by cask char during maturation.

Staves The wooden planks that make up a cask.

Tannins Group of free compounds present in oak wood. Responsible for imparting bitterness and astringency. For example, ellagic acid and gallic acid.

Tears Description of the trails of whisky left on the side of the glass when the glass it tilted or angled. Also called "legs".

Toasting The heat treatment of oak wood during cask manufacture, which produces aroma-active compounds, eg. vanillin (sweet) and guaiacol (spicy). These develop as the structural components of the wood, eg, its lignin, are degraded.

Triple distillation Description of a distillery that operates with a third set of stills, allowing for further purification.

Uisge beatha (pronounced ooska bar) Gaelic translation of the Latin "aqua vitae".

Valinch Traditional metal tube-like device for extracting whisky samples from a cask.

Vanillin Compound produced by the thermal degradation of lignin during the heat treatment of wood, such as in the charring or re-charring of casks. It is extracted by the liquid during maturation and responsible for whisky's sweet, vanilla-like aroma.

Wash The "beer" created by the addition of yeast to the wort, normally between 6–8% ABV.

Wash still The first set of stills, where fermented wash is heated, and the resulting alcohol vapour is cooled and condensed into a low-alcohol liquid of 22–25% ABV, known as low wines.

Wheat Common grain used for the production of Scottish grain whiskies and some US whiskeys. Biological name: Triticum vulgare.

White dog The US description of new-make spirit.

Weight Sometimes used to help describe the mouthfeel of a whisky.

Worm tub A traditional style of condenser that utilizes a long pipe that winds through a wooden tub of cold water.

Wort Solution of malted barley dissolved in warm water. It contains soluble sugar, and as the wort is fermented those sugars are converted to alcohol.

Whisky/Whiskey Alcohol distilled from a cereal-based mash and matured in wooden casks.

Wood finishing Whisky moved from one cask to another, perhaps more active, cask. This occurs later in the maturation process, with the objective being to extract further flavours from the second cask.

Yeast A single-celled organism, which is a type of fungus. When added to the mash in liquid or solid form, it acts as a catalyst to convert sugar into alcohol. The most common yeast used in whisky production is Saccharomyces cerevisiae.

INDEX

Page numbers in bold indicate a Tasting; those in italics refer to illustrations and captions.

PICTURE CREDITS

The publisher would like to thank the following for their kind permission to reproduce their photographs:

(Key: a–above; b–below/bottom; c–centre; f–far; l–left; r–right; t–top)

ABOUT THE AUTHOR

Eddie Ludlow developed his love for whisky while working as a sales assistant and van driver for Oddbins in the late 1990s.

After becoming UK Brand Ambassador for Ardbeg and Glenmorangie from 2005 until 2007, in 2008 Eddie and his wife Amanda co-founded The Whisky Lounge. Its mission is to convert, entertain, and educate all those with an interest in, or a burgeoning love for, whisky.

The Whisky Lounge now hosts thousands of people annually across the UK in its regular tastings, festivals, schools, and other events. One of UK whisky's best-known figures, Eddie Ludlow is a Keeper of the Quaich, a member of the Worshipful Company of Distillers, and an IWSC chair judge. This is his first book.

To find out more about Eddie Ludlow, follow The Whisky Lounge on Facebook, Instagram, and Twitter. You can also visit The Whisky Lounge website at: www.thewhiskylounge.com

ACKNOWLEDGMENTS

The author and the publisher would like to thank the following individuals and organizations for their help, advice, and products, without which this book would not have been possible:

The Whisky Exchange (www.thewhiskyexchange.com), for invaluable help with whisky images.
Master of Malt (www.masterofmalt.com) for help with whisky samples.

For help with samples:
Amathus Drinks, Celtic Whisky Compagnie Diageo Plc, Edrington-Beam Suntory, Hellyers Road Distillery, Interbev Group, MPR Communications, Reservoir Distillery, Smarts Communicate, Speciality Brands Spirit Cartel, Story PR, Taylor Strategy.

For editorial support:
Jamie Ambrose, Jürgen Deibel, Rona Skene, Marie Lorimer, for the Index, John Friend, for proofreading.

For practical and technical information:
Forsyths, The Scotch Whisky Association, Canadian Whisky: The New Portable Expert - Davin de Kergommeaux, Andy Watts, Angus Macraild, Billy Abbot.

Eddie would also like to thank the following people for fanning the flames:

The Oddbins Newcastle crew of the late 1990s - you know who you are!
Graeme "The Captain" Wright, Colin Dunn, Charles MacLean, Dr Andrew Forrester, Dave Broom, Sukhinder Singh, Dr Bill Lumsden, Douglas Murray, Ashok Chokalingam, The late Dr Jim Swan, Mickey Heads, Jackie Thompson, Doug McIvor, Graham Eunson, Dr Nick Morgan, Dr Ian Chang, Michael Morris, Joe Clark, Tim Forbes, Oliver Chilton, Helen Stewart, Julie Hamilton and the Glasgow crew, DC, Jonny McMillan, my fellow IWSC judges, Allen Gibbons, all of the fantastic whisky industry folks I get to work with throughout the year that I can't fit in here, customers and friends of The Whisky Lounge, The Whisky Lounge team (for putting up with me over the last year,) my family (particularly my Dad for his help on the grammar and punctuation!) and finally...

My wife and biggest supporter, Amanda, without whom none of this would have happened.